Leadership Development Transformational Future

An essential resource for leaders seeking to thrive in ambiguity, this book explores the pressing need for vertical leadership development in a world defined by rapid change, digital revolution, and complexity.

Traditional horizontal leadership development focuses on skills but falls short in helping leaders navigate complexity, ambiguity, and exponential technological advances. What's needed now is vertical development that emphasizes expanding leaders' capacity to think strategically, manage complexity, and lead with empathy. This book bridges the gap between traditional leadership development and modern demands by providing practical tools for vertical development and, uniquely, integrating digital coaching platforms. Backed by case studies and insights from global leaders who have successfully applied vertical development, it offers actionable frameworks and strategies and introduces AI-driven coaching solutions to enhance leadership growth.

Ideal for senior executives, leadership coaches, HR professionals, organizational consultants, and postgraduate leadership students, this book will help readers cultivate the mindset and skills necessary to succeed in a complex and rapidly changing world.

Sheila M. Boysen-Rotelli, PhD, PHR, MCC, is Professor of Organizational Leadership and Business Administration, Master Certified Coach, Leadership Development Consultant and the founder/owner of Professional Success Coaching.

Leadership Development for a Transformational Future

The Vertical Edge

Sheila M. Boysen-Rotelli

Routledge
Taylor & Francis Group
NEW YORK AND LONDON

Designed cover image: Getty

First published 2026
by Routledge
605 Third Avenue, New York, NY 10158

and by Routledge
4 Park Square, Milton Park, Abingdon, Oxon, OX14 4RN

Routledge is an imprint of the Taylor & Francis Group, an informa business

ISBN: 978-1-041-08338-2 (hbk)
ISBN: 978-1-041-08337-5 (pbk)
ISBN: 978-1-003-64494-1 (ebk)

DOI: 10.4324/9781003644941

Typeset in Sabon
by Apex CoVantage, LLC

To my family, whose unwavering love, support, and belief in me inspire every step of this journey.

To the leaders who embrace growth with courage, resilience, and a vision for a better future—this is for you.

And to my mentors and colleagues, whose guidance and partnership have shaped the path to this work. May we continue to evolve together.

Contents

Preface

In a world that is increasingly interconnected and constantly evolving, the challenges faced by leaders today are more complex, urgent, and multifaceted than ever before. The rapid pace of technological advancements, the shifting dynamics of globalization, and the changing expectations of a new generation of workers are pushing organizations and their leaders into uncharted territory. In this landscape, the traditional approaches to leadership development—those that focus merely on skills, behaviors, and tools—are no longer sufficient to address the complexities leaders now face.

As we navigate an era marked by brittleness, anxiety, nonlinearity, and incomprehensibility (BANI), it is clear that the way we approach leadership must evolve. Leadership cannot simply be about surviving disruption—it must be about thriving in it. This requires a deep, systemic shift in how we think about leadership, how we lead, and how we prepare leaders for the future.

Vertical Leadership Development (VLD) offers a transformative and dynamic approach to leadership development—one that moves beyond superficial change and focuses on the depth of transformation needed for leaders to truly navigate today's challenges. VLD is not just about adding new tools to a leader's toolbox but about fundamentally expanding how leaders think, perceive, and respond to the world around them. It's about evolving leadership from the inside out, fostering resilience, adaptability, and the wisdom needed to lead with clarity, empathy, and integrity in an ever-changing world.

This book represents a culmination of years of research, practice, and real-world application in the field of leadership development. It draws on the latest insights from the fields of emotional intelligence, systems thinking, and organizational change to offer leaders of all levels a roadmap for growth. This book is not just for executives or senior leaders but also for anyone who recognizes the need for deeper, more holistic growth to meet the demands of a rapidly transforming world.

Vertical development asks leaders to evolve their thinking—not just their skill sets. It challenges us to expand our capacity to navigate uncertainty, complexity, and change with a sense of purpose and resilience. It is about learning to make sense of an increasingly chaotic landscape while remaining grounded in our core values, connecting meaningfully with others, and leading with a deep sense of ethical responsibility. By embracing this developmental journey, leaders can begin to engage with the complexities of their organizations and communities in more profound and transformative ways.

As you read this book, my hope is that you will find not just strategies and frameworks but an invitation to embark on your own vertical development journey. I want to inspire you to think beyond the conventional boundaries of leadership development and embrace a more holistic, expansive approach that builds not only your competencies but also your character, mindset, and ability to effect systemic change.

Whether you are a seasoned executive, a rising leader, or someone invested in developing future leadership, this book offers something for everyone. It provides practical tools and exercises to support leaders in every stage of their journey, along with thought-provoking insights that will challenge you to rethink your approach to leadership. My goal is for you to finish this book feeling inspired, equipped, and ready to lead with greater impact and purpose in your organization, community, and beyond.

Leadership is not a static skill set; it is an ongoing journey of growth and discovery. The journey of VLD is one of deepening insight, expanding influence, and transforming how we connect with ourselves, others, and the world. By the end of this book, I hope you will have not only deepened your understanding of what it means to be a leader in today's world but also gained the tools to lead with greater clarity, resilience, and a sense of greater purpose.

Now, let's begin this journey together, toward becoming the kind of leaders our world so desperately needs.

Acknowledgments

This book would not have been possible without the incredible support of many individuals.

First and foremost, I would like to express my deepest gratitude to my family. To Graham, my unwavering partner in life and leadership, whose constant encouragement, love, and understanding have been the bedrock of my journey. He has always believed in the power of growth, both personally and professionally, and has supported me not only in the quiet moments but also in the moments of challenge, when true leadership is tested. His capacity for empathy, wisdom, and his innate ability to listen and coach me through the tough decisions mirror the very qualities I strive to cultivate in my own leadership and coaching practice. Graham exemplifies the kind of leadership that balances strength with tenderness, vision with humility, and action with reflection—qualities that inspire me daily as I work to guide others in their leadership journeys. I am endlessly grateful for his partnership, not only in this book but also in all aspects of our lives.

To the three brightest lights in my life, Finn, Blaney, and Declan, who remind me every day of the power of resilience, curiosity, and growth. You are my inspiration and my greatest teachers in the art of authentic leadership.

I am also profoundly grateful to my parents, whose love, guidance, and belief in me have been a guiding force in my life. To my mom and dad, your unwavering support and dedication to teaching me the importance of integrity, hard work, and compassion have shaped me in more ways than I can count. You taught me the value of nurturing both the mind and heart, and your example continues to guide me as I navigate my own leadership journey.

Dad, you've always shown me the power of unwavering support and presence—whether it was never missing one of my volleyball, basketball, or tennis games, or reading every one of my doctoral coursework papers before I submitted them! You cared so much about my future that you even cried at a few of my grade school parent–teacher conferences (I'm sorry I didn't take things more seriously in the third grade, but I did get it figured out eventually!). Your quiet but constant support has never gone unnoticed, and it has had a profound impact on who I am today. I'm forever grateful for your love, guidance, and steady presence.

And mom, I know you're immensely proud of me, even though, let's be honest, you still have no idea what it is that I actually do! But that's okay, because your belief in me has always been more than enough. Your constant appreciation and nurturing of my creativity shaped the way I approach leadership and helped me embrace my authentic self. You taught me to trust my intuition, to value my unique perspective, and to lead with heart—lessons that continue to guide me as I navigate both my personal and professional journey. Your unwavering support has allowed me to express myself fully, and for that, I will be forever grateful.

To my husband's parents who have been my bonus mom and dad since I was 13 years old, Mason and Donna, thank you for embracing me so authentically from the very beginning. Your kindness, generosity, and wisdom have been a constant source of support, and I am truly grateful for the love you have shown me. Dad, your steady presence and grounded perspective have taught me the power of patience and thoughtful action, while Mom, your warmth and nurturing always remind me of the importance of empathy and connection in leadership. I am so grateful to always have the two of you as sounding boards and cheerleaders in my corner.

I am also profoundly grateful to the mentors, colleagues, and thought leaders who have shaped my understanding of leadership. A special thanks to my current and past colleagues (who are also generous mentors and cherished friends), including Laura, Maria, Tara, Shannon, Karim, Scott, Mike, Tim, and Lesley for their partnership and unwavering commitment to supporting the growth and development of others. I am especially thankful to those who have shared their insights, research, and expertise, enriching this book in ways I could never have imagined on my own.

Thank you to the many leaders who have been part of my journey—those I've coached, worked alongside, and learned from. Your openness, dedication, and courage to evolve have inspired me every step of the way.

Finally, a heartfelt thank you to my siblings—Emily, Brian, Amy, Kevin, and Todd—who were, without a doubt, the very first recipients of my leadership skills practice. I'm sure they would agree that many of my "coaching moments" as a child were absolutely groundbreaking (if not completely unsolicited). Your patience, humor, and ability to handle my "leadership" have made me who I am today. Thank you for being my first—and possibly most challenging—leadership team (and best friends)!

I would also like to acknowledge the academic and professional communities that continue to push the boundaries of what it means to be a leader in today's world. Your work has laid the foundation for this book, and it will continue to guide leaders into the future.

About the Author

Sheila M. Boysen-Rotelli, is a Master Certified Executive Leadership Coach, facilitator, author, TEDx speaker, and professor, recognized as a thought leader in the fields of coaching and leadership development. She is deeply committed to advancing the profession of leadership coaching, blending innovative approaches with timeless principles to foster growth, transformation, and authentic leadership.

Sheila has designed and accredited numerous International Coaching Federation (ICF) coach training programs and personally trained hundreds of coaches across organizations and graduate-level academic settings. With over a decade of experience as a certified coach, she has worked with more than 2,000 clients from diverse industries including tech, finance, consumer packaged goods, education, government, and nonprofit sectors. Her coaching approach is authentic, compassionate, and results-oriented—empowering individuals and teams to uncover their leadership potential and live their values both personally and professionally.

Driven by a passion for helping leaders engage with courage and authenticity, Sheila focuses on enabling others to rise above challenges, create meaningful impact, and unlock their full potential. She empowers leaders to lead with empathy, insight, and resilience—skills critical in today's ever-evolving world.

Outside of her professional work, Sheila finds joy in spending quality time with her husband, Graham, and their three children—Finn, Blaney, and Declan—along with their seven-pound Yorkshire Terrier. Through her work and personal passions, she embraces the spirit of continuous growth and transformation, always striving to combine heart, insight, and dedication to help others achieve remarkable outcomes.

Sheila's unique blend of expertise, passion for human development, and commitment to the future of leadership makes her a visionary in coaching and leadership development. She encourages all leaders to embark on their own transformative journey, knowing that the power of continuous growth is the key to navigating complexity and uncertainty in the world ahead.

Chapter 1

Introduction to Vertical Leadership Development

In the rapidly evolving landscape of modern organizations, the traditional approaches to leadership development are showing significant limitations. Today's leaders face unprecedented complexity: global interconnectivity, fast-changing markets, diverse teams, and exponential advancements in technology. This kind of environment requires leaders who can think beyond immediate tasks and rigid hierarchies, ones who can interpret and adapt to multifaceted challenges with clarity and foresight.

Traditional Horizontal Versus Vertical Development

The majority of conventional leadership programs focus on building horizontal competencies—skills, knowledge, and tools for managing others effectively. This horizontal approach is practical and essential for developing capabilities like communication, task management, and decision-making within defined contexts.

However, as leadership researcher Nick Petrie and others in the field of leadership development have argued, horizontal skills alone are often insufficient (Petrie, 2018). Many leaders possess technical expertise and understand the theories of good leadership but struggle to implement them under complex, high-stakes conditions. Petrie highlights that despite being taught what they "should" do, leaders often find themselves unable to "be" the kind of leader their environments demand. In this sense, horizontal development can be likened to filling a container—the leader's mind—with information, while overlooking the potential to expand the container itself.

Vertical Development: The Pathway to Complexity and Resilience

Vertical Leadership Development (VLD) is a transformative approach that aims to increase a leader's capacity to handle complexity, ambiguity, and interdependent challenges by fostering growth in cognitive, emotional, and

DOI: 10.4324/9781003644941-1

interpersonal dimensions (Shavkun & Dybchinska, 2020). Instead of simply adding more tools to the leader's skill set, vertical development focuses on expanding how leaders think, perceive, and interpret the world around them. This transformational process aligns with psychological and developmental theories that map the progressive stages of adult development, such as those introduced by developmental psychologists Piaget (1971), Kegan (1982), and Erikson (1980). Through these theories, VLD challenges the notion that growth stops at adulthood, suggesting instead that leaders can continuously evolve, maturing in their abilities to handle increasingly complex situations with greater insight and flexibility.

The Stakes: Shifting From a VUCA World to a BANI World

A leader's ability to adapt and thrive in a VUCA world has become a defining factor in organizational success. Petrie shares that leaders often feel overwhelmed not because of an excessive workload but due to the strain of trying to make sense of a world that outpaces their current mindset (Petrie, 2018). When operating from an earlier developmental stage, leaders may feel "in over their heads" and struggle to understand and address the broader impacts of their decisions. In contrast, those who progress through later stages of development—such as those described in frameworks by developmental psychologist Robert Kegan, leadership scholar Bill Torbert, and others—gain the ability to view complex situations through multiple perspectives, embrace uncertainty, and lead in a way that fosters collaborative problem-solving and long-term strategic thinking (Kegan, 1994).

The language we use to describe the world reflects how we perceive and respond to its challenges. For decades, the term **VUCA**—volatile, uncertain, complex, and ambiguous—provided a framework for understanding and addressing the increasingly dynamic and unpredictable nature of global systems. Originally developed in military contexts and later adopted by organizational leaders and strategists, VUCA captured the essence of a world where change was constant, uncertainty pervasive, and complexity an ever-present challenge.

However, as the 21st century unfolds, the limitations of VUCA have become apparent. While it accurately describes the characteristics of a dynamic world, it fails to convey the deeper, more disruptive realities that define the current global landscape. The COVID-19 pandemic, climate crises, geopolitical tensions, technological disruption, and social inequities have highlighted the inadequacy of traditional frameworks. In response, a new paradigm—BANI—has emerged, offering a more nuanced and actionable understanding of the modern era. BANI, an acronym for brittle, anxious, nonlinear, and incomprehensible, captures the fragility, emotional toll, and chaotic nature of our interconnected world.

Understanding the Shift From VUCA to BANI

VUCA became a dominant lens for leaders navigating a rapidly changing world. It described the following:

- **Volatility**: The rate and pace of change
- **Uncertainty**: The lack of predictability and reliable information
- **Complexity**: The interconnected nature of systems and challenges
- **Ambiguity**: The difficulty in interpreting and making sense of unclear or conflicting signals

The term VUCA—volatile, uncertain, complex, and ambiguous—captured the essence of modern organizational life. In this context, the demands placed on leaders stretch beyond traditional managerial skills. Leaders needed to navigate fast-paced technological changes, unpredictable markets, and shifting social and cultural dynamics.

Consider, for instance, the example of Nelson Mandela, who, upon being released from prison, chose not to seek retribution but instead aimed to unify South Africa through a shared vision of diversity and reconciliation. His actions were not driven by content knowledge or techniques but by an advanced capacity for empathy, resilience, and strategic foresight. Mandela's approach demonstrated that in a VUCA world, it was not just what a leader knew but how they thought that determined their effectiveness.

VUCA encouraged leaders to develop agility, adaptability, and resilience. Its solutions often emphasized forecasting, strategic planning, and system optimization—approaches suited to mitigating risk and exploiting opportunities in a dynamic but still comprehensible environment.

Yet, as global crises multiplied and intensified, the VUCA framework struggled to address deeper systemic breakdowns and the emotional and psychological impact of a world in constant upheaval. Leaders and organizations required a new lens—one that acknowledged not just external challenges but also their destabilizing effects on people and institutions.

BANI: A New Lens for a Fractured World

BANI, introduced by futurist Jamais Cascio, offers a more visceral understanding of the modern world's challenges (Olkowicz et al., 2024). It shifts the focus from managing uncertainty to grappling with the fragility and emotional turbulence of contemporary systems.

Brittle

Brittle systems appear robust but are prone to sudden and catastrophic failure when stressed. The interconnectedness of global supply chains, for example, creates efficiency but leaves systems vulnerable to collapse when a single link breaks.

Implications: Leaders must prioritize resilience over-optimization, designing systems that can flex and recover rather than merely function efficiently.

Anxious

Anxiety reflects the emotional and psychological toll of living in a world where threats—real or perceived—are pervasive. Whether due to health crises, economic instability, or social unrest, individuals and organizations face heightened stress and decision paralysis.

Implications: Addressing anxiety requires empathy, clear communication, and psychological safety, enabling individuals and teams to navigate challenges without succumbing to fear.

Nonlinear

In a nonlinear world, cause and effect are disconnected or disproportionate. Small events can trigger massive consequences, as seen in viral social movements or cascading failures in digital networks.

Implications: Leaders must embrace ecosystems thinking and scenario planning, recognizing that outcomes often defy traditional logic or linear models.

Incomprehensible

Incomprehensibility describes a world where complexity has reached a level that defies understanding. Information overload, conflicting narratives, and opaque technologies like artificial intelligence leave individuals feeling disoriented and powerless.

Implications: Leaders need humility and collaborative intelligence, leveraging diverse perspectives to make sense of challenges that no single individual or organization can fully grasp.

Why the Shift Matters?

The transition from VUCA to BANI reflects a broader evolution in how we understand and approach global challenges. VUCA emphasized external forces and the strategic responses they demanded. In contrast, BANI highlights the fragility and emotional impact of these forces, demanding deeper introspection and systemic transformation.

From Stability to Fragility: VUCA assumed that systems were stable but subject to disruption. BANI recognizes that systems themselves are inherently fragile, requiring continuous reinforcement and adaptation.

From Rationality to Emotionality: VUCA focused on rational responses to uncertainty. BANI acknowledges the emotional toll of living in a world where uncertainty feels existential, requiring leaders to address not just systems but also the human experience within them.

From Predictability to Unpredictability: While VUCA acknowledged complexity, it often sought to predict and manage it. BANI embraces unpredictability, encouraging leaders to build agility and resilience rather than rely on forecasts.

Adapting Leadership for a BANI World

The shift from VUCA to BANI demands a corresponding evolution in leadership. Leaders must develop new mindsets and capabilities to navigate a world that feels increasingly fragile, emotionally charged, and incomprehensible. Key shifts include the following:

- **Building Resilience:** Leaders must design systems and cultures that can absorb shocks and recover quickly. This involves redundancy, adaptability, and an acceptance of failure as a learning opportunity.
- **Fostering Psychological Safety:** In a world of heightened anxiety, leaders need to create environments where individuals feel supported, valued, and empowered to act without fear of retribution or judgment.
- **Embracing Complexity and Ambiguity:** Leaders must develop the cognitive capacity to hold multiple perspectives, understand systems dynamics, and act decisively despite incomplete information.
- **Communicating With Empathy:** In times of incomprehensibility, clear and empathetic communication helps build trust and provides clarity in the midst of confusion.
- **Practicing Humility and Collaboration:** No leader can fully grasp the intricacies of a BANI world alone. Effective leadership requires humility, openness, and a willingness to collaborate across disciplines and perspectives.

As we transition from a VUCA to a BANI world, the challenges we face are not merely strategic or operational—they are deeply human and systemic. Leaders must move beyond traditional frameworks of prediction and control, embracing resilience, empathy, and adaptability as core principles. The BANI paradigm is not just a new vocabulary but also a call to action for leaders to reimagine how they navigate uncertainty and complexity in an ever-changing world. By adapting to this new reality, leaders can foster innovation, build trust, and guide their organizations with clarity and purpose.

Through this book, readers will be introduced to the frameworks, practices, and tools that underpin VLD, emphasizing its role as a process of transformation rather than mere skill acquisition. By reshaping the very lens through which leaders see their roles, challenges, and relationships, VLD equips leaders to transcend conventional limitations and drive meaningful impact within their organizations.

The Importance of Vertical Growth in Modern Organizations

As organizations increasingly operate within complex, interconnected environments, the ability of leaders to grow and adapt beyond traditional skill sets has become vital. The challenges facing today's leaders are no longer limited to isolated issues; they involve multifaceted, often unpredictable situations that require them to think strategically across various dimensions. Vertical Leadership Development (VLD) addresses this need by advancing leaders' cognitive and emotional capacities, enabling them to understand and influence complex systems effectively.

Complexity Beyond Competence

In most conventional models, leadership development emphasizes competencies that are relatively static—specific skills, techniques, and knowledge that leaders can apply within their roles. This approach, however, assumes that the knowledge and skills a leader acquires will continue to be effective as they encounter new challenges. In reality, as the environment grows more complex, the sheer addition of skills and information is often insufficient. The gap between what leaders know and what they need to navigate complex, nuanced situations grows wider. Vertical development fills this gap by emphasizing adaptability, encouraging leaders to advance through stages of maturity, empathy, and strategic insight.

Developmental Stages as a Framework for Modern Leadership

Pioneers in developmental psychology, such as Robert Kegan (1982) and Bill Torbert (2005), identified that adults progress through distinct stages of cognitive and emotional maturity. In leadership contexts, these stages translate into how leaders understand themselves and others, how they view the organization and its mission, and how they approach decision-making under pressure. According to Kegan's Subject-Object Theory, for example, leaders evolve from a "socialized mind"—where they are shaped by others' expectations—to a "self-authoring mind," where they form their own belief systems and values (2009). In the latest stages, leaders adopt a "self-transforming mind," in which they can hold multiple perspectives, integrating diverse viewpoints to make holistic, systems-oriented decisions. This research by developmental psychologist Robert Kegan and organizational psychologist Lisa Lahey suggests that leaders evolve from being shaped by others' expectations to forming their own unique worldview—a progression we'll examine in detail in Chapter 2.

Additionally, Nick Petrie's work underscores how critical these shifts in mindset are for leaders today. Leaders operating from advanced developmental stages are more likely to interpret complex issues in innovative ways, see long-term patterns amid ambiguity, and make sense of change not as a threat but as an integral of progress (Petrie, 2018). In a BANI environment, this ability to think fluidly, learn continuously, and adapt without losing focus becomes the distinguishing factor of an effective leader.

A Transformational Approach to Leadership Development

In today's organizations, leaders who lack the adaptive, growth-oriented mindset that VLD cultivates are often at risk of plateauing in their roles. The shift from conventional skill-based training to a developmentally focused approach is therefore not just a beneficial addition but a strategic imperative. Vertical development not only equips leaders to meet the demands of their roles but also prepares them to inspire and support others in an increasingly complex world.

In the chapters that follow, we will explore how VLD provides leaders with a path to grow their capacity for nuanced decision-making, deep self-awareness, and transformative influence. This shift from knowing more to thinking differently is at the heart of VLD and serves as the foundation for leaders who aspire to make a meaningful impact in today's BANI landscape.

Defining Vertical Leadership Development

Vertical Leadership Development (VLD) represents a significant shift from traditional, horizontal leadership training. While horizontal development focuses on "what" leaders know and can do, vertical development is concerned with "how" leaders think and process experiences. Rather than adding competencies, vertical development enhances the leader's ability to integrate diverse perspectives, understand greater complexity, and adapt in an increasingly interconnected world. In essence, VLD is about growing the leader's internal capacity to make sense of complexity and to lead with insight, resilience, and agility.

Beyond the Skills: Developing Cognitive and Emotional Capacity

Horizontal development is competency-based, often resembling a checklist of knowledge and skills that can be acquired through training programs, workshops, and academic study. Horizontal development is undoubtedly essential—it provides leaders with the tools they need to communicate effectively, manage resources, and set goals. However, in a BANI environment, even the most highly trained leaders may find themselves limited by their level of cognitive and emotional complexity.

Vertical development, by contrast, is concerned with enhancing a leader's psychological maturity and adaptive capacity. This process is based on frameworks in adult development theory, which suggest that adults can grow through successive levels of maturity, each expanding their capacity to understand and engage with complex situations. For instance, developmental psychologist Robert Kegan's Subject-Object Theory that we will explore further in Chapter 2 illustrates how leaders can move from a "socialized mind" shaped by external expectations, to a "self-authoring mind" that is internally directed, and ultimately to a "self-transforming mind" capable of holding and integrating contradictory ideas and perspectives.

A Framework for Transformation

Vertical development is not a single technique but rather a framework for deep transformation that encompasses several domains of growth: cognitive, emotional, and relational. This framework involves moving through distinct stages, each characterized by progressively greater levels of cognitive sophistication and emotional resilience. Vertical development frameworks—such as Robert Kegan's orders of consciousness, Bill Torbert's Action Logics, and Susanne Cook-Greuter's (1999) ego development theory—are central to understanding how VLD unfolds.

Although they use differing terminology for each stage, these frameworks generally describe three to seven broad stages that leaders move through as they advance vertically:

- **Dependent Stages:** In the initial stages of leadership development, individuals heavily rely on external guidance, rules, and validation. Their behaviors and decisions align closely with established norms, primarily

aimed at gaining approval, maintaining harmony, and avoiding conflict or criticism.
- **Independent Stages:** As leaders advance, they begin to establish and trust their own internal principles and values. Decision-making becomes more autonomous, with leaders emphasizing personal achievement, independent problem-solving, and the pursuit of individual goals and standards.
- **Interdependent Stages:** At this stage, leaders recognize the interconnectedness between their own actions and broader organizational or societal systems. They demonstrate advanced collaborative skills, effectively engage with diverse stakeholders, embrace complexity and ambiguity, and use relational intelligence to address multifaceted challenges.
- **Systemically Transformational Stages:** At the highest stages of development, leaders adopt an integrative, visionary perspective that transcends conventional organizational boundaries. They actively promote systemic innovation, ethical reflection, and sustainable global impact, adeptly balancing paradoxes and transforming complexity into opportunities for growth and long-term change.

To better understand these developmental stages, consider how they manifest in everyday leadership scenarios. The following examples illustrate real-world situations that mirror the characteristics of each stage, helping to clarify how leaders evolve from being primarily dependent on external validation to becoming transformative change agents:

- **Dependent Stage Example:**

  Imagine a newly promoted supervisor in a retail store who closely adheres to existing protocols and guidelines. Their primary concern is to follow policies precisely, seeking frequent reassurance from management and colleagues to confirm they're meeting expectations. For example, if a customer raises a concern not covered by standard procedures, this supervisor would escalate the issue immediately, hesitant to act independently for fear of criticism or mistakes.

- **Independent Stage Example:**

  Consider a project manager in a marketing agency who proactively establishes clear goals and independently develops processes to streamline campaigns. They confidently initiate improvements based on their experience and personal insights, often implementing changes without waiting for approval. However, their focus remains mostly internal, prioritizing immediate objectives or specific project outcomes, and sometimes overlooking broader organizational implications.

- **Interdependent Stage Example:**

  Think of a senior department head in a healthcare organization who consistently works across teams, facilitating discussions among doctors, nurses, administrators, and support staff to enhance patient care. They proactively build consensus, encourage diverse viewpoints, and regularly coordinate meetings to address complex issues such as patient safety, operational efficiency, or community health outcomes. This leader demonstrates a clear shift from individual to collective success, embracing complexity and navigating uncertainty through collaboration and systems thinking.

- **Systemically Transformational Stage Example:**

  Envision a senior executive at a global technology firm who initiates strategic shifts that fundamentally change the company's approach to innovation, sustainability, and corporate responsibility. They skillfully integrate diverse viewpoints from internal teams, industry experts, and external communities, ensuring alignment between organizational actions and broader societal values. This leader continually reflects on their impact, encourages others to question assumptions, and actively fosters a culture of continuous learning and ethical decision-making that extends beyond immediate business goals.

In the VLD framework, this type of stage framework offers a roadmap for how leaders can advance through progressively greater levels of complexity, transforming not only what they do but fundamentally how they view themselves and the world around them.

Transformation Over Information

The essential difference between horizontal and vertical development lies in the outcome: while horizontal development results in more knowledge or skills, vertical development results in transformation. This transformation process allows leaders to shift how they interpret and respond to the challenges they face. Through VLD, leaders don't just acquire new strategies; they begin to think with a deeper awareness of systems, relationships, and interdependencies. In a volatile, ambiguous world, the ability to perceive and hold multiple perspectives becomes invaluable, positioning these leaders to guide their organizations through periods of uncertainty with clarity and purpose.

In the upcoming chapters, we will examine the various stages of vertical development in greater detail, exploring how leaders can progress through each stage and the specific practices and mindsets that support this growth. VLD challenges leaders to see development as an ongoing journey, one that transforms how they engage with their teams, tackle complex issues, and contribute to their organizations.

Differentiating Horizontal Versus Vertical Development

In today's leadership programs, a common distinction is made between horizontal and vertical development. While both approaches play important roles in cultivating effective leaders, they address different dimensions of growth shown in Table 1.1. Horizontal development expands a leader's skills and knowledge, adding competencies that enhance immediate performance. Vertical development, however, seeks to transform the leader's ability to think critically, adapt to complexity, and integrate diverse perspectives. By understanding the unique value each approach offers,

Table 1.1 Horizontal Versus Vertical Development

Dimension	*Horizontal Development*	*Vertical Development*
Focus	Expanding what leaders know (skills and competencies)	Transforming how leaders think and process experiences
Nature of Growth	Incremental; accumulates knowledge and techniques	Transformational; shifts mindset and increases cognitive complexity
Approach	Training programs, workshops, courses	Reflective practices, challenging experiences (e.g., heat experiences), and developmental assignments
Outcome	Enhanced performance in familiar tasks and roles	Increased adaptability, resilience, self-awareness, and systemic thinking
Measurement	Quantifiable skills assessments and performance metrics	Developmental assessments, qualitative feedback, and longitudinal tracking of mindset shifts
Impact on Leadership	Improves operational and technical abilities	Fosters innovative, adaptive leadership capable of navigating complexity

organizations can develop balanced programs that not only prepare leaders for routine responsibilities but also equip them to face evolving challenges.

Horizontal Development: Adding Skills and Knowledge

Horizontal development focuses on expanding what leaders know and can do. This approach is often structured around specific competencies—communication skills, project management techniques, time management tools, and so forth. In horizontal development, growth is measured in terms of skill acquisition, new tools, and job-specific training. It is traditionally the foundation of most corporate leadership programs, as these skills are essential for leaders to fulfill their immediate responsibilities.

While horizontal development builds a leader's toolkit, it often falls short in equipping them to handle unfamiliar, complex situations. Leaders who are horizontally developed but not vertically may be technically proficient yet struggle to adapt when challenges extend beyond established protocols or require multifaceted, innovative thinking. They may focus on implementing existing solutions rather than exploring new ways of seeing a problem or approaching it holistically.

Vertical Development: Transforming Mindset and Complexity Capacity

Vertical development, by contrast, seeks to enhance the leader's capacity for understanding and navigating complexity. It is concerned not with adding more information but with expanding the leader's capacity to interpret, process, and respond to information. Vertical development can be seen as cultivating a broader and more nuanced perspective, in which leaders learn to think across contexts, consider the interconnected nature of organizational issues, and approach leadership from a systems thinking viewpoint.

This type of development moves leaders through progressive stages, each representing a higher level of cognitive and emotional maturity. Where horizontal development prepares leaders to "do" more, vertical development enables leaders to "be" more—to grow in self-awareness, flexibility, and empathy, qualities essential for navigating ambiguity and inspiring transformational change. Leaders developed vertically have the capacity to transcend immediate challenges, identify underlying patterns, and foster resilient, adaptive teams that are prepared to face an uncertain future.

Imagine you have a cup. That cup represents your capacity—your ability to understand, lead, and make sense of the world around you. Most traditional development focuses on filling the cup—pouring in more knowledge, skills, and expertise. It's about gaining experience, learning

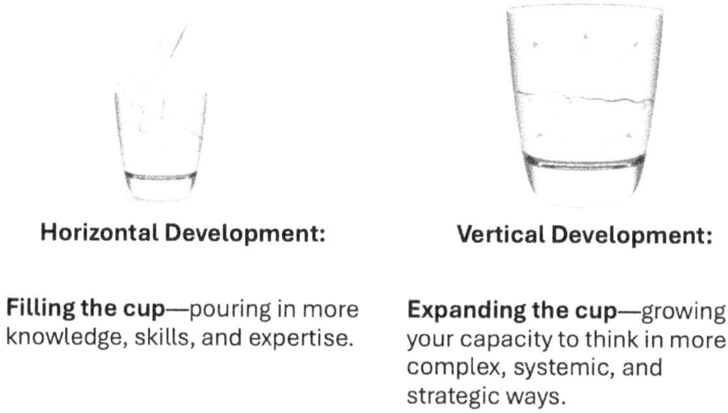

Figure 1.1 Horizontal Versus Vertical Development: Filling the Cup Versus Expanding the Size of the Cup.

new frameworks, and becoming more competent in what you do. This is horizontal development—and it's valuable. But what happens when the challenges you face require more than just what fits in your current cup?

This is where expanding the cup comes in. Vertical development isn't just about adding more information—it's about growing your capacity to think in more complex, systemic, and strategic ways. Instead of just knowing more, you begin to see differently—recognizing patterns, managing paradoxes, and navigating uncertainty with a new level of wisdom. The question isn't just: What do I need to learn next? It's also: How do I need to grow to handle the challenges ahead? Because at some point, filling the cup isn't enough—we need to expand it.

The Need for an Integrated Approach

While horizontal development provides a strong foundation, vertical development is increasingly seen as the differentiator for effective leadership in complex environments. An integrated approach that combines both dimensions ensures that leaders are not only technically capable but also prepared to evolve alongside the demands of their roles. Nick Petrie emphasizes that the future of leadership development lies at the intersection of these two approaches, where competencies are built upon a foundation of adaptive, growth-oriented mindsets.

In practice, combining horizontal and vertical development means supporting leaders in both skill acquisition and mindset transformation. For instance, a program may begin by teaching communication strategies (horizontal) while also challenging leaders to engage in reflective practices that enhance empathy and self-awareness (vertical). As a leader's mindset matures, the way they apply their competencies also changes, evolving from task-focused applications to strategic, long-term thinking that considers broader impacts.

By developing both horizontal and vertical dimensions, organizations can cultivate leaders who are technically adept, self-aware, and capable of guiding their teams through uncertain times with clarity and resilience. This combination represents the future of leadership development, where leaders are equipped not only to perform but also to transform.

The Cynefin Framework: Navigating Complexity and Vertical Growth

No discussion of preparing leaders for complexity would be complete without touching on the Cynefin framework, a sensemaking model that helps leaders diagnose the nature of the situations they face. Developed by Dave Snowden, Cynefin (a Welsh word for habitat) divides contexts into five domains: *Clear* (also known as Obvious), *Complicated*, *Complex*, *Chaotic*, and a center of *Confusion* (or Disorder) when the domain is unclear. Each domain requires a different leadership approach and decision-making style:

- In a Clear context, cause-and-effect relationships are well known; leaders should categorize the situation and apply established *best practices* (e.g., a routine process issue).
- In a Complicated context, there is a knowable relationship between cause and effect, but it may require expert analysis; here leaders rely on *good practices* and expert advice (e.g., engineering a new product feature—multiple right ways exist, and analysis is needed).
- In a Complex context, causes and effects can only be understood in retrospect; there are no right answers, only emergent patterns. Leaders must *probe–sense–respond*, encouraging experimentation and allowing solutions to emerge through safe-to-fail trials. This is the domain of unknown unknowns (e.g., navigating a market disruption or a public health crisis) where emergent practice is key.
- In a Chaotic context, there is high turbulence with no perceivable order; the leader must act decisively to establish some order (*act–sense–respond*), using *novel practices* to address the immediate chaos (e.g., crisis management in the first hours of a disaster).
- Confusion refers to not yet knowing which domain applies, requiring leaders to gather more information and rapidly triage the situation.

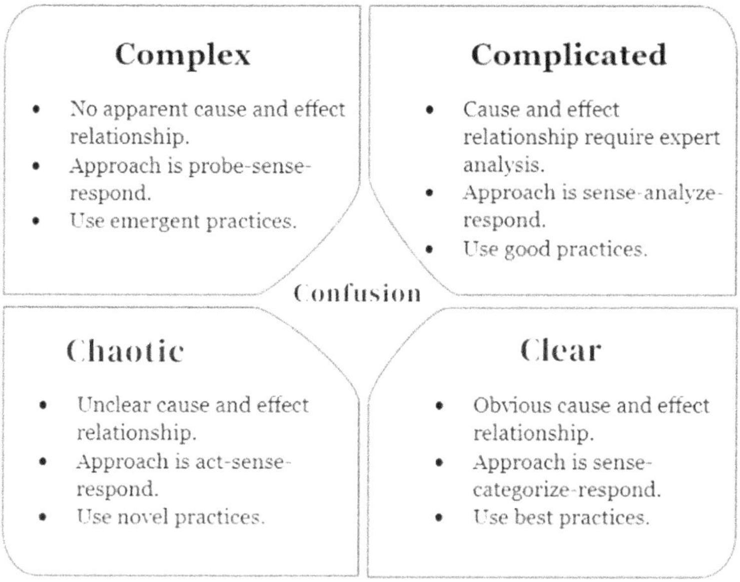

Figure 1.2 The Cynefin Framework.

So how does this tie to vertical development? VLD equips leaders to excel, especially in the Complex (and to some extent Chaotic) domain. In clear and complicated environments, a leader with solid horizontal skills and expertise may perform well—these contexts reward known solutions and analytical thinking. However, in complex contexts, rigid expertise or past experience often fails. Leaders must be comfortable with ambiguity, able to learn on the fly, integrate multiple perspectives, and shift mental models as patterns (The Cynefin Co., 2024). The Cynefin framework highlights that the leadership approach needs to shift from authoritative problem-solving in clear/complicated domains to adaptive sensemaking in complex/chaotic domains. This is precisely the shift that vertical development enables within a leader.

For example, a leader operating at an earlier developmental stage might approach a complex problem (say, declining employee morale in a fast-changing company) with a linear plan and best practices that worked in the past, becoming frustrated when those don't work. A more vertically developed leader, recognizing the problem as complex, would instead involve diverse team members, encourage experiments to see what improves morale, and be willing to iterate—behaviors aligned with *probe–sense–respond.*

They would also remain steady amidst uncertainty, not needing immediate clarity. Snowden and Boone (2007), in introducing Cynefin in HBR, noted that leaders must learn to shift their decision-making style to fit the domain—a cognitively demanding task that benefits from a higher level of sensemaking capacity. Indeed, vertical development contributes to what Snowden calls "leader's framework for decision-making" by expanding the leader's ability to discern context and adapt accordingly.

In practical terms, organizations leveraging Cynefin have found it useful to also invest in vertical development: they train leaders to recognize complex situations *and* help them develop the cognitive agility and open mindset required to respond effectively. The connection is intuitive: in increasingly complex work and life contexts, vertical development becomes essential. Leaders with a growth mindset and advanced cognitive frameworks are more likely to excel in the complex domain by fostering innovation and adaptation rather than clinging to old paradigms. Thus, Cynefin provides the external roadmap of "what type of situation am I in and what approach is called for?" while vertical development is the internal capacity building that allows a leader to actually execute the adaptive, collaborative approaches needed in complexity. Together, they guide leaders to be both aware *and* capable: aware of the nature of problems, and capable of responding with the right leadership approach.

To illustrate, consider a technology company navigating a major industry disruption (a complex scenario). Using Cynefin, its leaders diagnose the situation as complex: the way forward is unclear, so they decide to run several pilot projects (experiments) to test new business models. Now, if those leaders have strong vertical development, they will likely embrace the learning process, remain flexible as results come in, and avoid the trap of searching for one "right" answer. They can hold contradictory data, delay closure on decisions until patterns emerge, and engage their teams in sensemaking discussions—behaviors consistent with higher-stage leadership. If, however, the leaders are not vertically developed enough, they might struggle with the ambiguity, perhaps prematurely converging on one strategy or resisting input from unconventional sources. In this way, the Cynefin framework and vertical development are complementary tools for leadership in complexity: one helps map the terrain, the other builds the vehicle (the leader's mind) to traverse it.

Leaders can pair Cynefin with vertical development, ensuring that they have both the external map to navigate complexity and the internal capacity to adapt and lead effectively. While Cynefin helps leaders diagnose the nature of challenges, vertical development determines their ability to respond—moving from rigid, rule-based approaches in Clear and Complicated contexts to adaptive, sensemaking strategies in Complex and Chaotic environments. By cultivating higher-order thinking, emotional resilience, and systems awareness, leaders can evolve beyond reactive decision-making and embrace the transformative leadership required in today's dynamic world. In this way, the journey of vertical development is not separate from Cynefin—it is what enables leaders to move fluidly across its domains, shifting perspectives and strategies as complexity demands.

The Cynefin framework is one of several established and emerging theories that can coexist alongside VLD to enrich our understanding of leadership in complex environments. While Cynefin provides a valuable lens for diagnosing external challenges, it serves as an illustrative example rather than a competing model. Alongside other frameworks such as adaptive leadership and complexity science, it highlights that the internal growth fostered through VLD remains essential. These complementary approaches underscore that while external analytical tools help map the landscape, the transformative journey of vertical development is crucial for cultivating the resilience, adaptability, and systems awareness required to navigate today's dynamic world.

Overview of Book Structure and Purpose

The field of leadership development is in the midst of a significant shift. Traditional approaches, which focused primarily on skill acquisition and role-specific training, no longer provide leaders with the resilience and adaptability they need to thrive in complex, fast-changing environments. Vertical Leadership Development (VLD) addresses this gap, emphasizing transformation over information, and enabling leaders to grow in ways that align with the multifaceted demands of a BANI world. This book aims to guide readers through the theory, practice, and application of VLD, creating a comprehensive framework for cultivating leaders who are prepared to make a lasting impact.

Purpose and Goals of This Book

The primary goal of this book is to provide readers with a deep, actionable understanding of VLD. It not only explains the theory behind developmental stages but also offers practical tools, frameworks, and real-world examples to illustrate how vertical growth occurs in organizational settings. This book is written for leaders, HR professionals, executive coaches, and organizational change agents who are committed to fostering transformational growth, both in themselves and in others.

By moving through each chapter, readers will gain insights into how to design and implement VLD programs within their organizations, learn the key practices that support vertical growth, and understand how to create a culture that sustains continuous development. The ultimate purpose is to equip readers with the knowledge and tools to cultivate leaders who are resilient, adaptable, and capable of navigating the complexities of modern leadership.

Book Structure

This book is organized into eight chapters, with each focusing on a core aspect of VLD:

Chapter 1 Introduction to Vertical Leadership Development (VLD): This chapter introduces VLD as a framework for navigating increasing complexity in leadership. It explores the shift from traditional horizontal development to vertical growth, highlighting how leaders must evolve in response to today's VUCA (Volatile, Uncertain, Complex, Ambiguous) and BANI (Brittle, Anxious, Nonlinear, Incomprehensible) environments. Readers will gain an understanding of why vertical growth is essential for resilience and adaptive leadership and how this book provides a transformational roadmap for leadership development.

Chapter 2 Theoretical Foundations of Vertical Leadership Development: This chapter explores the historical evolution of leadership development theories, leading to the emergence of Vertical Development as a core leadership framework. It introduces systems thinking, interdependence, and collective leadership, positioning collaborative mindsets as the foundation for advanced leadership. Readers will learn why shifting from individual leadership to collective leadership is key to addressing modern organizational complexity.

Chapter 3 Stages of Vertical Leadership Development: Leadership development unfolds through distinct stages of increasing complexity. This chapter introduces the stages model, outlining the journey from dependent (rules and roles), to independent (self-authorship), to interdependent (collaborative and systemic thinking), and ultimately to transformational leadership with global consciousness. Readers will gain insights into how leaders progress through these stages and the developmental challenges they face at each level.

Chapter 4 Assessing Vertical Growth: Assessment is critical to understanding and tracking vertical development. This chapter examines key developmental assessment tools, including their benefits and challenges, while exploring how technology is expanding access to leadership assessments. It also presents strategies for assessing vertical development at the individual and organizational levels, ensuring that leaders can measure and apply insights to their growth journey.

Chapter 5 Turning Up the Temperature With Heat Experiences: True leadership transformation occurs through heat experiences—intense challenges that push leaders beyond their comfort zones. This chapter explores what defines a heat experience, its role in disrupting habitual thinking, and how it accelerates vertical growth. It provides practical strategies for individuals and organizations to intentionally create and embrace these experiences, ensuring that they are leveraged as catalysts for transformation.

Chapter 6 Perspectives—Expanding Worldviews for Vertical Growth: Colliding perspectives are crucial for breaking out of cognitive echo chambers and fostering growth. This chapter explores how exposure to diverse viewpoints challenges leaders' existing assumptions, accelerating their ability to think more broadly and integrate complexity. Readers will gain tools for creating and embracing these perspective collisions, using them as fuel for deeper learning, adaptability, and leadership transformation.

Chapter 7 Elevated Sensemaking: As leaders move through vertical stages, sensemaking becomes a critical skill for navigating uncertainty and ambiguity. This chapter explores how leaders at different stages interpret complexity, the key characteristics of elevated sensemaking, and practical strategies for fostering this skill. Readers will learn how to integrate diverse perspectives, identify hidden patterns, and make more informed, adaptive decisions in an ever-changing landscape.

Chapter 8 Overcoming the Challenges and Criticisms of Vertical Development: Despite its transformative potential, Vertical Development faces resistance at both individual and organizational levels. This chapter addresses common critiques, including Snowden's challenges to the model, fear of change, and corporate inertia. Readers will gain strategies for overcoming misconceptions, embedding vertical growth into organizational culture, and ensuring sustainable long-term development through partnerships and communities of practice.

Chapter 9 The Future of Vertical Development and Its Evolving Role in Leadership: As leadership challenges continue to evolve, so too must Vertical Development frameworks. This chapter explores emerging trends, technological innovations, and the impact of globalization and remote work on leadership growth. It presents recommendations for the future of Vertical Development programs and reinforces the idea of lifelong leadership transformation as a journey of continuous learning and impact.

How to Use This Book

Each chapter is designed to build upon the previous one, offering both academic insight and practical guidance. Readers are encouraged to take an active approach, engaging in reflective exercises and applying the tools introduced in each section to their own leadership contexts. Whether you are a leader looking to grow personally, an HR professional developing leadership programs, or a coach guiding others through vertical growth, this book provides a comprehensive roadmap for understanding and applying VLD principles.

As we move forward, remember that vertical development is not a one-time process but a continuous journey. This book will equip you with the frameworks and strategies to support this journey, helping you and your organization cultivate leaders who are prepared to make thoughtful, transformative contributions in an increasingly complex world. In Chapter 2, we will ground these ideas in psychological theory, exploring how adults grow through developmental stages.

References

Cook-Greuter, S. R. (1999). *Postautonomous ego development: A study of its nature and measurement* [Doctoral dissertation, Harvard University].

The Cynefin Co. (2024). *Stairways to heaven*. The Cynefin Company. https://thecynefin.co/stairways-to-heaven/

Erikson, E. H. (1980). *Identity and the life cycle*. W. W. Norton & Company (Original work published 1959).

Kegan, R. (1982). *The evolving self: Problem and process in human development*. Harvard University Press.

Kegan, R. (1994). *In over our heads: The mental demands of modern life*. Harvard University Press.

Olkowicz, J. U., Jarosik-Michalak, A., & Kozłowski, A. (2024). The role of a leader in shaping employee behaviour in the VUCA/BANI world. *Journal of Management Studies*, *56*(2), 503–534. https://doi.org/10.13166/jms/188913

Petrie, N. (2018). *Lessons in vertical leadership development*. https://dragonfly-recorder-nty9.squarespace.com/s/Lessons-in-Vertical-Leadership-Development_Nick-Petrie.pdf.

Piaget, J. (1971). The theory of stages in cognitive development. In D. R. Green, M. P. Ford, & G. B. Flamer (Eds.), *Measurement and Piaget* (pp. 1–11). McGraw-Hill.

Shavkun, I., & Dybchinska, Y. (2020). Vertical leadership development: Problems of conceptualization and implementation. *Management and Entrepreneurship: Trends of Development*, *1*(11), 67–80. https://doi.org/10.26661/2522-1566/2020-1/11-05

Snowden, D. J., & Boone, M. E. (2007). A leader's framework for decision making. *Harvard Business Review*, *85*(11), 68–76.

Torbert, William R. (2005). Seven Transformations of Leadership. *Harvard Business Review*, *83*(4), 66–76.

Chapter 2

Theoretical Foundations of Vertical Leadership Development

Historical Perspectives on Leadership Development Theories

Now that we've introduced what vertical development is and why it matters (Chapter 1); we turn to the theories that underpin these concepts. The concept of vertical development in leadership is rooted in psychological theories that date back to the early 20th century. These theories explore how individuals grow through increasingly complex stages of cognitive, emotional, and interpersonal capacity (Day, 2000). By understanding this progression, leaders gain insights into how they can develop the internal capabilities necessary to address the complex challenges of modern organizational life.

Early Foundations: Cognitive Development in Children and Adolescents

One of the earliest contributions to the study of developmental growth came from Swiss psychologist Jean Piaget, who, in the 1930s, introduced his Piaget's model focused primarily on children, detailing how they progress through distinct cognitive stages, each enabling more complex forms of thought (Piaget, 1971). His work laid the foundation for understanding development as a staged process, with each stage representing a new level of maturity in perception and reasoning.

Piaget's model, though focused on childhood, established a key insight: development occurs in structured stages, and each stage builds on the previous one. This concept of structured progression provided a framework that later theorists adapted to study adult development. It introduced the idea that cognitive abilities could evolve over time, becoming increasingly sophisticated as individuals encounter and adapt to more complex life situations. In the context of leadership, this staged model of growth suggests that leaders, too, can develop through progressive levels of thinking, with each level equipping them to handle higher-order challenges (Piaget, 1971).

DOI: 10.4324/9781003644941-2

Table 2.1 Piaget's Stages of Cognitive Development

Piaget's Stage	*Age Range*	*What Happens at This Stage?*
Sensorimotor	0–2 years old	Coordination of senses with motor responses, strong curiosity about the world, language used for demands and categorizing, and emergence of object permanence
Preoperational	2–7 years old	Symbolic thinking develops. Children use more sophisticated language and imagination, but abstract thinking is still limited. They rely heavily on intuition rather than logical reasoning
Concrete Operational	7–11 years old	Concepts become attached to concrete situations. Children begin to understand time, space, and quantity more logically, though these ideas are applied mainly to tangible or familiar contexts
Formal Operational	11 years and older	Theoretical, hypothetical, and counterfactual thinking emerge. Abstract logic and reasoning are possible, and individuals can transfer concepts from one context to another

Extending Development to Adulthood: Erikson's Psychosocial Model

Building on the idea of developmental stages, psychologist Erik Erikson expanded Piaget's framework by focusing on psychosocial development throughout life. Introduced in the 1950s, Erikson's model emphasized that growth continues well into adulthood, with each life stage involving a specific psychosocial challenge or "crisis" that individuals must confront. Erikson's work was pioneering in showing that development does not stop at adolescence; rather, adults encounter different stages that shape their personality, values, and capacity to engage with the world (Erikson, 1980).

Erikson's contributions provided a critical foundation for understanding how leaders, as adults, face challenges that shape their development. His

Table 2.2 Erikson's Stages of Psychosocial Development

Approximate Age	*Psychosocial Crisis/Task*	*Virtue Developed*
Infant–18 months	Trust vs. mistrust	Hope
18 months–3 years	Autonomy vs. shame/doubt	Will
3–5 years	Initiative vs. guilt	Purpose
5–13 years	Industry vs. inferiority	Competency
13–21 years	Identity vs. confusion	Fidelity
21–39 years	Intimacy vs. isolation	Love
40–65 years	Generativity vs. stagnation	Care
65 years and older	Integrity vs. despair	Wisdom

model suggested that each stage requires resolving a fundamental conflict (e.g., autonomy vs. shame, integrity vs. despair), and the way individuals address these conflicts shapes their maturity and interpersonal effectiveness. For leadership development, Erikson's theory underscores the role of life experiences in shaping a leader's ability to understand, influence, and motivate others, suggesting that each stage in a leader's life journey adds layers of complexity to their worldview (Erikson, 1980).

Moral and Ethical Development: Lawrence Kohlberg's Stages of Moral Reasoning

In the 1970s and 1980s, Lawrence Kohlberg built upon Piaget's work, extending developmental theory into the moral domain. Kohlberg's theory of moral development outlined stages of moral reasoning, showing how individuals progress from basic, self-interested forms of morality to more principled, justice-oriented thinking (Kohlberg, 1981). His work emphasized that moral reasoning evolves in a staged sequence, with each stage representing a more comprehensive understanding of ethical principles and the impact of one's actions on others.

Kohlberg's model has implications for leadership, particularly in how leaders approach ethical dilemmas and balance competing interests. Leaders operating from higher stages of moral development are better equipped to consider the broader social and ethical implications of their decisions (Kohlberg, 1981). They can navigate morally complex situations with a greater sense of responsibility and equity, which is increasingly critical in organizations that prioritize ethical leadership and social responsibility. Kohlberg's model aligns with vertical development's emphasis on growth in values and ethics, suggesting that advanced stages of leadership maturity involve a more nuanced, morally sophisticated understanding of one's role.

Table 2.3 Kohlberg's Stages of Moral Reasoning

Level/Stage	*Age Range*	*Description*
I: Obedience/Punishment	Infancy	No difference between doing the right thing and avoiding punishment
II: Self-Interest	Pre-school	Interest shifts to rewards rather than punishment; effort is made to secure the greatest benefit for oneself
III: Conformity and Interpersonal Accord	School age	The "good boy/girl" level; effort is made to secure approval and maintain friendly relations with others
IV: Authority and Social Order	School age	Orientation toward fixed rules; the purpose of morality is maintaining social order; interpersonal accord expands to the entire society
V: Social Contract	Teens	Mutual benefit, reciprocity; morally right and legally right are not always the same; utilitarian rules make life better for everyone
VI: Universal Principles	Adulthood	Morality is based on principles that transcend mutual benefit

Shifting From Information to Transformation: A Developmental Perspective

These foundational theories laid the groundwork for what would become the constructive-developmental view of adult growth, a perspective popularized by developmental psychologist Robert Kegan in the 1980s. Kegan's Subject-Object Theory represents a pivotal shift from cognitive and moral development to a holistic framework that considers how adults make meaning of their experiences. According to Kegan, development involves moving from being "subject" to certain beliefs and assumptions—meaning one is embedded in them—to making these beliefs and assumptions "object," or something that one can reflect upon and modify.

Kegan's theory underscores a key principle of vertical development: the capacity to question and reframe one's own beliefs, values, and assumptions. Leaders who advance through Kegan's stages move from being shaped by external expectations (the "socialized mind") to creating and following their own beliefs (the "self-authoring mind"). In the most advanced stages, leaders adopt a "self-transforming mind," where they see themselves as part of a larger, interdependent system and embrace multiple perspectives. This transformative approach to development, focused on reshaping how leaders interpret their experiences, lies at the core of Vertical Leadership Development (VLD).

Laying the Foundation for Vertical Leadership Development

These early theories in cognitive, psychosocial, moral, and constructive-developmental psychology form the backbone of VLD, illustrating how leaders can evolve through progressive stages of maturity and perspective-taking. As leaders advance, they become more adept at handling complexity, understanding interconnectedness, and acting with both empathy and strategic foresight. Each of these foundational theories contributes unique insights into how leaders can develop beyond technical competence, growing into roles that require resilience, adaptability, and transformative influence.

In the next section, we will explore Robert Kegan's Subject-Object Theory in greater detail, examining how this model specifically informs the stages of vertical growth that define leadership maturity. By understanding Kegan's framework, we gain insight into the processes through which leaders can move from conventional, externally driven mindsets to self-transforming perspectives that empower them to thrive in complex, unpredictable environments.

Adult Development and Constructive-Developmental Psychology

One of the most influential frameworks within the realm of adult development theory is Robert Kegan's Subject-Object Theory. Developed in the 1980s, this theory provides a foundational understanding of how adults grow through increasingly complex stages of sensemaking and self-awareness. Unlike models focused solely on cognitive or moral growth, Kegan's framework explores the transformative process by which individuals shift their perspectives—moving from being deeply embedded in their assumptions to viewing them as objects that can be examined and revised. In the context of Vertical Leadership Development (VLD), Kegan's model offers invaluable insights into how leaders can progress through developmental stages that enhance their capacity to navigate complexity, lead authentically, and foster organizational resilience (Kegan, 1982).

Kegan's Subject-Object Theory: A Transformational Approach to Growth

Kegan's theory suggests that adult development is characterized by a progressive shift in how people understand themselves and the world around them. At each stage, individuals move from being "subject" to their assumptions—taking them for granted—to treating those assumptions as "object," which allows for critical reflection and the integration of more complex perspectives (Kegan, 1982). In leadership, this process supports the evolution from reactive, self-focused mindsets toward more expansive, systemic thinking that enables leaders to engage effectively with ambiguity and diversity.

Kegan's Subject-Object Theory describes five orders of consciousness, or stages, through which individuals evolve in their cognitive, emotional, and relational capacities. At each stage, what was previously experienced subjectively ("Subject," meaning unquestioned assumptions or ways of seeing the world) shifts to something that can be viewed objectively ("Object," meaning something one can reflect upon, question, and intentionally change). In the First Order (Impulsive Mind), individuals are entirely subject to their immediate impulses, unable yet to reflect upon their impulses objectively. Moving to the Second Order (Instrumental Mind), individuals can now reflect upon impulses but remain subject to their own needs and desires, acting primarily from self-interest. At the Third Order (Socialized Mind), individuals become capable of reflecting upon personal desires, but their sense of self remains subject to external relationships, roles, and societal expectations. Progressing to the Fourth Order (Self-Authoring Mind), they develop the ability to critically reflect on these external influences and create an internal framework of self-defined values, beliefs, and goals. Finally, at the Fifth Order (Self-Transforming Mind), even one's internal framework becomes object, allowing leaders to reflect continuously on their own perspectives, embrace ambiguity, and integrate multiple, even contradictory viewpoints in their thinking and actions.

Implications for Vertical Leadership Development

The progression from external validation to self-transformation is critical for leadership in complex environments. Leaders who remain attached to their existing assumptions may struggle to respond flexibly to new challenges. By developing the ability to observe and question their beliefs, they gain the capacity to integrate new insights, adapt to changing circumstances, and make decisions that reflect a broader understanding of interconnected systems.

Table 2.4 Kegan's Subject-Object Theory Stages

Order	*Stage Name*	*Subject (Cannot See or Reflect Upon)*	*Object (Can Reflect Upon)*	*Characteristics*
First	**Impulsive mind**	Immediate impulses, perceptions, sensations	None	Driven entirely by impulses and immediate experiences; no reflection or awareness of consequences
Second	**Instrumental mind** (*self-centered stage*)	Personal needs, wants, and immediate desires	Immediate impulses, sensations	Behaviors driven by self-interest; sees relationships transactionally ("What's in it for me?")
Third	**Socialized mind**	External expectations, relationships, social roles	Personal needs, desires, and immediate goals	Seeks approval; identity shaped by group norms and expectations; struggles with conflict or criticism
Fourth	**Self-authoring mind**	Internal values, beliefs, self-defined identity	External expectations, relationships, social roles	Operates from internal standards and principles; can critically assess external pressures; capable of autonomous decision-making and accountability
Fifth	**Self-transforming mind**	Ongoing transformation, interdependence, and dynamic systems	Own internal framework (values, beliefs, worldview)	Holds multiple perspectives simultaneously; comfortable with paradox, ambiguity, and self-reflection; transcends personal and organizational boundaries

Vertical development practices—such as reflective exercises, mentorship, and exposure to diverse perspectives—are designed to support these shifts. As leaders move from a socialized mindset toward self-authoring and, eventually, a self-transforming mindset, they become better equipped to align their actions with both personal values and long-term organizational objectives.

Tolbert's Action Logics and the Bridge to Practice

Complementing Kegan's framework, Bill Tolbert's Action Logics translate these abstract developmental stages into observable leadership behaviors. Tolbert's model categorizes leadership mindsets—from early-stage Diplomat or Expert mindsets to more advanced Achiever, Strategist, and Alchemist mindsets—illustrating how leaders evolve from reactive problem-solving to strategic, systems-oriented thinking (Tolbert & Rooke, 2005). This framework provides a practical roadmap for recognizing and fostering developmental growth in real-world leadership contexts.

Table 2.5 Torbert's Action Logics

Action Logic	*Primary Mindset/ Focus*	*Characteristic Leadership Behaviors*	*Potential Limitations*
Opportunist	Self-centered, immediate gains	Seeks quick wins and personal advantage Reacts impulsively Views others mainly as obstacles or opportunities	May break rules or norms Tends to ignore longer-term impacts Limited trust from others
Diplomat	Social approval, harmony	Strives to fit in and avoid conflict Maintains positive relationships Often defers to authority	Avoids tough decisions or dissent May not challenge the status quo Limited strategic focus
Expert	Technical competence, expertise	Focuses on precision and correctness Solves problems by applying specialized knowledge Relies on logic and facts	May struggle with ambiguity or interpersonal complexity Tends to undervalue collaboration

(Continued)

Table 2.5 (Continued)

Action Logic	*Primary Mindset/ Focus*	*Characteristic Leadership Behaviors*	*Potential Limitations*
Achiever	Goal-oriented, results-driven	Sets ambitious targets and measures success Uses project management and strategic planning Emphasizes efficiency	May focus too narrowly on metrics Risks overlooking systemic issues Can be impatient with slower processes
Individualist	Self-awareness, exploring multiple viewpoints	Questions own assumptions Welcomes diverse perspectives Adapts style to different contexts	Can appear inconsistent to others May challenge norms in ways that unsettle the organization
Strategist	Systems thinking, transformative leadership	Integrates short-term and long-term objectives Seeks to align diverse stakeholder interests Fosters culture of learning	Efforts can be slowed by complexity May become frustrated with less advanced peers
Alchemist	Global, ethical, and systemic transformation	Inspires profound change across multiple systems Integrates contradictory viewpoints fluidly Embodies high moral purpose	Rarely encountered in practice Can seem enigmatic or distant Challenging to sustain momentum without broad support

These theories provide the foundation for understanding the leadership maturity stages we'll explore in Chapter 3.

Cognitive and Emotional Complexity in Leadership

In the journey of VLD, cognitive and emotional complexity play crucial roles. As leaders advance through the stages of development, they cultivate the capacity to think in increasingly complex ways while managing emotions with greater resilience and empathy. Together, these dimensions enable leaders to understand intricate systems, navigate uncertainty, and build strong, supportive relationships. Understanding how cognitive and emotional complexity contribute to vertical growth provides insight into why certain leaders are better equipped to handle high-stakes, complex situations and inspires a roadmap for fostering these capacities.

Cognitive Complexity: Expanding How Leaders Think

Cognitive complexity refers to the ability to perceive and process information in sophisticated ways, integrating diverse perspectives and understanding nuanced relationships. Leaders with high cognitive complexity can think across multiple dimensions, consider various possibilities, and recognize patterns in ambiguity. They are less likely to see situations in binary terms and are more capable of embracing "both/and" rather than "either/or" thinking.

At earlier stages of cognitive complexity, leaders may view problems as straightforward and solutions as fixed. They may focus on immediate outcomes without considering the broader implications of their actions. However, as leaders grow vertically, they begin to see issues as interconnected and multidimensional. They realize that decisions often have ripple effects across different areas of the organization and require a balanced approach that considers various stakeholders.

Vertical development programs often encourage cognitive complexity by exposing leaders to diverse viewpoints, challenging them to reflect on their assumptions, and fostering systems thinking. Leaders who think systemically are able to recognize that the elements of an organization—people, processes, policies—are interrelated, and a change in one area can influence the entire system. This understanding enables leaders to make informed decisions that consider both short-term and long-term impacts, fostering organizational resilience and alignment.

Emotional Complexity: Developing Resilience and Empathy

While cognitive complexity expands what leaders can think, emotional complexity deepens how leaders feel and respond. Leaders with emotional complexity have a heightened ability to manage their own emotions, understand the emotions of others, and navigate interpersonal challenges with empathy and composure. This capacity is essential in high-stress environments, where leaders frequently encounter uncertainty, conflicting demands, and potential conflicts.

In early stages of emotional development, leaders may react impulsively to stress or conflict, interpreting situations in a self-centered way. They may struggle with feedback, seeing it as criticism rather than an opportunity for growth. However, as they advance, they develop emotional resilience—the ability to remain calm and composed in challenging situations. They also become more empathetic, recognizing the perspectives and feelings of others, which allows them to lead with compassion and build trust.

Empathy is particularly critical in leadership, as it enables leaders to connect with diverse team members, understand their needs, and foster an inclusive environment. Leaders with high emotional complexity not only are capable of managing their own responses but can also encourage emotional growth in others by modeling open communication, active listening, and supportive engagement. This emotional maturity contributes to a positive organizational culture where individuals feel valued, motivated, and aligned with shared goals.

The Interplay Between Cognitive and Emotional Complexity

In effective leadership, cognitive and emotional complexity are deeply interconnected. Leaders who can think in complex ways but lack emotional depth may struggle to connect with their teams or to inspire trust. Conversely, leaders who are emotionally aware but limited in cognitive complexity may be supportive but may not possess the strategic insight needed for high-level decision-making. Vertical development nurtures both dimensions, enabling leaders to navigate complex situations with clear, strategic thinking and to do so in a way that respects and elevates others.

Nick Petrie's research highlights that in VUCA (volatile, uncertain, complex, ambiguous) and now BANI (brittle, anxious, nonlinear, and Incomprehensible) environments as discussed in Chapter 1, leaders who thrive are those who combine these qualities: they can make sense of complex information while simultaneously building strong relationships and supporting their team's emotional well-being. For instance, in times of organizational change, leaders must not only understand the strategic implications but also empathize with team members who may feel uncertain or anxious. Leaders with developed cognitive and emotional complexity can address these concerns effectively, guiding their teams through transition with both clarity and compassion.

Fostering Complexity in Leadership Development

Organizations that aim to cultivate vertical development can support cognitive and emotional complexity through specific practices and program structures. For cognitive growth, programs may include complex problem-solving exercises, exposure to diverse perspectives, and training in systems thinking. Leaders might work on interdisciplinary projects that require them to step out of their comfort zones and address problems from multiple angles.

For emotional development, programs often incorporate feedback loops, coaching, and reflective exercises. Feedback, especially 360-degree feedback, allows leaders to see themselves through the eyes of others and identify areas for growth in their interpersonal approach. Coaching sessions provide a safe space for leaders to discuss challenges and receive guidance on managing their emotions, deepening self-awareness and resilience. Reflective practices, such as journaling or mindfulness exercises, can further help leaders understand and regulate their emotional responses, fostering a balanced and grounded approach to leadership.

The Foundation of Resilient, Adaptive Leadership

Cognitive and emotional complexity are fundamental to VLD, enhancing leaders' capacity to interpret and respond to complex challenges thoughtfully and empathetically. By cultivating both, leaders can navigate ambiguity with insight, inspire trust and engagement, and contribute to a resilient organizational culture. As we continue to explore the theoretical foundations of VLD, these dimensions will remain central, guiding leaders through stages of growth that prepare them for the complexities of today's organizations.

In the following section, we will explore how systems thinking and an awareness of interdependence play a critical role in vertical development, enabling leaders to approach challenges with a broad, interconnected perspective.

Systems Thinking and Vertical Development

As leaders progress through stages of vertical development, they increasingly recognize the interconnected nature of their roles, decisions, and the broader organizational environment. Systems thinking—the ability to see relationships and patterns within complex systems—becomes a defining feature of effective leadership at advanced stages. This approach allows leaders to identify not only isolated challenges but also the underlying structures, relationships, and dynamics that drive organizational behavior. By adopting a systems-oriented perspective, leaders move beyond narrow, role-specific thinking and begin to address challenges holistically, creating sustainable solutions and fostering an adaptive organizational culture.

What Is Systems Thinking?

Systems thinking is an approach to problem-solving that views challenges as part of a larger, interdependent network rather than as isolated events.

Leaders who think systemically understand that changes in one part of the organization can have ripple effects across other areas. For example, a decision to implement a new technology might initially appear to be a straightforward technical upgrade, but leaders who use systems thinking recognize that this change will also impact workflows, employee roles, and even the organization's culture (Senge, 1990). Systems thinking encourages leaders to consider these interconnected elements, predict potential side effects, and manage outcomes more effectively.

In the context of VLD, systems thinking is not merely a skill; it represents a transformative way of perceiving the organization that emerges as leaders grow in cognitive complexity. Leaders at advanced developmental stages tend to adopt a holistic view, considering both the visible and invisible connections that shape organizational life. They understand that lasting change requires addressing not only the symptoms of problems but also their root causes, which are often embedded in the organization's structure and processes.

Expanding to Ecosystems Thinking

Building upon traditional systems thinking, many contemporary leaders are now embracing ecosystems thinking. This approach expands the focus beyond the boundaries of the organization to include the external environment—such as economic, social, environmental, and technological systems. Ecosystems thinking recognizes that organizations are part of larger, dynamic networks where external forces—from global supply chains and environmental sustainability to community relationships and regulatory landscapes—play a significant role in shaping organizational outcomes (Meadows, 2008).

Ecosystems thinking challenges leaders to consider how their decisions affect both internal operations and external stakeholders. For instance, when a company decides to adopt a new manufacturing process, ecosystems thinking encourages leaders to evaluate the environmental implications, potential community impacts, and long-term sustainability of that decision. Leaders who incorporate this broader perspective are better equipped to foster resilience and innovation, ensuring that the organization not only thrives internally but also contributes positively to its external context.

Integrating Systems and Ecosystems Thinking

Integrating systems thinking with ecosystems thinking provides leaders with a comprehensive toolkit for addressing both internal and external complexities. This integration requires a mindset shift—leaders must see their organization as both a self-contained system and part of a wider, interconnected ecosystem. By doing so, they are able to:

- **Identify Cross-Domain Interactions:**

  Leaders become adept at spotting connections between internal processes and external trends. For example, they may recognize that shifts in consumer behavior driven by environmental awareness can influence product design, supply chain management, and marketing strategies.

- **Anticipate Ripple Effects:**

  Understanding that decisions made within the organization can have far-reaching consequences in the external environment enables leaders to anticipate and mitigate negative impacts while capitalizing on opportunities. This might involve implementing sustainable practices that not only reduce costs but also enhance brand reputation and stakeholder trust (Senge et al., 2015).

- **Foster Collaborative Networks:**

  Ecosystems thinking promotes a collaborative approach where organizations engage with partners, communities, and even competitors to address systemic challenges. Such networks can drive innovation and shared solutions to common issues like climate change or technological disruption.

- **Enhance Adaptive Capacity:**

  Leaders who view their organization as part of a larger ecosystem are better positioned to respond to external shocks. This broader perspective helps in crafting strategies that are flexible and adaptive, ensuring the organization can sustain growth in a rapidly changing world.

Recent studies underscore the importance of integrating ecosystems thinking into leadership. Research by Senge et al. (2015) emphasizes that leaders who adopt both systems and ecosystems perspectives are more effective in driving sustainable innovation and achieving long-term competitive advantage. These leaders not only improve internal efficiencies but also build resilient networks that can withstand external uncertainties (Senge et al., 2015).

Practical Implications of Systems and Ecosystems Thinking

For practitioners, integrating systems and ecosystems thinking into VLD translates into several actionable strategies:

1. **Conduct Holistic Impact Assessments:**

   Evaluate decisions not only on immediate internal benefits but also on potential external impacts. Use tools like stakeholder mapping and environmental impact assessments to capture a broad range of effects.

2. **Develop Cross-Functional and Cross-Sector Collaboration:**

   Create initiatives that bring together leaders from different departments, as well as external partners such as suppliers, community representatives, and regulatory bodies. This collaborative approach helps develop a more comprehensive view of challenges and opportunities.

3. **Implement Scenario Planning:**

   Use scenario planning exercises to simulate both internal system changes and external environmental shifts. These exercises help leaders prepare for diverse futures and reinforce the importance of adaptability.

4. **Embed Sustainability into Strategy:**

   Integrate sustainability and social responsibility into the core strategic framework of the organization. Encourage leaders to consider long-term environmental and social outcomes as critical components of business success.

5. **Leverage Technology for Integrated Insights:**

   Utilize advanced analytics and digital tools to monitor both internal processes and external trends. Data-driven insights can help leaders identify emerging patterns and make more informed decisions that benefit both the organization and its broader ecosystem.

6. **Create Reflective Learning Opportunities:**

   Incorporate regular reflective practices that prompt leaders to assess how their decisions are affecting both internal systems and external stakeholders. Journaling, debrief sessions, and peer discussions can be instrumental in integrating these complex insights into daily leadership practice.

For example, consider an organization planning to introduce a new product line. A leader using integrated systems and ecosystems thinking would analyze market trends, internal production capabilities, environmental impact, supply chain sustainability, and potential community feedback. This comprehensive approach might lead to adopting greener materials, improved waste management practices, and ultimately, a more sustainable business model.

Enhancing Organizational Culture Through Integrated Thinking

Leaders who embrace both systems and ecosystems thinking can drive cultural change within their organizations. By modeling a comprehensive approach to problem-solving, they can inspire a culture that values collaboration, sustainability, and continuous learning. Such a culture is better equipped to adapt to change, innovate, and create long-term value for all stakeholders. Organizations can support this cultural shift by the following:

- **Promoting Storytelling:**

  Share success stories that illustrate how integrated thinking led to innovative solutions and positive impacts.

- **Facilitating Workshops and Training:**

  Offer training sessions that emphasize the principles of systems and ecosystems thinking.

- **Encouraging a Learning Mindset:**

  Create forums for ongoing dialogue about the interconnected nature of business challenges, fostering an environment where continuous improvement is the norm.

The Role of Interdependence in Vertical Leadership Development

An awareness of interdependence—the understanding that individuals, teams, and departments are interconnected—is central to systems thinking. Leaders who recognize interdependence are better equipped to foster collaboration, resolve conflicts, and align diverse stakeholders around shared goals. In early stages of development, leaders may approach problems with a narrow focus on their immediate goals or the needs of their department. As they progress through vertical development, they begin to see how their work contributes to and depends upon other parts of the organization.

Interdependence also affects how leaders view their relationships with colleagues and team members. Leaders with a strong sense of interdependence understand that individual success is linked to collective success. This mindset allows them to lead in a way that builds bridges between departments, encourages teamwork, and creates an environment where everyone feels responsible for the organization's outcomes. For instance, when addressing a complex issue, such leaders are more likely to seek input from diverse departments, recognizing that other perspectives can offer valuable insights that might not be visible from their own position.

Systems Thinking as a Path to Sustainable Change

One of the most powerful applications of systems thinking in leadership is its capacity to drive sustainable change. Leaders who approach change with a systems-oriented mindset consider how decisions will impact not only the immediate issue but also the organization's long-term health and resilience. For example, when implementing new policies, they analyze how these changes will influence team dynamics, morale, and the organization's adaptability in the face of future challenges. This holistic approach contrasts with more limited, reactive approaches that often result in unintended consequences or require repeated interventions to address the same problem.

A well-known example of systems thinking in leadership comes from the late W. Edwards Deming, whose philosophy of continuous improvement transformed quality management in organizations worldwide. Deming advocated for leaders to focus not on isolated outcomes, such as production targets, but on the entire system that contributes to these outcomes (Deming, 1986). By understanding how each part of the organization influences others, leaders can create processes that support long-term success rather than quick fixes.

Practical Steps for Cultivating Systems Thinking in Leadership

Organizations that aim to develop systems thinkers can do so through intentional practices and developmental opportunities. For instance, exposure to cross-functional teams allows leaders to engage with colleagues from various departments, broadening their understanding of organizational interdependence. When leaders work on projects that span multiple departments, they see firsthand how different functions contribute to a common goal, helping them appreciate the importance of collaboration and shared accountability.

Leadership development programs can also incorporate specific training in systems thinking techniques. Methods such as causal loop diagrams—which map out cause-and-effect relationships within a system—enable leaders to visualize complex interdependencies and anticipate the impacts of their decisions. Workshops on scenario planning, where leaders explore potential future outcomes and their implications, further enhance their ability to think in terms of interconnected systems.

Mentorship from leaders who already embody systems thinking can play a transformative role as well. Experienced leaders can model how to identify and address root causes of problems, guiding mentees to consider how their actions influence the organization as a whole. This guidance helps emerging leaders practice seeing the "big picture" and encourages them to approach issues with a mindset that values sustainable, long-term solutions.

Systems Thinking as a Hallmark of Advanced Leadership

In VLD, systems thinking represents a significant shift from task-oriented management to strategic, interconnected leadership. Leaders who develop this capacity make decisions that honor the complexity of their organizations, recognizing that every action influences a broader system. This perspective enables leaders to drive change in ways that are not only effective in the short-term but also beneficial for long-term resilience and adaptability. By fostering systems thinking, organizations empower leaders to understand their roles within a larger context, leading to more thoughtful, impactful decisions.

This shift toward an interconnected view of leadership is essential as organizations face complex, global challenges that demand holistic solutions. When combined with ecosystems thinking—where external environmental factors are also considered—leaders are better prepared to innovate, collaborate, and create adaptive organizational cultures that thrive in today's rapidly changing world.

Collaborative Mindsets and Collective Leadership

As leaders advance through vertical development, they gain a deeper appreciation for collaboration and shared purpose. The ability to lead collectively, rather than solely from an individualistic perspective, becomes a hallmark of advanced leadership maturity. Leaders who embrace collective leadership understand that their role is not only to make decisions but also to foster an environment where diverse perspectives, skills, and contributions can flourish. This approach, which integrates the principles of systems thinking and interdependence, creates a foundation for adaptive, resilient organizations equipped to meet complex challenges through a unified, inclusive approach.

From Individual Contribution to Collective Empowerment

Early in their development, leaders often approach leadership as an individual endeavor. They may focus on setting personal goals, achieving targets, and gaining recognition for their contributions. This approach is effective for certain roles but can create limitations as leaders encounter increasingly complex situations that require collaboration across departments, functions, or even geographical regions.

As they progress through vertical development, leaders shift from an individualistic mindset to one that values collective input and shared responsibility. They begin to see leadership as a process of empowering others, building on diverse strengths to create a cohesive, adaptable organization. This shift is particularly relevant in today's interconnected world, where the speed and scale of change require leaders to think beyond their personal objectives and consider how to foster collective success.

Leaders with collaborative mindsets actively seek out diverse perspectives, understanding that innovation and effective problem-solving often emerge from the interplay of different ideas. They create environments where team members feel safe to share insights, experiment with new approaches, and contribute to shared goals. In this way, collaborative leaders enhance the organization's adaptability and resilience, positioning it to respond effectively to both opportunities and challenges.

Creating a Culture of Collective Leadership

The principles of collective leadership extend beyond the actions of individual leaders; they shape the culture of the organization itself. Organizations that prioritize collective leadership encourage shared accountability and align individual and team efforts with the organization's mission and values. This culture of collaboration fosters a sense of ownership and purpose across all levels, empowering employees to act with initiative and responsibility.

In practice, collective leadership means that leadership roles and responsibilities are distributed rather than centralized. Leaders work not only as decision-makers but also as facilitators, guiding team members to take ownership of their tasks and supporting them in their development. In such organizations, authority is flexible and dynamic, with leaders stepping forward as needed while also allowing others to lead when their expertise or perspective is most relevant.

Collective leadership is particularly valuable in organizations that operate in complex, unpredictable environments. By distributing leadership, these organizations ensure that they can respond quickly to changes, with multiple leaders who are capable of making informed, contextually aware decisions. This adaptability is essential for organizations facing global, multifaceted challenges where a single leader's perspective is often insufficient.

Building Collaborative Skills in Leadership Development

To cultivate collective leadership, organizations must focus on developing collaborative skills and mindsets within their leadership programs. VLD often includes experiential learning opportunities where leaders practice working in teams, taking on different roles, and building trust across diverse groups. Team-based projects, cross-functional rotations, and group problem-solving exercises are common methods for fostering these collaborative skills.

Feedback and reflection are also crucial in helping leaders adopt a collaborative mindset. Through structured feedback, leaders gain insight into how their behavior affects others and learn to identify areas where they can enhance their approach to collaboration. Reflective exercises, such as journaling or guided self-assessment, help leaders internalize the importance of shared purpose and collective accountability, encouraging them to adopt these values in their everyday interactions.

Mentorship and peer coaching further support the development of collaborative skills. Experienced leaders who already embody a collective mindset can model inclusive decision-making, empathy, and mutual respect for emerging leaders. Peer coaching, where leaders provide support and accountability to one another, reinforces the concept of shared responsibility and demonstrates that leadership is not a solitary journey but a mutual, supportive process.

The Benefits of Collective Leadership for Organizational Success

Organizations that cultivate collective leadership benefit from a workforce that is engaged, resilient, and aligned with shared goals. Collective leadership not only enhances productivity and innovation but also strengthens morale, as employees feel valued and empowered to contribute meaningfully. Leaders who operate from a collaborative mindset create inclusive environments where everyone feels a sense of purpose and connection to the organization's mission.

Furthermore, collective leadership prepares organizations for the complexities of a globalized world, where decisions often require input from multiple areas of expertise and understanding of diverse perspectives. By fostering collective leadership, organizations build a culture of adaptability, equipping themselves to respond effectively to emerging challenges and to harness the full potential of their teams.

Collective Leadership as the Pinnacle of Vertical Development

In VLD, collaborative mindsets and collective leadership represent the pinnacle of advanced leadership maturity. Leaders who embrace collective approaches understand that their role is not only to lead but to create an environment where others can lead as well. This mindset shifts the focus from individual achievement to shared success, creating an organizational culture that values inclusivity, adaptability, and continuous growth.

As we move forward, we will explore the specific stages of vertical development in leadership, examining how leaders progress from early, self-focused stages to the advanced, collaborative mindsets discussed here. Understanding these stages offers a roadmap for organizations seeking to cultivate leaders who are prepared to guide their teams through complexity, inspire collective resilience, and contribute to long-term organizational success. With these developmental models in mind, Chapter 3 will translate theory into practice by mapping out the distinct stages of vertical leadership growth.

References

Day, D. V. (2000). Leadership development: A review in context. *The Leadership Quarterly*, *11*(4), 581–613. https://doi.org/10.1016/S1048-9843(00)00061-8

Deming, W. E. (1986). *Out of the crisis*. MIT Center for Advanced Educational Services.

Erikson, E. H. (1980). *Identity and the life cycle*. W. W. Norton & Company (Original work published 1959).

Kegan, R. (1982). *The evolving self: Problem and process in human development*. Harvard University Press.

Kohlberg, L. (1981). *Essays on moral development, Vol. I: The philosophy of moral development*. Harper & Row.

Meadows, D. H. (2008). *Thinking in systems: A primer*. Chelsea Green Publishing.

Piaget, J. (1971). The theory of stages in cognitive development. In D. R. Green, M. P. Ford & G. B. Flamer (Eds.), *Measurement and Piaget* (pp. 1–11). McGraw-Hill.

Senge, P. M. (1990). *The fifth discipline: The art and practice of the learning organization*. Doubleday.

Senge, P. M., Smith, B., Kruschwitz, N., Laur, J., & Schley, C. (2015). *The necessary revolution: How individuals and organizations are working together to create a sustainable world*. Doubleday.

Tolbert, W. R., & Rooke, D. (2005). Seven transformations of leadership. *Harvard Business Review*, *83*(4), 66–76.

Chapter 3

Stages of Vertical Leadership Development

Introducing the Stages Model of Vertical Leadership Development

In today's rapidly evolving global environment, leadership is no longer solely about possessing a set of technical or interpersonal skills. Instead, true leadership transformation requires an evolution in the way leaders think, feel, and act—an evolution that enables them to navigate complex challenges, engage diverse stakeholders, and drive systemic change. Vertical Leadership Development (VLD) offers a compelling framework for this transformative process, emphasizing a progressive journey of internal growth. Unlike horizontal development, which adds skills and competencies incrementally, vertical development transforms a leader's mindset, allowing them to see beyond immediate tasks and adopt a more adaptive, reflective, and integrative approach.

In an era characterized by VUCA (volatility, uncertainty, complexity, ambiguity) and BANI (brittle, anxious, nonlinear, incomprehensible), traditional skill-based training methods often fall short. Globalization and digital disruption further amplify the need for leaders to develop more adaptive mindsets. Leaders who remain confined to a fixed set of behaviors or narrow thinking patterns struggle to meet the multifaceted challenges of modern organizations. In contrast, those who develop vertically gain the capacity to interpret their experiences in new ways, challenge their assumptions, and ultimately lead with a vision that aligns with the complex realities of the 21st century.

This chapter introduces the stages model of leadership development—a framework that describes how leaders evolve through increasingly sophisticated levels of cognitive, emotional, and relational complexity. At its heart lies the work of Bill Torbert (introduced in Chapter 2), whose Action Logics model provides a practical roadmap to understand how leaders interpret challenges, make decisions, and interact with others as they progress through various stages. By integrating insights from developmental

DOI: 10.4324/9781003644941-3

psychology with practical leadership models, VLD proposes that as leaders mature, they shift from a self-focused, rule-bound approach to a more globally conscious, systems-aware, and ethically grounded mindset.

In the following pages, we will explore the four major levels of vertical development stages—dependent, independent, interdependent, and systemically transformational. We will discuss how these categories and the correlated Action Logics mindsets reflect changes in a leader's ability to handle complexity, how they influence decision-making, and why these shifts are crucial for organizational success. While later sections will delve into the nuances of each stage and mindset, this first part provides an overview of the overall model and sets the conceptual foundation for understanding the transformative journey that leaders undertake.

The Rationale Behind a Stages Model

Vertical development models propose that leadership growth is not a mere accumulation of skills but a fundamental transformation in how leaders perceive themselves and the world. This transformation is akin to what developmental psychologists have long observed in other domains of human growth. Early theories by Piaget (1971) and Erikson (1980) showed that as individuals mature, their cognitive and psychosocial capacities change qualitatively. Similarly, leaders too undergo a transformation: they begin by operating within the confines of externally imposed rules and expectations, but as they progress, they internalize new ways of thinking that allow them to synthesize diverse perspectives and navigate ambiguity.

Building on these foundations, Bill Torbert's Action Logics model (introduced in Chapter 2) translates abstract developmental concepts into leadership mindsets. Each "Action Logic" represents a specific set of these leadership mindsets—a way of interpreting and interacting with the world that becomes progressively more complex as leaders mature. As we focused on in Chapter 2, leaders initially operate from mindsets that are heavily influenced by external rules and the need for social approval. Over time, as they accumulate experience and self-reflection, they develop the capacity for independent thought, collaborative problem-solving, and ultimately, transformative leadership that transcends traditional boundaries.

This model is particularly useful because it not only explains why leaders behave the way they do at different stages but also offers insights on how to invite developmental leadership shifts. By understanding one's current Action Logics mindset, leaders can identify areas for growth and engage in targeted development activities designed to move them to the next stage and mindset. In essence, the stages model serves as both an indicator and a guiding tool—it indicates where a leader currently stands and guides the stretches needed to advance their leadership capabilities and capacity.

This understanding provides context for the staged model that follows, reinforcing why each leadership stage marks a meaningful shift, not just an incremental step.

Overview of the Four Developmental Stage Levels

The stages model of VLD is typically divided into four primary stage levels: dependent, independent, interdependent, and systemically transformational. Each level represents a distinct way of thinking and operating that builds upon the previous one.

Dependent

At the dependent level, leadership behavior is primarily driven by external structures. Leaders at this level rely heavily on rules, roles, and authority figures. Their actions are guided by the need to conform to established norms and expectations. They tend to be reactive, focusing on immediate tasks and following directives without questioning underlying assumptions. In Torbert's model, early Action Logics mindsets such as the Opportunist and Diplomat are characteristic of this stage level. While these stages provide necessary foundational skills, they also limit a leader's capacity to handle ambiguity and innovate.

Independent

As leaders progress to the independent level stages, they begin to internalize their own set of values and principles. These stages are characterized by self-authorship—the development of an internal compass that guides decision-making. Leaders become more confident in their abilities to solve problems independently and set personal as well as team goals. In Torbert's framework, the Expert and Achiever Action Logics mindsets exemplify this stage level. Leaders start to see beyond external validation and focus on developing their expertise and achieving results, though they may still operate largely from an individualistic perspective.

Interdependent

The interdependent level marks a shift from solitary achievement to collaborative and systems-oriented thinking. Leaders at this level recognize that their success is intertwined with the success of others. They begin to appreciate the value of diverse perspectives and the importance of building cohesive teams. This level is reflected in the Individualist and Strategist

Action Logics mindsets, where leaders embrace relationships, foster team collaboration, and develop a holistic understanding of organizational dynamics. They are better equipped to navigate complex problems that require coordinated efforts across different functions.

Self-Transforming

At the self-transforming level, leaders transcend traditional organizational boundaries. They adopt a globally conscious and ethically driven mindset, prioritizing systemic impact over individual or even organizational gains. These leaders are characterized by a transformative approach that is both integrative and adaptive. In Torbert's model, this level is epitomized by the Alchemist Action Logics mindset. Leaders at this level not only are adept at handling complexity but also inspire profound, long-term change by addressing the deeper, often systemic, challenges facing their organizations and societies. Before examining each stage in depth, we'll look at how Bill Torbert's Action Logics model underpins these stages.

The Role of Torbert's Action Logics Model

Torbert's Action Logics model provides a structured framework that maps the evolution of leadership through these developmental stages. It offers a practical perspective on the theoretical foundations discussed in earlier chapters by categorizing observable behaviors and decision-making styles that correspond with each stage of development. For instance, in the dependent stages, leaders often exhibit behaviors such as rule following and a high reliance on authority. As they progress, their decision-making evolves from reactive to more strategic and collaborative forms. Ultimately, at the self-transforming stage, leaders demonstrate an ability to hold multiple, sometimes contradictory, perspectives simultaneously—a hallmark of advanced cognitive complexity.

Torbert's model is particularly valuable because it connects the dots between theory and practice. It shows that as leaders evolve, their capacity to handle ambiguity, complexity, and change increases dramatically. For instance, a leader at an early Action Logic might struggle to reconcile conflicting feedback, whereas an advanced Action Logic leader can integrate contradictory perspectives into a coherent strategy. This evolution is not just about acquiring more knowledge but about transforming one's entire approach to leadership. As leaders move through these stages and corresponding Action Logics mindsets, they become more capable of creating environments that encourage innovation, resilience, and ethical decision-making.

Linking Developmental Theory With Organizational Practice

Understanding the stages model is essential for designing effective leadership development programs. Organizations that wish to cultivate adaptive, transformational leaders must first recognize that leadership is a developmental process. This means that training programs should be designed not just to impart skills but to facilitate deeper changes in how leaders think and approach challenges. The stages model provides a roadmap for this journey, offering insights into where a leader currently stands and what steps are necessary for growth.

For example, a leader operating in the dependent stages may benefit from developmental assignments that challenge them to make decisions independently and encourage them to reflect on their own values. Similarly, a leader in the independent stages might benefit from stretch opportunities to collaborate across departments, thereby gradually shifting their focus from individual achievement to team-oriented outcomes. As

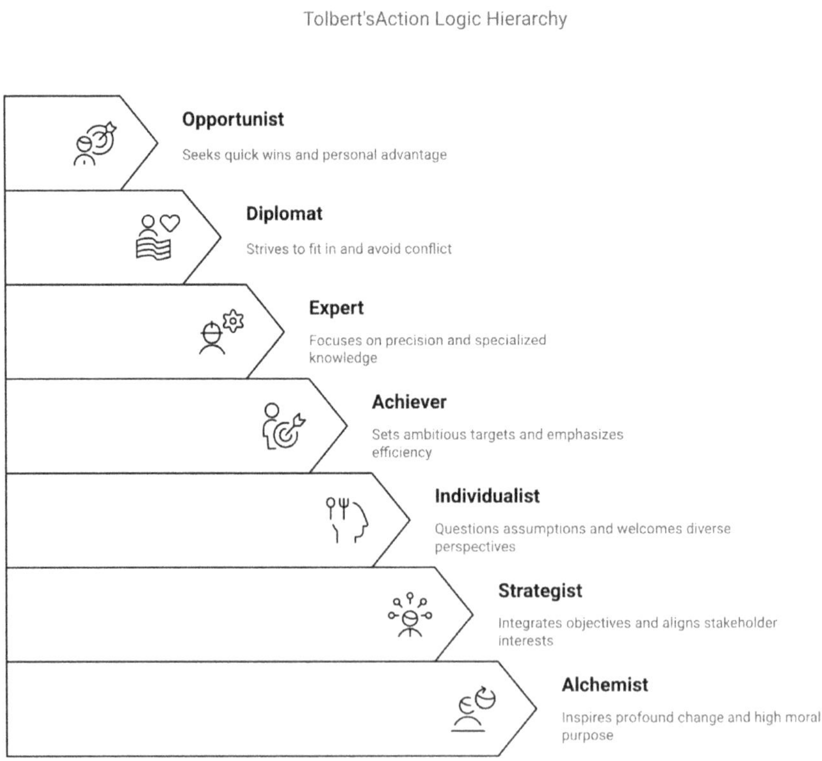

Figure 3.1 Torbert's Action Logics.

leaders progress to higher stages, they require increasingly sophisticated interventions that promote self-awareness, ethical reasoning, and systemic thinking (see Figure 3.1 for a visual representation of Torbert's Action Logics, and Table 3.1 for a summary of each stage and its Action Logic characteristics).

In practice, integrating the stages model into leadership development involves a combination of assessments, coaching, experiential learning, and reflective practices. Tools such as the Leadership Maturity Framework and 360-degree feedback mechanisms can help diagnose a leader's current developmental stage and mindset. These diagnostic tools, when paired with targeted interventions—such as coaching sessions focused on self-reflection or cross-functional team projects—enable organizations to create personalized developmental pathways. Over time, this integrated approach helps build a resilient leadership pipeline capable of navigating the complexities of modern business environments.

Emerging Research and Theoretical Integration

Recent research in leadership development further underscores the importance of vertical growth. Studies have shown that leaders who achieve later developmental stages are more effective at managing complex, uncertain environments. For instance, McCauley et al. (2006) found that leaders with greater cognitive and emotional complexity are better at adaptive decision-making, which in turn leads to improved organizational performance. Similarly, research by Day (2000) indicates that transformational leadership practices are correlated with advanced developmental stages, highlighting the practical benefits of moving beyond rule-bound, reactive behaviors.

These findings support the idea that leadership transformation is not merely a function of increased knowledge or technical expertise but of a fundamental shift in how leaders perceive and engage with their environment. By integrating insights from developmental psychology with practical frameworks like Torbert's Action Logics, organizations can create a more robust model for leadership growth—one that is both theoretically sound and practically relevant.

The stages model of VLD offers a comprehensive framework for understanding how leaders evolve from relying on external validation and rule-based behaviors to developing internal, transformative capacities that enable them to drive systemic change. Through the integration of theoretical insights from developmental psychology and practical frameworks such as Torbert's Action Logics, this model underscores the transformative journey that leaders must undertake to meet the demands of modern, complex organizations.

Table 3.1 The Development Stages and Action Logics Mindsets

Developmental Stages	*Action Logics Mindsets*	*Description*
Dependent—Leaders at these stages rely on external guidance, rules, and validation. They focus on self-protection or conformity and social approval	**Opportunist**	Leaders focus on personal gain, are reactive, and often seek immediate, short-term wins. Behavior is primarily self-centered and driven by personal benefit or survival
	Diplomat	Leaders rely heavily on external validation, prioritizing conformity, group harmony, and adherence to established norms. They avoid conflict and seek approval from authority or peers
Independent—Leaders at these stages develop internal expertise and drive results autonomously. They are guided by personal principles and goals, seeking individual success and mastery	**Expert**	Leaders prioritize mastering their own area of expertise. They make decisions independently based on specialized knowledge, emphasizing accuracy, efficiency, and technical proficiency
	Achiever	Leaders set clear goals, demonstrate initiative, and focus on achieving measurable results. They develop internal standards and personal principles to drive outcomes and innovation but may still focus narrowly on immediate objectives
Interdependent—Leaders begin valuing multiple perspectives and collaborative success, demonstrating advanced systems thinking skills. They embrace ambiguity and complex problem-solving	**Individualist**	Leaders value diverse perspectives and question established norms. They see ambiguity and complexity as opportunities for growth, though they may occasionally resist traditional structures or constraints
	Strategist	Leaders adopt collaborative systems thinking, embracing complexity, and viewing their actions as interconnected within broader organizational or societal contexts. They excel at integrative, strategic problem-solving
Self-transforming—Leaders transcend traditional boundaries by fostering deep inquiry, ethical responsibility, and collective learning, enabling profound, sustainable change that positively impacts both their organizations and society	**Alchemist**	Leaders transcend organizational and personal boundaries, demonstrating global consciousness, ethical clarity, and transformative vision. They integrate diverse viewpoints, drive systemic innovation, and lead with purpose for broad societal impact

As we have seen in this section, the journey from dependency to self-transforming involves significant shifts in cognitive, emotional, and relational capacities. The early stages—characterized by reliance on rules and external structures—set the foundation for later growth, while the later stages empower leaders to adopt a holistic, systems-oriented approach. These advanced stages not only enhance decision-making and innovation but also foster a culture of continuous improvement and ethical leadership.

Dependent Stages—Rules and Roles

The dependent stages represent the starting point in the journey of VLD. At this earliest staging, leaders rely heavily on external structures such as established rules, formal roles, and authoritative guidance. Their behaviors and decision-making processes are primarily shaped by the need to conform to predefined expectations, which, while necessary for initial organizational functioning, can restrict creativity and independent thought. In these stages, the leader's focus is largely on maintaining stability and following established procedures rather than questioning underlying assumptions.

Understanding the dependent stages is critical because they form the bedrock upon which later developmental stages are built. Although leaders in this phase may display competence in executing tasks and upholding organizational norms, they are often limited by a lack of internal direction. This section will explore the defining characteristics, strengths, and limitations of the dependent stages, drawing upon Bill Torbert's Action Logics model as well as insights from developmental theories by Piaget (1971), Erikson (1980), and Kohlberg (1981). Additionally, we will discuss practical strategies for profiling dependent leadership and initiating the journey toward more autonomous, innovative thinking. The next sections examine each stage—from Dependent to Self-transforming—in detail, including their characteristic mindsets and how leaders can progress through them.

The Dependent Stages: A Theoretical Overview

At the dependent stages, leadership is characterized by a reliance on external validation and adherence to rules. These stages are often marked by a low tolerance for ambiguity, as individuals rely on clearly defined structures to guide their actions. In many ways, this developmental phase mirrors the early stages of cognitive and moral development observed in broader psychological research. For example, Piaget's early developmental phases indicate that individuals initially operate within concrete, rule-bound frameworks, a concept that extends into leadership behaviors at this stage (Piaget, 1971). Likewise, Erikson's psychosocial model highlights that early developmental tasks focus on conforming to external expectations before the emergence of self-driven identity (Erikson, 1980).

In the context of leadership, the dependent stages are crucial for establishing basic operational competence. Leaders in these stages are often seen as reliable and consistent because they closely adhere to established norms. However, the very strengths that define these stages can also be limitations. A strict adherence to rules can stifle creativity, and the reliance on external authority may prevent leaders from developing the internal reflection necessary for later transformational growth. In short, early-stage leaders tend to think in black-and-white terms and look to authority for direction.

Action Logics in the Dependent Stage: Opportunist and Diplomat

Bill Torbert's Action Logics model provides a practical framework for understanding the dependent stages through the identification of two specific mindsets: the Opportunist and the Diplomat. Each of these Action Logics mindsets encapsulates distinct behavioral patterns and cognitive orientations that reflect the limitations and potentials of dependent leadership.

Opportunist Action Logics Mindset

At this staging, leaders are driven primarily by self-interest and the pursuit of immediate, short-term gains. Their decisions are typically reactive and focused on preserving personal control. Opportunist leaders view challenges as threats to their authority and prioritize quick, decisive action. This mindset, while sometimes effective in high-stakes, competitive scenarios, often results in impulsive decision-making without due consideration for long-term consequences. Research indicates that while the opportunist mindset can produce rapid responses (a strength in crisis situations), its self-centered orientation typically undermines teamwork and sustainable growth (McCauley et al., 2006).

Diplomat Action Logics Mindset

In contrast, the diplomat mindset reflects a strong desire for social approval and group harmony. Diplomat leaders are adept at maintaining positive interpersonal relationships and ensuring that the team functions smoothly. However, their reliance on established norms and a need for external validation can result in a resistance to change and a reluctance to challenge the status quo. As a result, while they excel in creating cohesive, stable work environments, diplomats may struggle when faced with situations that demand independent thought or innovative approaches.

An Opportunist leader might, for instance, take credit for quick wins and bypass protocols if it means a personal victory, whereas a Diplomat leader might always defer to their boss's opinion and strive to keep team meetings agreeable at the cost of honest debate.

Characteristics of Dependent Leaders

Leaders operating from the dependent stages exhibit several common characteristics that influence both their strengths and limitations within organizational settings. These characteristics can be broadly grouped into three main categories: reliance on external structures, behavioral tendencies, and the resulting strengths and weaknesses.

Reliance on External Structures

Dependent leaders typically look outward for guidance. They rely on the following:

- **Rules and Regulations:** They adhere strictly to policies and procedures, often without questioning whether these guidelines are optimal in all contexts.
- **Hierarchical Authority:** They tend to defer to authority figures and expect clear directives from superiors, which can limit their ability to act independently.
- **Social Approval:** Their decisions are influenced by the need to gain approval from peers and supervisors, leading them to avoid actions that might lead to conflict.

This heavy reliance on external structures ensures that dependent leaders maintain order and consistency in their teams. However, it also means that these leaders may struggle to innovate or adapt when the established norms become outdated or insufficient for dealing with new challenges.

Behavioral Tendencies and Cognitive Patterns

At the dependent stages, cognitive and behavioral patterns are characterized by the following:

- **Rule-Focused Thinking:** Leaders think in terms of rules, roles, and clear expectations, which can limit their capacity to engage with ambiguous or complex situations.
- **Reactive Decision-Making:** Their approach to challenges is often reactive rather than proactive, as they default to familiar procedures rather than exploring novel solutions.

- **Low Tolerance for Ambiguity:** Uncertainty and change are typically viewed as threats rather than opportunities, which can inhibit learning and growth.

Such tendencies make dependent leaders reliable in routine operations, but they also restrict the leader's ability to move beyond the status quo. This narrow focus, while providing stability, does not foster the innovative, adaptive thinking required in rapidly changing environments.

Strengths and Limitations

Strengths:

- **Consistency and Reliability:** Dependent leaders are dependable because they adhere closely to established norms and procedures. This consistency can build trust in environments that value stability.
- **Efficiency in Structured Environments:** In settings where rules and roles are clearly defined, dependent leaders can excel in executing tasks with minimal deviation.
- **Quick Responsiveness in Familiar Contexts:** When faced with routine challenges, dependent leaders can act quickly and decisively based on well-known protocols.

Limitations:

- **Inflexibility in the Face of Ambiguity:** Their reliance on established norms makes it difficult for them to adapt when confronted with novel challenges or uncertain situations.
- **Limited Innovation:** The focus on rules and external validation often stifles creativity and independent problem-solving, limiting long-term growth.
- **Dependency on Authority:** This dependency restricts their capacity to develop self-direction and internal judgment, which are essential for higher levels of leadership.

Reflections on the Dependent Stages

While the dependent stages are essential for establishing foundational skills, its limitations become evident as organizational complexity increases. Leaders who remain mired in dependency risk stifling innovation and hindering long-term growth. However, the dependent stage also offers crucial learning opportunities. It provides a safe starting point where individuals can learn the value of rules and structure, which are necessary for operational consistency. The challenge, then, is to leverage these strengths as a springboard for further development.

Organizations must carefully design developmental interventions that gradually encourage leaders to move beyond dependency. By providing targeted feedback, coaching, and experiential learning opportunities, organizations can help leaders build the internal capacity needed for more advanced stages of development.

The dependent stages are characterized by a strong adherence to external structures and norms, resulting in reliable but limited leadership. The strengths of these stages—such as consistency and operational efficiency—lay the groundwork for later development. However, to thrive in complex and dynamic environments, leaders must evolve beyond this stage. Practical strategies such as developmental assessments, targeted coaching, stretch assignments, and reflective practices are essential for helping dependent leaders transition to higher levels of autonomy and strategic thinking.

The dependent stage serves as the essential foundation for VLD. Leaders at this stage rely on external structures to guide their behavior, ensuring consistency and stability within their organizations. However, the same reliance on external validation that makes dependent leaders effective in stable environments also limits their capacity for independent thought and innovation. By understanding the characteristics, strengths, and limitations of this stage—illustrated through Torbert's Opportunist and Diplomat Action Logics—organizations can implement targeted interventions designed to move leaders toward greater self-authorship and adaptive capacity.

Through practical strategies such as developmental assessments, coaching, stretch assignments, and reflective practices, organizations can facilitate the transition from dependency to a more independent and ultimately transformative leadership style. As leaders begin to internalize their own values and challenge established norms, they pave the way for a more collaborative, systems-oriented, and ultimately, higher-level leadership that is essential in today's complex world.

Independent Stages—Self-Authorship and Personal Values

The independent stages represent a critical turning point in VLD. At these stages, leaders begin to shift away from an over-reliance on external validation and predefined roles, moving instead toward self-authorship. This shift is marked by the emergence of an internal compass—a set of personal values, beliefs, and principles—that guides decision-making and action. Leaders in the independent stage increasingly take responsibility for shaping their own identity, goals, and strategies, rather than simply adhering to externally imposed expectations.

The transition to self-authorship is transformative. It not only enables leaders to operate more autonomously but also empowers them to innovate, challenge the status quo, and drive organizational change. The independent stages build upon the foundational skills developed during the dependent stages, such as operational competence and adherence to rules. However, as leaders evolve, the emphasis shifts from compliance and consistency to independent thought, creative problem-solving, and strategic goal setting.

Next, we explore the characteristics, strengths, and limitations of leaders in the independent stages. We will discuss how this stage is represented within Bill Torbert's Action Logics model—specifically through the Expert and Achiever Action Logics—and examine how these mindsets foster an internal drive for excellence and innovation.

The Independent Stages: A Theoretical Overview

The independent stages of VLD are rooted in several foundational theories that describe the evolution of human cognition and moral reasoning. Early work by Piaget (1971) and Erikson (1980) established that individuals gradually move from concrete, externally driven thought processes toward more abstract and self-determined ways of thinking. Kohlberg's (1981) stages of moral reasoning further illustrate how individuals progress from a focus on external approval to embracing internal principles that guide ethical decision-making. However, it is Robert Kegan's Subject-Object Theory (1982) that most directly informs the concept of self-authorship in leadership.

Kegan's Subject-Object Theory and Self-Authorship

Kegan (1982) posits that adult development is characterized by a shift from being "subject" to one's beliefs—where those beliefs remain unquestioned and largely imposed by external forces—to making these beliefs "object," where individuals gain the capacity for self-reflection and critical evaluation. In the context of leadership, this shift manifests as self-authorship, whereby leaders begin to define their own values, set personal goals, and act with greater autonomy. At the independent stages, the leader is less dependent on external structures for validation and more focused on internal standards and principles. This evolution is critical because it fosters a mindset that is both innovative and adaptive, enabling leaders to tackle complex challenges with confidence.

The transformation from a dependent to an independent mindset is a gradual process. Initially, leaders might rely on established protocols and the opinions of authority figures. Over time, however, they develop an internal framework that guides their actions—one that is built on personal experience, reflection, and a willingness to challenge existing norms. This internalization of values and decision-making criteria is what characterizes the independent stage.

Action Logics in the Independent Stages: Expert and Achiever

Two key Action Logics emerge during this stage: the Expert and the Achiever.

Expert Action Logics Mindset

At the Expert level, leaders focus primarily on developing and demonstrating technical or domain-specific expertise. They derive satisfaction from mastering their field and applying their knowledge to solve clearly defined problems. Expert leaders are self-reliant in their problem-solving, often preferring to operate independently and relying on their technical acumen to drive success. Characteristics of this mindset include a strong emphasis on accuracy, precision, and efficiency. However, while the Expert Action Logic fosters technical proficiency, it may also lead to a narrow focus that limits the ability to see the broader strategic context.

Achiever Action Logics Mindset

The Achiever mindset marks a natural progression from the Expert stage. While still valuing expertise, Achievers begin to set ambitious goals and prioritize outcomes that benefit both themselves and their teams. They are driven by measurable results and are more inclined to collaborate and seek feedback. Achiever leaders start integrating strategic thinking with operational execution; they recognize the importance of aligning personal objectives with broader organizational goals. In doing so, they move toward a more balanced approach that values both independence and interdependence. Achievers are often characterized by their proactive approach, resilience, and commitment to continuous improvement. Nonetheless, a potential limitation of this stage is the risk of focusing too narrowly on short-term results without sufficiently considering long-term, systemic impacts.

Characteristics and Behaviors of Independent Leaders

Leaders in the independent stages exhibit several key characteristics that distinguish them from those operating in the dependent stages. These characteristics can be grouped into three primary areas: the development of an internal value system, independent decision-making, and a heightened focus on personal growth and self-improvement.

Internal Value System and Self-Reflection

One of the hallmarks of the independent stages is the emergence of an internal value system. Unlike dependent leaders, who rely on external validation, independent leaders begin to derive their actions from internal principles. They develop a clearer sense of identity and purpose, which guides their decision-making processes. This internal compass is built through self-reflection, critical analysis, and a willingness to challenge existing paradigms. Regular self-reflection, whether through journaling, meditation, or reflective coaching sessions, plays a crucial role in solidifying this internal framework.

As leaders gain self-awareness, they are better able to articulate what is important to them and align their behaviors with their core values. This alignment not only enhances their authenticity but also builds trust among team members, as others perceive their decisions as being grounded in well-considered principles rather than external pressures.

Independent Decision-Making

Independent leaders are distinguished by their ability to make decisions autonomously. They are comfortable with ambiguity and willing to take calculated risks when traditional guidelines fall short. This decision-making process is characterized by the following:

- **Analytical Rigor:** Leaders rely on data, personal insights, and critical thinking to assess complex situations.
- **Innovative Problem-Solving:** They are more open to exploring unconventional solutions, drawing on both intuition and analytical reasoning.
- **Accountability:** Independent leaders take responsibility for their decisions, viewing mistakes as opportunities for learning rather than failures.

This increased autonomy fosters a proactive approach. Instead of waiting for instructions or seeking constant validation, independent leaders initiate change and drive projects forward based on their internal judgment.

Emphasis on Personal Growth

A significant component of the independent stages is a commitment to personal growth. Leaders in this phase actively seek out opportunities for learning and self-improvement. They set ambitious personal and professional goals and are willing to invest time and resources in their development. This proactive engagement in continuous learning often manifests in:

- **Pursuit of Advanced Knowledge:** Whether through formal education, mentorship, or self-directed learning, independent leaders prioritize expanding their expertise.
- **Feedback Orientation:** They actively solicit and incorporate feedback, viewing constructive criticism as a tool for further refinement.
- **Resilience:** Leaders demonstrate a willingness to persevere through setbacks, using challenges as catalysts for growth.

This orientation toward growth not only improves individual capabilities but also contributes to a broader culture of continuous improvement within organizations.

Reflections on the Independent Stages

The independent stages are a period of significant transformation. Leaders who successfully navigate these stages develop a robust internal framework that enables them to act autonomously and strategically. However, the journey is not without its challenges. The shift from reliance on external validation to internal self-guidance requires significant introspection, willingness to embrace uncertainty, and a commitment to continuous learning.

One key challenge at these stages is balancing independence with the need for collaboration. While independent leaders are more self-directed, they must also learn to integrate their insights with the broader organizational context. This balance is critical because overemphasis on independence can lead to isolation, whereas premature reliance on external validation can stunt growth. Organizations must, therefore, create environments where leaders are encouraged to pursue autonomy while still engaging in collaborative efforts.

Another challenge is the potential for overconfidence. As leaders become more self-assured in their decision-making, they may risk neglecting the value of feedback or ignoring alternative perspectives. Continuous development programs that incorporate regular assessments, coaching, and reflective practices are essential to mitigate this risk. By maintaining a structured approach to feedback and self-reflection, organizations can ensure that independent leaders remain open to learning and adaptable in the face of new challenges.

The independent stages are characterized by the emergence of self-authorship, the development of an internal value system, and the capacity for independent decision-making. Leaders at this stage begin to redefine their roles, challenge conventional wisdom, and set the foundation for later developmental stages. The transition from a dependent mindset to an independent one is both challenging and transformative, laying the groundwork for a leadership style that is innovative, adaptive, and aligned with long-term strategic goals.

The independent stages of VLD are pivotal. They mark the transition from externally driven behaviors to a more self-directed, reflective, and internally guided leadership approach. Drawing on theoretical insights from developmental psychology—particularly Kegan's Subject-Object Theory—and illustrated through Torbert's Action Logics (Expert and Achiever), these stages highlight the emergence of self-authorship as a critical component of effective leadership.

Leaders in the independent stages are characterized by their ability to make decisions autonomously, innovate in response to challenges, and continuously seek personal and professional growth. However, these stages also present challenges, such as balancing independence with collaboration and avoiding overconfidence. Practical strategies, including developmental assessments, targeted coaching, stretch assignments, reflective practices, and educational workshops, are essential for facilitating the shift to self-authorship.

Ultimately, the independent stages lay the groundwork for subsequent developmental stages by establishing a foundation of internal values, autonomy, and strategic thinking. As leaders progress beyond dependency, they become better equipped to contribute to their organizations in meaningful ways, paving the path for higher-level leadership that is collaborative, systemic, and transformative.

Interdependent Stages—Collaborative Mindsets and Systems Awareness

The interdependent stages mark a transformative shift in VLD, where leaders begin to view themselves not as isolated decision-makers but as integral parts of a larger, interconnected system. At these stages, the focus moves away from individual achievement and toward building relationships, fostering collaboration, and developing a systems-oriented perspective. Leaders in these stages recognize that organizational success relies on leveraging diverse perspectives and integrating the strengths of various stakeholders. As a result, they adopt mindsets that emphasizes inclusivity, mutual accountability, and collective problem-solving.

The progression into the interdependent stages builds on the foundations laid in the dependent and independent stages. Whereas earlier stages were characterized by a reliance on external rules and the development of internal self-authorship, the interdependent stages challenges leaders to transcend personal achievements and consider the broader impact of their decisions. These stages are marked by increased emotional and cognitive complexity, enabling leaders to navigate organizational dynamics with a deep understanding of interdependence. In this part, we examine the theoretical underpinnings of the interdependent stages and present practical strategies for developing collaborative mindsets and systems awareness.

The Interdependent Stages: A Theoretical Overview

The transition from the independent to the interdependent stages is a critical developmental leap. At the independent stages, leaders develop an internal compass and become adept at self-directed decision-making. However, this autonomy—while empowering—can sometimes lead to siloed thinking. The interdependent stages, by contrast, require leaders to shift their focus from self-sufficiency to collective success.

This shift echoes theoretical perspectives from developmental psychology. For instance, Kegan's (1982) Subject-Object Theory highlights that true transformation involves not just self-reflection but also the ability to see oneself in relation to others. As leaders advance, they become capable of integrating multiple viewpoints, thus fostering a more inclusive, holistic approach to leadership.

Similarly, Erikson's (1980) emphasis on the interplay between individual identity and social context reinforces the idea that effective leadership is rooted in the ability to navigate complex interpersonal dynamics. Leaders who embrace the interdependent stage not only are concerned with their own success but also recognize that their decisions have far-reaching effects on their teams, departments, and the organization as a whole. This recognition is vital for creating a culture where collaboration and collective accountability are paramount.

Action Logics in the Interdependent Stages: Individualist and Strategist

In these stages, leaders typically transition into Action Logics characterized by a broader, more integrative perspective. The two Action Logics associated with the interdependent stage are the Individualist and the Strategist.

Individualist Action Logics Mindset

At the Individualist level, leaders begin to question established norms and explore alternative ways of thinking. They appreciate diversity and challenge assumptions, which often leads to creative problem-solving and innovative approaches. However, Individualists may still operate with a strong sense of autonomy, even as they start valuing diverse perspectives. Their ability to see the unique contributions of each team member sets the stage for more collaborative behavior.

Strategist Action Logics Mindset

The Strategist mindset represents a more advanced form of interdependence. Strategist leaders integrate individual insights with a systemic understanding of organizational dynamics. They are capable of aligning personal, team, and organizational goals by recognizing how different parts of the system interact. Their approach is characterized by a long-term, transformative vision that balances immediate operational needs with broader strategic objectives. Research by McCauley et al. (2006) has shown that such systems-oriented thinking is essential for adaptive decision-making in complex environments.

These mindsets reinforce the idea that the interdependent stages are about moving beyond isolated achievements toward a collaborative framework where every decision is informed by an understanding of interconnections. Leaders in these stages are more likely to foster environments of trust and mutual respect, which are crucial for organizational innovation and resilience.

Integration With Systems and Ecosystems Thinking

As discussed in Chapter 2, systems thinking plays a critical role in vertical development. In the interdependent stage, this approach is extended to embrace not only internal organizational systems but also external ecosystems. Leaders begin to understand that their organizations do not operate in a vacuum. They see how internal dynamics—such as team collaboration and cross-functional initiatives—are intertwined with external factors like market trends, regulatory changes, and social dynamics.

Ecosystems thinking encourages leaders to expand their perspective further, considering how decisions made within the organization impact the larger network of stakeholders and the environment (Senge et al., 2015). This comprehensive outlook is central to the interdependent stage, as it compels leaders to act with a sense of shared purpose and collective responsibility. The integration of systems and ecosystems thinking fosters a leadership style that is both adaptive and resilient, capable of driving sustainable change in a complex world.

Characteristics and Behaviors of Interdependent Leaders

Leaders who operate in the interdependent stages exhibit several defining characteristics that set them apart from those in earlier developmental stages. These traits not only enhance their effectiveness but also contribute to the overall health and adaptability of their organizations.

Emphasis on Collaboration and Inclusivity

Interdependent leaders value collaboration as a fundamental element of effective leadership. They understand that leveraging the diverse skills, experiences, and perspectives of their teams leads to more innovative and sustainable solutions. In practice, these leaders

- Actively seek input from a broad range of stakeholders.
- Encourage open communication and facilitate inclusive discussions.
- Build cross-functional teams that harness the collective intelligence of the organization.

This collaborative mindset is crucial for addressing complex challenges that require multifaceted solutions. By fostering an environment where every team member's voice is valued, interdependent leaders build trust and drive a culture of mutual support.

Systems-Oriented Thinking

A hallmark of interdependent leadership is a deep appreciation for systems thinking. Leaders in this stage view the organization as an interconnected whole, recognizing that changes in one area can have significant ripple effects throughout the system. They are skilled at

- Mapping out relationships and interdependencies within the organization.
- Identifying potential bottlenecks and root causes of systemic issues.
- Designing solutions that address both immediate problems and long-term strategic goals.

Such a holistic perspective not only improves decision-making but also enhances the organization's ability to adapt to changing circumstances. Leaders who can see the bigger picture are better equipped to integrate diverse viewpoints and create strategies that promote resilience and innovation.

Adaptive and Transformational Mindset

Interdependent leaders are characterized by their ability to navigate ambiguity and drive transformational change. They are not satisfied with incremental improvements; instead, they seek to fundamentally reimagine processes, structures, and strategies to meet evolving challenges. This adaptive mindset is reflected in their willingness to

- Embrace uncertainty as an opportunity for growth.
- Challenge traditional practices and explore innovative alternatives.
- Align short-term actions with long-term, systemic objectives.

By fostering a culture of continuous learning and experimentation, these leaders inspire their teams to pursue innovative solutions and drive positive organizational change.

The Strategic Impact of Interdependent Leadership

The benefits of cultivating interdependent leadership extend far beyond individual growth. When leaders operate with a collaborative mindset, organizations as a whole become more agile, innovative, and resilient. The strategic impacts include the following:

- **Enhanced Problem-Solving Capabilities:**

  Collaborative, systems-oriented leaders are better equipped to tackle multifaceted challenges because they can integrate insights from diverse sources. This leads to more comprehensive and sustainable solutions.

- **Improved Organizational Alignment:**

  When leaders work interdependently, they create a culture of shared purpose and collective accountability. This alignment fosters greater coherence in strategy and execution, ultimately improving organizational performance.

- **Increased Adaptability:**

  Organizations led by interdependent leaders are more agile in responding to external disruptions. By leveraging cross-functional collaboration and external engagement, these organizations can quickly adapt to market changes and emerging trends.

- **Stronger Innovation Culture:**

  A collaborative approach encourages creativity by bringing together diverse viewpoints. Leaders who value interdependence are more likely to experiment, take calculated risks, and drive continuous improvement.

Renaming for Resonance

Nick Petrie and other practitioners shifted Bill Torbert's original terms—*Individualist* and *Strategist*—to *Redefining* and *Transforming*, respectively, to create clearer, more relatable language for organizational leaders and executives. Torbert's original terms, rooted in academic precision, were sometimes perceived as abstract or challenging for practical, business-oriented audiences. By renaming *Individualist* to *Redefining*, Petrie emphasized a leader's developmental shift toward actively questioning and reshaping personal and organizational assumptions. Similarly, *Strategist* became *Transforming* to highlight the leader's capacity for fostering systemic, transformational change. These adaptations made the stages intuitive, actionable, and accessible, significantly contributing to the widespread integration of vertical development concepts into leadership development programs and coaching engagements.

Reflections on the Interdependent Stages

The interdependent stages are both challenging and transformative. Leaders must learn to balance their growing autonomy with the need for collective input, and they must continually adapt to the evolving demands of a complex organizational environment. The transition from independent self-authorship to collaborative leadership requires not only changes in mindset but also the development of new skills—such as advanced communication, conflict resolution, and systems thinking.

As leaders mature, they begin to appreciate that true success is not achieved in isolation but through the combined efforts of diverse teams working toward common goals. This realization is crucial in today's interconnected world, where challenges are rarely confined to a single department or function. Leaders who embrace interdependence foster a culture of mutual respect, inclusivity, and continuous learning—attributes that are essential for long-term organizational resilience.

The interdependent stages lay the groundwork for the subsequent self-transforming stage. By building strong collaborative networks and honing their systems-oriented mindset, leaders create a solid foundation for further personal and organizational transformation. In the next part of this chapter, we will explore how leaders transition from interdependence to self-transformation, adopting a global consciousness and a commitment to systemic impact.

The interdependent stages represent a critical evolution in VLD. It is at these stages that leaders begin to transcend the boundaries of individual achievement and embrace a collective, systems-oriented approach to leadership. Drawing on theoretical foundations from developmental psychology and practical frameworks such as Torbert's Action Logics, this stage is characterized by a commitment to collaboration, inclusivity, and strategic alignment.

Leaders in the interdependent stages are marked by their ability to integrate diverse perspectives, navigate complex organizational dynamics, and drive systemic change.

They recognize that the success of the organization hinges on the interconnectedness of its parts and are adept at building networks that span both internal and external boundaries. Through targeted interventions—such as cross-functional projects, systems mapping exercises, reflective practices, and mentorship programs—organizations can facilitate this vital transition.

In essence, interdependent leadership is not just about working together but about reimagining leadership as a dynamic, integrative process that aligns individual capabilities with collective goals. This holistic approach empowers organizations to respond effectively to external disruptions, foster innovation, and create sustainable competitive advantage.

As we transition to the next stage in our exploration of VLD, the focus will shift to the self-transforming stage, where leaders further expand their influence by adopting a globally conscious and ethically driven mindset. The journey from interdependence to self-transformation marks the culmination of the developmental process, setting the stage for leadership that is as visionary as it is pragmatic.

Self-Transforming Stage—Global Consciousness and Transcendent Thinking

The self-transforming stage represents the pinnacle of VLD, where leaders not only refine their internal frameworks but also transcend traditional organizational boundaries. At this stage, leadership is characterized by a profound sense of global consciousness, ethical commitment, and an integrative mindset that addresses challenges on a systemic scale. Leaders in the self-transforming stage are driven by purpose and an unwavering commitment to long-term societal well-being. They see themselves as stewards of change, capable of inspiring transformation that goes beyond short-term organizational success to create lasting, positive impact on communities, industries, and even global systems.

In the journey toward self-transformation, leaders begin to view their personal and organizational goals through a lens that transcends self-interest. This stage is marked by a heightened awareness of the interconnectedness between an organization and its broader socio-economic and environmental context. As such, self-transforming leaders are adept at integrating diverse perspectives, managing ambiguity, and harnessing innovation to address complex global challenges. This section delves into the defining characteristics of the self-transforming stage, outlines the transformative nature of the Alchemist Action Logic, and presents practical strategies for cultivating this advanced level of leadership.

The Self-Transforming Stage: A Theoretical Overview

At the self-transforming stage, leaders move beyond the confines of individual expertise and collaborative success to embrace a transcendent approach. Drawing on developmental psychology theories—particularly Kegan's Subject-Object Theory (1982)—self-transforming leaders have reached a point where they can view their own beliefs, assumptions, and biases as objects of reflection rather than as absolute truths. This ability to hold multiple, sometimes contradictory, perspectives simultaneously is a critical hallmark of the self-transforming mindset. It enables leaders to approach complex problems with a comprehensive, integrative vision that considers long-term implications and systemic interdependencies.

This level of cognitive and emotional complexity is essential in today's dynamic and interconnected world. Research by McCauley et al. (2006) suggests that leaders who achieve higher developmental stages, characterized by self-transformation, are better equipped to handle the unpredictable and multifaceted challenges of modern organizations. By transcending their own limitations, self-transforming leaders foster an environment where learning and adaptation are continuous processes.

Ethical and Global Orientations

Self-transforming leadership is also defined by a strong ethical foundation and a commitment to global consciousness. In this stage, leaders no longer focus solely on achieving short-term organizational gains but prioritize ethical considerations and societal impact. Their decision-making is guided by an internalized set of values that emphasize inclusivity, justice, and sustainability. This ethical orientation is not an abstract ideal; it manifests in concrete actions such as prioritizing corporate social responsibility initiatives, engaging in transparent stakeholder communication, and driving policies that promote environmental sustainability.

Self-transforming leaders are globally conscious. They recognize that organizations do not operate in isolation; rather, they are part of a larger ecosystem that includes diverse cultures, economies, and ecological systems. This broader perspective enables them to anticipate and respond to global trends, aligning their strategic vision with the needs of the wider community. Such an orientation is critical in an era marked by rapid globalization and environmental challenges, where decisions made at the organizational level can have far-reaching consequences.

Action Logics in Self-Transforming Stage: Alchemist

Leaders operating from the Alchemist stage embody a transformative, integrative approach that transcends traditional leadership paradigms. Alchemists are visionary and adaptive, using their advanced cognitive and emotional capacities to catalyze systemic change.

The Alchemist Action Logics Mindset

- **Visionary and Ethical Leadership:** Alchemists are motivated by a clear, purpose-driven vision that prioritizes the well-being of both the organization and the broader society. They approach leadership with an ethical framework that values transparency, inclusivity, and sustainability.
- **Holistic and Integrative Thinking:** Leaders in this stage view challenges through multiple lenses, integrating insights from diverse fields and perspectives. They are capable of holding seemingly contradictory ideas simultaneously and reconciling them into a coherent strategy.
- **Transformational Capacity:** Alchemists drive change not by incremental adjustments but through transformative initiatives that address systemic issues. Their approach often involves rethinking established processes, fostering innovation, and leading strategic realignments that have a lasting impact.

Research and case studies have shown that organizations led by Alchemists are more likely to achieve sustainable success because they balance short-term operational demands with long-term visionary goals (Senge et al., 2015).

Characteristics and Behaviors of Self-Transforming Leaders

Leaders who reach the self-transforming stage exhibit several defining characteristics that distinguish them from those at earlier stages:

Profound Self-Awareness: Self-transforming leaders possess a high degree of self-awareness. They continuously reflect on their own values, beliefs, and behaviors, recognizing the limitations of their previous mindsets. This self-reflection enables them to learn from experience and adapt their approaches over time.

Ethical Clarity and Social Responsibility: These leaders prioritize ethical decision-making and consistently consider the broader impact of their actions on society and the environment. Their decisions are guided by an internal moral compass that transcends organizational boundaries, reflecting a deep commitment to social justice and sustainability.

Global Consciousness: Self-transforming leaders are acutely aware of the global context in which their organizations operate. They understand that local decisions can have global repercussions, and they actively seek to align organizational strategies with broader societal trends and environmental imperatives.

Transformative Vision: With a forward-thinking perspective, self-transforming leaders articulate a compelling vision for change. They are not satisfied with maintaining the status quo; instead, they strive to create innovative, disruptive solutions that drive systemic improvement.

Resilience and Adaptability: These leaders excel in the face of uncertainty and complexity. Their ability to navigate ambiguity and remain agile under pressure is a testament to their advanced developmental stage. They view challenges as opportunities for growth and are skilled at turning setbacks into catalysts for innovation.

Integrative Decision-Making: By synthesizing diverse perspectives and leveraging cross-disciplinary insights, self-transforming leaders make decisions that are both holistic and strategic. They consider the short-term and long-term implications of their actions, ensuring that solutions are sustainable and ethically sound.

Strategic Impact and Organizational Benefits

Leaders who reach the self-transforming stage drive profound, systemic change. Their ability to integrate diverse perspectives, think holistically, and act ethically not only enhances individual performance but also transforms organizational culture.

The strategic impacts of self-transforming leadership include the following:

- **Sustainable Competitive Advantage:**

  Organizations led by self-transforming leaders are better positioned to anticipate and respond to global trends. Their capacity for ethical decision-making and systemic innovation creates a sustainable competitive advantage that endures in dynamic environments.

- **Enhanced Organizational Resilience:**

  By embedding a deep sense of ethical responsibility and global consciousness, self-transforming leaders foster a culture of resilience. This enables the organization to weather disruptions, adapt to change, and maintain long-term viability.

- **Innovation and Adaptability:**

  The holistic, integrative approach of self-transforming leaders sparks innovation by encouraging cross-functional collaboration and creative problem-solving. Their ability to synthesize complex information leads to breakthrough ideas and transformative solutions.

- **Improved Stakeholder Engagement:**

  Leaders who operate from a self-transforming mindset build strong, trusting relationships with internal and external stakeholders. Their transparent, ethical approach enhances organizational reputation and fosters lasting partnerships.

Reflections on the Self-Transforming Stage

The self-transforming stage is the latest stage of a leader's developmental journey, where internal values, ethical principles, and a global perspective converge to create a profoundly transformative leadership style. However, this stage also poses challenges. The very qualities that define self-transforming leaders—such as an unwavering commitment to ethical integrity and a willingness to embrace ambiguity—can sometimes lead to tension with traditional organizational structures.

Self-transforming leaders often challenge long-standing norms, which can be met with resistance from those accustomed to more conventional approaches.

Nonetheless, the benefits of self-transforming leadership far outweigh the challenges. Organizations that nurture self-transforming leaders build cultures of continuous learning, ethical decision-making, and systemic innovation. The transformational impact of these leaders extends beyond individual performance, shaping the overall direction and resilience of the organization in a rapidly changing world.

The self-transforming stage represents the apex of VLD, where leaders transcend conventional boundaries and adopt a globally conscious, ethically driven mindset. Grounded in the theoretical frameworks of Kegan (1982) and operationalized through practical models such as Torbert's Alchemist Action Logic, self-transforming leadership embodies a comprehensive transformation in cognitive, emotional, and ethical capacities. Leaders at this stage demonstrate profound self-awareness, embrace complexity, and drive systemic change that benefits not only their organizations but also the broader society.

Through targeted developmental interventions—ranging from advanced assessments and personalized coaching to global immersion projects and reflective practices—organizations can facilitate the journey toward self-transformation. The strategic impact of such leadership is significant: enhanced innovation, improved stakeholder engagement, greater organizational resilience, and a sustainable competitive advantage in an increasingly interconnected global landscape.

As organizations face unprecedented challenges and opportunities in the 21st century, the cultivation of self-transforming leaders becomes not only a strategic imperative but also a cornerstone of sustainable success. The self-transforming stage is where leadership truly evolves from being reactive and self-focused to becoming proactive, integrative, and visionary—a transformation that holds the promise of lasting, positive impact on both organizations and society.

Stage models have played a critical role in helping us understand how adults grow and make meaning over time. They offer a helpful map of the developmental terrain, illustrating how leadership capacity can deepen through distinct transformations of perspective. These models give us language to describe the complex journey of becoming—illuminating what more expanded meaning-making might look like.

Yet while stage models are valuable, the aim of this book is not to advocate for a race to the highest stage or to treat development as a linear climb. Vertical development is not about arriving at a final destination of leadership maturity. Rather, it's about cultivating **vertical range**—the ability to access and integrate multiple ways of making sense of the world and leading within it. This broader range allows leaders to respond more skillfully to the complexity, uncertainty, and relational nuance of today's challenges.

True leadership development means learning to move fluidly between action, reflection, and deeper sensemaking. It means expanding one's capacity to hold paradox, navigate competing perspectives, and lead with both clarity and care. It's not about discarding earlier ways of thinking but honoring and incorporating them—building an inner repertoire that grows more versatile and wise.

Understanding these stages is crucial, but development doesn't happen automatically. In Chapter 4, we will explore assessing vertical development.

References

Day, D. V. (2000). Leadership development: A review in context. *The Leadership Quarterly*, *11*(4), 581–613. https://doi.org/10.1016/S1048-9843(00)00061-8

Erikson, E. H. (1980). *Identity and the life cycle*. W. W. Norton & Company (Original work published 1959). Flamer (Eds.), *Measurement and Piaget* (pp. 1–11). McGraw-Hill.

Kegan, R. (1982). *The evolving self: Problem and process in human development*. Harvard University Press.

Kohlberg, L. (1981). *Essays on moral development, Vol. I: The philosophy of moral development*. Harper & Row.

McCauley, C. D., Drath, W. H., Palus, C. J., O'Connor, P. M., & Baker, B. A. (2006). The use of constructive-developmental theory to advance the understanding of leadership. *The Leadership Quarterly*, *17*(6), 634–653. https://doi.org/10.1016/j.leaqua.2006.09.007

Piaget, J. (1971). The theory of stages in cognitive development. In D. R. Green, M. P. Ford & G. B. Flamer (Eds.), *Measurement and Piaget* (pp. 1–11). McGraw-Hill.

Senge, P. M., Smith, B., Kruschwitz, N., Laur, J., & Schley, C. (2015). *The necessary revolution: How individuals and organizations are working together to create a sustainable world*. Doubleday.

Torbert, W. R., & Rooke, D. (2005). Seven transformations of leadership. *Harvard Business Review*, *83*(4), 66–76.

Chapter 4

Assessing Vertical Growth

Assessment and Evaluation of Vertical Growth

Because vertical development changes mindsets (unlike conventional skill training, as discussed in Chapter 1), measuring progress is challenging; yet robust assessment is valuable for understanding the true impact of leadership development initiatives and for guiding future efforts. Next, we dive deeper into how to use assessment, alongside observations and feedback, to gauge vertical growth. Without systematic assessment, organizations risk investing in programs without clear evidence of their effectiveness, and leaders may miss critical opportunities to refine their growth. To capture the subtle shifts in cognitive, emotional, and relational capacities that define vertical development, organizations need tools and methods that extend beyond standard performance metrics. This section provides a comprehensive framework for assessing vertical leadership growth through developmental assessments, behavioral observations, qualitative feedback, and longitudinal data tracking.

The Value of Assessing Vertical Development

Assessing vertical development is important because it provides valuable insights into how individuals and organizations think, interpret experiences, and approach complexity—qualities crucial for navigating today's rapidly changing environment. Vertical development assessments inform both personal growth and organizational strategies, highlighting the transformative impact this type of development has on overall capability and resilience.

Through assessment practices, individuals can clearly identify their developmental baselines, understanding their current cognitive complexity, emotional resilience, and adaptive behaviors. This self-awareness empowers individuals to recognize their strengths and pinpoint areas for personal growth, enhancing their effectiveness and readiness to tackle increasingly

DOI: 10.4324/9781003644941-4

complex challenges. Organizations benefit from these assessments by gaining a deeper understanding of their leaders' developmental capacities.

By recognizing unique developmental profiles, both individuals and organizations can design customized development plans tailored to specific growth opportunities. Personalized interventions increase relevance, engagement, and effectiveness (Emam et al., 2024).

Vertical development assessments also enable ongoing monitoring of individual and organizational developmental progress, tracking growth and shifts in meaning-making and complexity over time. Regular evaluations provide concrete evidence of growth, allowing organizations to refine and adapt leadership development programs continually. Individuals, in turn, gain clarity and encouragement from seeing growth as well.

Vertical assessments promote continuous learning through structured feedback loops at both individual and organizational levels. Individuals gain valuable perspectives on their evolving thought processes and adaptive capacities, which encourages reflection, learning, and proactive engagement in their developmental journeys. At the organizational level, this continuous learning loop reinforces a culture that values adaptability, resilience, and growth.

Ultimately, assessing vertical development equips both individuals and organizations to better anticipate, adapt, and respond to future challenges, cultivating the deeper capacities required for sustained success in complex and dynamic environments.

What Does Research Say About Measuring Vertical Development?

Vertical development can indeed be assessed using several validated psychometric tools and structured interview methods. Instruments such as the Subject-Object Interview (SOI) developed by Robert Kegan, the Leadership Development Profile (LDP) and Global Leadership Profile (GLP) created by Bill Torbert, and the Maturity Assessment Profile (MAP) by Susanne Cook-Greuter have all demonstrated reliability and validity in capturing vertical developmental progression. These assessments focus on evaluating how individuals interpret their experiences, make sense of complexity, navigate ambiguity, and reason about themselves and their interactions with the world around them. Rather than measuring discrete skills, knowledge, or personality traits alone, these tools seek to capture underlying patterns of meaning-making and cognitive complexity that influence an individual's worldview and leadership behaviors (Geerts, 2024).

However, despite their demonstrated validity, researchers consistently emphasize that vertical development is a profoundly intricate, dynamic, and nuanced construct. As a result, no single assessment can fully encapsulate the entirety of an individual's developmental complexity. Assessments can capture snapshots of developmental stages or action logics, but individuals often exhibit fluidity across multiple stages depending on context, personal growth experiences, and situational demands. Consequently, experts advocate using assessments as starting points or guides rather than definitive indicators, underscoring the importance of combining multiple methods and perspectives to gain a comprehensive understanding of an individual's developmental capacity (Garvey et al., 2012).

Key Developmental Assessment Tools

Developmental assessments are the cornerstone of evaluating Vertical Leadership Development (VLD). Several assessment tools have been developed specifically for this purpose:

Maturity Assessment Profile (MAP)

The MAP is rooted in Jane Loevinger's Washington University Sentence Completion Test (WUSCT), further expanded by Dr. Susanne Cook-Greuter's research at Harvard to include later, post-conventional stages of adult ego development. It is administered as a sentence completion test, where participants provide written endings to prompts that are then scored by expert evaluators using a refined scoring manual based on Cook-Greuter's ego development framework. The MAP assesses an individual's level of ego development (meaning-making maturity), supporting self-awareness and growth in both personal and leadership contexts. Targeting professionals and leaders, it is widely used in executive coaching and adult development research. The Vertical Development Academy (VeDA) offers the MAP, aligning with Cook-Greuter's Leadership Maturity Framework.

Vertical Mindset Indicator (VMI)

The VMI leverages the same theoretical foundation as the MAP—Loevinger and Cook-Greuter's ego development framework—but simplifies the approach through digital administration and AI-driven scoring. Participants complete an online questionnaire consisting of open-ended prompts, with results quickly analyzed by artificial intelligence. The primary purpose is to provide an accessible, cost-effective snapshot of an individual's developmental stage for leadership coaching and developmental conversations. The VMI was co-created by Nick Petrie and Jan Rybeck and is offered through Adeption, aimed at leaders seeking an introductory assessment of their developmental mindset.

STAGES Assessment

Developed by Dr. Terri O'Fallon, the STAGES Assessment integrates Ken Wilber's Integral Theory with traditional developmental stage research, presenting a comprehensive model of 12 developmental stages. Administered through a sentence completion test, responses are evaluated by certified coaches to identify the participant's stage within O'Fallon's framework. The assessment supports nuanced, detailed personal and leadership development, particularly within integral and developmental coaching communities. STAGES International offers this assessment, emphasizing complex and advanced developmental insights.

Lectical Assessments (Lectica)

Lectical Assessments, developed by Dr. Theo L. Dawson, are grounded in Kurt Fischer's Dynamic Skill Theory and assess developmental complexity in specific cognitive and reasoning domains. Administered through essay-style responses to complex prompts, results are scored using Lectica's developmental scoring system, often supported by computerized algorithms. Primarily designed to guide educational interventions and leadership development, Lectica assessments measure reasoning skills and complexity growth over time. Initially prominent in educational contexts, Lectica has expanded to organizational settings, offering domain-specific assessments for leadership and decision-making.

Shifting Horizons

The Shifting Horizons assessment integrates insights from established vertical development theories, including those of Cook-Greuter and Torbert, identifying an individual's predominant action logic within specific contexts. Delivered digitally through reflective exercises, the assessment provides immediate results that highlight an individual's developmental stage and personalized growth opportunities. Geared toward leaders managing complexity and change, Shifting Horizons is particularly useful in leadership coaching contexts. Developed collaboratively by senior vertical development experts, it is offered through the Vertical Development Institute (VDI).

Subject-Object Interview (SOI)

The SOI, based on Robert Kegan's Constructive-Developmental theory, employs a semi-structured interview format to identify the individual's stage of mental complexity. Conducted one-on-one by trained interviewers, it involves guided discussions around specific topics, with transcripts analyzed to determine developmental stages. Widely validated and extensively used in research and executive coaching, the SOI provides rich qualitative insights into how individuals interpret their experiences and complexity. Developed by Robert Kegan and Lisa Lahey, the SOI is closely affiliated with Harvard University and Minds at Work.

Growth-Edge Interview

The Growth-Edge Interview, created by Dr. Jennifer Garvey Berger, is a practical adaptation of Kegan's approach tailored for leadership coaching. It involves qualitative, exploratory conversations aimed at identifying a person's current developmental "growth edge," rather than assigning a precise stage score. Primarily used in coaching contexts, it helps leaders explore their meaning-making patterns and identify opportunities for developmental advancement. Popular among executive coaches, it is taught through Berger's platforms such as Cultivating Leadership and the Growth Edge Network.

Washington University Sentence Completion Test (WUSCT)

The WUSCT, developed by Jane Loevinger, is the original empirical measure of adult ego development. Participants respond to 36 sentence stems, with responses scored according to Loevinger's detailed developmental stages manual. Initially designed for research, the WUSCT is foundational in adult development literature and remains widely respected in academic and clinical contexts. While less frequently used directly in organizational settings today, it provided the basis for many contemporary vertical assessments.

Leadership Circle Profile (LCP)—360° Assessment

The LCP integrates multiple leadership theories, including vertical development models, into a comprehensive 360-degree feedback tool. Participants receive feedback from multiple raters, highlighting their leadership competencies and developmental stage, identifying Reactive versus Creative orientations. Primarily used with executives and senior leaders, the LCP is popular for leadership development programs aiming for transformative growth. Developed by Bob Anderson and Bill Adams, it is offered by The Leadership Circle (now part of Wiley).

Leadership Evolution and Actualization Profile (LEAP)

LEAP aligns with Cook-Greuter and Torbert's developmental models, translating vertical development stages into accessible business language.

Administered via a sentence completion test tailored for organizational contexts, results inform leaders about their developmental stage and implications for their leadership effectiveness. LEAP is specifically targeted at corporate leadership development and coaching programs, developed by The Holos Group to bridge developmental theory and practical application in business environments.

Table 4.1 gives an overview of each of these assessments. These tools serve as a diagnostic baseline for leadership development programs. When administered at the beginning of a program, they help leaders understand their current stage and identify specific areas where targeted interventions are needed.

Preferred Terminology: Staging, Profiling, Assessing, or Measuring?

The terminology used to describe evaluations in vertical development varies based on the theoretical foundations and researcher preferences, each emphasizing different nuances and application contexts:

- **Staging:** This terminology is prevalent among developmental psychology theorists, including Robert Kegan and Susanne Cook-Greuter. The term "staging" emphasizes clearly defined developmental milestones or significant shifts in an individual's cognitive complexity and meaning-making processes. Examples include Kegan's "orders of consciousness" and Cook-Greuter's "ego development stages."
- **Profiling:** Often linked specifically to Bill Torbert's Global Leadership Profile (GLP), "profiling" emphasizes creating individualized developmental profiles. Rather than assigning a leader rigidly to a single developmental stage, profiling highlights the fluidity of development, acknowledging that individuals often span multiple action logics or stages simultaneously, with varying levels of intensity.
- **Assessing:** Broadly applied across structured methodologies like structured interviews (e.g., Subject-Object Interview—SOI) or written sentence completion tests (e.g., Maturity Assessment Profile—MAP). The term "assessing" highlights the evaluative, often qualitative nature of these methodologies, focusing primarily on understanding and interpreting developmental complexity through narrative or written responses.
- **Measuring:** Used predominantly in psychometric and quantitative contexts within vertical development research. This term underscores the focus on the reliability, validity, numerical scoring, and statistical analysis of developmental data. Examples include scoring systems used in tools like the MAP or GLP, which quantify developmental complexity into measurable stages or scores.

Table 4.1 Overview of Vertical Leadership Assessments

Theoretical Foundation	*Delivery Method*	*Assessment Type*	*Primary Purpose*	*Target Audience*	*Key Organizations/ Individuals*
Global Leadership Profile (GLP)	Torbert's Action Logics	Sentence completion test	Leadership development; assess action logics	Leaders, executives	Bill Torbert; Global Leadership associates
Maturity Assessment Profile (MAP)	Cook-Greuter/ Loevinger Ego Development	Sentence completion test	Personal and leadership maturity; Ego development	Leaders, professionals	Susanne Cook-Greuter; Vertical Development Academy (VeDA)
Vertical Mindset Indicator (VMI)	Ego development, simplified MAP stages	Digital AI-scored assessment	Cost-effective developmental snapshot	Leaders, coaches	Nick Petrie, Jan Rybeck; Adeption
STAGES Assessment	Terri O'Fallon's STAGES Model (Integral Theory)	Sentence completion test	High-resolution developmental profiling	Leaders, coaches, integral practitioners	Terri O'Fallon; STAGES International
Lectical Assessments (Lectica)	Kurt Fischer's Dynamic Skill Theory	Essay-based open-ended response	Cognitive complexity and skill growth	Leaders, professionals, students	Theo Dawson; Lectica, Inc.
Shifting Horizons	Action Logics (contextualized stage model)	Digital self-assessment; scenario-based	Contextualized developmental insights	Leaders, coaches, organizations	Vertical Development Institute (VDI)
Subject-Object Interview (SOI)	Kegan's Subject-Object Theory	Structured interview	Assess stage of adult meaning-making	Leaders, researchers, educators	Robert Kegan, Lisa Lahey; Minds at Work, Harvard
Growth-Edge Interview	Kegan's Constructive Developmental Theory (simplified)	Qualitative developmental coaching interview	Identifying developmental "edges" for coaching	Leaders, coaches	Jennifer Garvey Berger; Cultivating Leadership

(Continued)

Table 4.1 (Continued)

Theoretical Foundation	*Delivery Method*	*Assessment Type*	*Primary Purpose*	*Target Audience*	*Key Organizations/ Individuals*
Washington University Sentence Completion Test (WUSCT)	Loevinger's Ego Development Theory	Sentence completion test	Ego development research and measurement	General adult population, researchers	Jane Loevinger; Washington University
Leadership Circle Profile (LCP)	Universal Model (vertical and horizontal integration)	360-degree feedback survey	Leadership mindset and competencies	Leaders, executives, organizations	Bob Anderson, Bill Adams; The Leadership Circle
Leadership Evolution and Actualization Profile (LEAP)	Cook-Greuter and Torbert stage theories (business-focused)	Sentence completion test (business context)	Practical leadership developmental insights	Organizational leaders	The Holos Group
Leadership Agility 360	Joiner and Josephs' Leadership Agility Stages	360-degree feedback survey	Measuring leadership agility stages	Mid- to senior-level leaders	Bill Joiner; ChangeWise Consulting
Constructive-Developmental Framework (CDF)	Kegan's Social–Emotional and Basseches' Dialectical Cognitive Development	Multi-method (interviews: social–emotional, cognitive; personality questionnaire)	Holistic developmental diagnosis (cognitive, emotional)	Leaders, senior executives, coaches	Otto Laske; Interdevelopmental Institute (IDM)

Currently, the most widely accepted terms in contemporary research and practice include the following:

- **Assessing:** For general evaluations of vertical development, encompassing both qualitative and quantitative methodologies.
- **Profiling:** Specifically related to Torbert's methodology and individualized development profiles.
- **Staging:** Typically used within developmental psychology contexts to emphasize distinct developmental stages or milestones.
- **Measuring:** Applied primarily within psychometric and research-driven contexts emphasizing quantitative evaluation and statistical rigor.

Understanding and carefully selecting appropriate terminology is crucial, as it ensures clarity, precision, and effective communication among practitioners, researchers, and organizations engaged in vertical development.

Challenges With Vertical Development Assessments

There are a number of challenges with these assessments highlighted in Table 4.2. While vertical development assessments provide essential insights into a leader's meaning-making maturity and cognitive complexity, it's important to acknowledge several practical challenges and limitations associated with their use. One significant consideration is the cost and resource intensity of many established assessments.

Tools like the Leadership Maturity Assessment Profile (MAP), Global Leadership Profile (GLP), and the Subject-Object Interview (SOI) require trained raters and certified practitioners to interpret nuanced responses, making them both resource-intensive and expensive. These assessments are often time-consuming, involving detailed interviews or extensive written responses, thus typically being more appropriate for executive-level or targeted leadership interventions rather than broader organizational use. However, newer digital tools such as the Vertical Mindset Indicator (VMI) or Shifting Horizons aim to simplify and democratize vertical assessment through artificial intelligence and automated scoring.

Consequently, assessments should be carefully selected by balancing practical considerations such as cost, intended use, and scale, against the depth and precision of developmental insight required. Ultimately, the effectiveness of vertical development assessments depends significantly on skilled interpretation and appropriate contextual application, emphasizing the importance of training, certification, and ongoing support for those utilizing these tools.

In practice, these assessments are most effective when combined with coaching. For instance, after an initial assessment, a leader might engage in

Table 4.2 Common Challenges in Vertical Development Assessments

Challenge/Consideration	*Explanation and Impact*	*Example Assessments Most Impacted*
Time Intensity and Complexity	Many vertical assessments (especially those using interviews or open-ended sentence completion tests) require extensive time to administer, analyze, and interpret, making them resource-intensive and difficult to scale broadly	Subject-Object Interview (SOI), Growth-Edge Interview, MAP (Cook-Greuter), GLP (Torbert)
Cost and Resource Intensity	Intensive scoring methods (often manual and expert-driven) lead to higher costs. Requires certified raters or trained facilitators, making them expensive for mass use	MAP, GLP, SOI, Growth-Edge Interviews, STAGES, Lectica
Complexity and Accessibility	Some assessments are complex or abstract, which can reduce usability in practical organizational contexts or limit accessibility for participants unfamiliar with developmental concepts	SOI, MAP, Lectica assessments, CDF
Time Commitment	In-depth interview-based assessments or written response assessments can require significant time commitments from both participants and assessors	Subject-Object Interview (SOI), Growth-Edge Interview, Lectica
Validation and Reliability	Some newer or digitally simplified assessments may lack extensive validation or research compared to established tools	VMI, Shifting Horizons, LEAP (newer tools typically less validated compared to MAP or WUSCT)
Accessibility and Scalability	More comprehensive, qualitative, or interview-based assessments are difficult to scale widely across large groups or organizations due to complexity of administration	SOI, Growth-Edge Interview, MAP, GLP
Complexity of Interpretation	Developmental assessments yield rich, nuanced results that require expert interpretation. Without proper training, insights might be misunderstood or misused	GLP, MAP, SOI, Lectica, LEAP
Context Specificity	Results may vary depending on the context or state of the respondent when taking the assessment, potentially impacting validity if not contextualized appropriately	Shifting Horizons, Leadership Circle Profile (LCP), LEAP

one-on-one coaching sessions with a trained coach to interpret the results and set actionable developmental goals.

How Technology Is Increasing Assessment Access

Technology is playing a pivotal role in democratizing and making VLD assessments more accessible and scalable than ever before. A prime example of such innovation is Adeption's Vertical Mindset Indicator (VMI), an assessment rooted in ego or vertical development theory. The Adeption assessment is based on vertical development theory initially articulated by Jane Loevinger and further refined by researchers like Susanne Cook-Greuter.

The Vertical Mindset Indicator (VMI) leverages technology—specifically artificial intelligence to efficiently assess a leader's vertical development stage. VMI participants complete a set of nine carefully selected sentence stems originally derived from the Washington University Sentence Completion Test (WUSCT), a seminal assessment in ego development theory developed by Loevinger and later modified by Cook-Greuter. Each participant's responses are initially analyzed by Adeption's AI algorithm. Following this automated scoring, an expert scorer reviews the results to validate and refine the outcomes, ensuring both accuracy and nuanced human interpretation.

The VMI assesses leaders across the seven distinct developmental stages: Opportunist, Diplomat, Expert, Achiever, Redefining, Transforming, and Alchemical. Significantly, the AI-driven methodology of the VMI has shown remarkable accuracy and correlation with traditional assessments, such as the MAP (Maturity Assessment Profile). Recent Adeption validation studies demonstrate that the VMI algorithm produces results consistent with full MAP profiles, with 91.89% exact stage match rate, surpassing the typical inter-rater reliability target of 80% for human scorers. Additionally, participant feedback confirms the VMI's face validity, with 81% of users rating their results as highly accurate reflections of their own developmental stage.

The technological foundation of the VMI is integral to its accessibility and scalability. Built on the Adeption Leadership Development Platform, the assessment capitalizes on cloud-based infrastructure provided by Microsoft Azure, allowing scalability for large cohorts or leaders. This infrastructure not only enables handling thousands of simultaneous assessments but also ensures high-level security, reliability, and compliance, meeting stringent GDPR standards and undergoing regular third-party audits.

Integration with enterprise technologies further enhances its usability. The VMI utilizes secure single sign-on (SSO) integration methods, such as OAuth, Azure Active Directory, and SAML, facilitating easy and secure access for organizational participants. Comprehensive technology audits, including internal disaster recovery drills and third-party evaluations, underline Adeption's commitment to reliability, security, and performance excellence, ensuring the VMI meets rigorous corporate standards.

Organizations such as Novartis, Accenture, Walmart, Cardinal Health, and McDonald's, among others, have integrated the VMI within their leadership development initiatives, recognizing its robustness and practicality for assessing and enhancing leadership maturity at scale. These enterprises have recognized the value of the VMI's technologically enabled approach, allowing them not only to support individual leaders but also to strategically evaluate and influence organizational leadership culture.

The VMI exemplifies how technology can profoundly enhance the assessment of VLD. Through AI-driven scoring combined with human oversight, robust technological architecture, and secure integration capabilities, the VMI makes advanced developmental insights both broadly accessible and practical for individuals and large organizations alike.

Assessing Vertical Development in Organizations

Research into measuring vertical development at an organizational level remains relatively sparse and underexplored within the field of organization development (OD). Despite growing recognition of the value of vertical complexity—capturing how groups collectively evolve in their cognitive complexity and meaning-making capabilities—empirical methods and validated instruments to assess vertical development at a collective or organizational level are still emerging. Consequently, organizations have historically relied upon methods that primarily measure horizontal development. These traditional assessments typically emphasize improvements in operational effectiveness, strategic alignment, and structural maturity rather than explicit developmental progressions.

Horizontal Assessments in Organizational Development: The Current Landscape

In today's organizations, the prevailing methods for assessing growth, effectiveness, and progress have traditionally focused on horizontal development—that is, expanding skills, capabilities, and operational improvements within existing ways of thinking. Most mainstream OD practices emphasize measurable enhancements in specific competencies, process efficiency, and structural maturity, without explicitly assessing the deeper cognitive and developmental shifts described by vertical growth models.

For instance, organizations frequently use competency frameworks to gauge whether leaders have developed skills such as effective communication, time management, decision-making proficiency, and strategic execution. These assessments typically result in targeted training or interventions to fill skill gaps and enhance productivity.

Similarly, many organizations rely on well-established organizational typologies—such as models that categorize companies based on cultural attributes (innovative, bureaucratic, market-driven)—or organizational life cycle models (start-up, growth, maturity, decline). These frameworks aim to identify where the organization currently stands operationally and strategically, and what actions might be needed to move forward. However, they primarily address operational improvements or adjustments to business models rather than examining deeper shifts in cognitive or emotional capacities needed to thrive in complex or uncertain conditions.

This horizontal orientation has become prevalent because it aligns closely with conventional business needs: organizations often prioritize clear, immediate, and quantifiable improvements in processes, financial results, or market positioning. As a result, measurement approaches predominantly focus on performance metrics, strategic alignment indicators, and operational benchmarks. While these horizontal assessments are valuable for tracking incremental improvements, their focus remains fundamentally different from assessments of vertical development, which seek to understand and promote growth in individual and collective mindsets, capacities for complexity, and adaptive resilience.

In essence, horizontal assessments dominate organizational development today because they provide familiar, quantifiable, and immediate ways to gauge performance. But as organizations encounter more unpredictable and interconnected challenges, the limitations of purely horizontal frameworks—particularly their inability to measure or nurture more complex, integrative ways of thinking and being—are becoming increasingly apparent.

Assessments of Organizational Change

Mainstream organizational development often equates "development" with "change," typically viewing it as a planned, strategic initiative aimed at achieving specific business outcomes. In fact, in common practice and in many OD educational resources, the terms "organizational development" and "organizational change" are frequently used interchangeably. This association emphasizes implementing new processes, restructuring departments, or adopting new technologies—activities oriented around managing transitions rather than explicitly facilitating cognitive or vertical growth.

Most widely used OD frameworks for assessing and managing organizational change revolve around linear, sequential stages. For instance, Kurt Lewin's classic three-stage model—unfreeze, change, and refreeze—still underpins many modern change initiatives. This model describes an organization's current state, the desired future state, and outlines how to transition between the two effectively. Although simple and practical, this approach tends to focus exclusively on tangible, visible changes in organizational structures, processes, or practices. It does not explicitly address underlying developmental progressions—how teams' and leaders' fundamental ways of thinking and making sense of their environments might evolve in response to complex challenges.

Other well-known change models also prioritize horizontal shifts. For example, Weisbord's six-box model helps diagnose areas for improvement across domains like structure, rewards, and processes. Nadler and Tushman's congruence model assesses alignment between strategy, work processes, and culture. Similarly, methodologies and models center around conversational and relational change processes—yet they predominantly frame these in terms of cultural alignment or communication effectiveness rather than explicitly fostering developmental complexity.

Even within OD frameworks that explicitly reference "stages," these stages are usually prescriptive phases in a planned change sequence rather than descriptions of developmental growth. For instance, phrases like "moving from a reactive to a proactive state" or "progressing from siloed to collaborative operations" appear frequently. While helpful for managing organizational shifts, such stages do not assess deeper vertical development—the transformation in how individuals and teams perceive complexity, uncertainty, and interconnectedness.

Current organizational change assessment practices heavily emphasize horizontal perspectives—focusing on clearly defined transitions, measurable incremental improvements, and concrete structural adjustments. These methods are essential for managing day-to-day organizational effectiveness and practical change management but fall short of fully capturing or facilitating the deeper developmental shifts increasingly required in today's complex, dynamic business environments. The growing recognition of this limitation is prompting interest in assessment approaches explicitly designed to identify, nurture, and measure vertical developmental growth in organizations.

Approaches of Vertical Organization Development Assessment

Stage-based vertical development assessments for organizations represent an emerging and innovative field within OD. As organizations face increasingly complex and rapidly evolving environments, interest in understanding not just skill acquisition but deeper shifts in leaders' and teams' capacities to navigate complexity has grown significantly.

Some progressive organizations have begun introducing individual-level assessments of VLD, recognizing the value of supporting their leaders in advancing through increasingly complex stages of thinking and behaving. These assessments provide valuable insights into individual leaders' developmental stages, offering guidance on how leaders might better adapt to ambiguity and complex decision-making scenarios. However, while these individual assessments deliver critical insights into personal developmental trajectories, they differ substantially from organization-level vertical assessments. Individual assessments primarily reflect personal cognitive and emotional maturity without directly capturing how collective dynamics and systemic interactions influence or reflect organizational maturity.

Organization-level vertical assessments focus explicitly on collective behaviors, interactions, and patterns emerging from groups and organizational systems. Unlike individual assessments, these methods analyze how teams collectively approach complexity, manage tensions, and integrate diverse perspectives. Thus, organization-level assessments uniquely account for relational dynamics, cultural patterns, decision-making processes, and shared understandings that arise specifically within group contexts. Assessing VLD within organizations involves various methodologies, each with its strengths and challenges. There are five predominant approaches that we will review next.

Assessment by Aggregating Individual Scores

This method involves assessing individual developmental stages within a group and then aggregating the individual scores (using mean, median, or mode) to represent the group's overall developmental stage. For example, each team member might individually complete an assessment like the Vertical Mindset Indicator (VMI), and the results would be combined to create a single, averaged score for the team.

However, aggregating individual scores presents considerable challenges. It significantly simplifies the complex dynamics of collective development by reducing a group's maturity to mere arithmetic summaries of its members. This approach overlooks the critical nuances of interpersonal interactions, emergent group behaviors, and collective dynamics, potentially leading to misleading interpretations of a group's actual developmental capacity.

Assessment by a Single-Expert Rater

This approach relies on a single developmental expert's qualitative evaluation of a group's developmental stage through direct observation, structured interviews, or analyses of recorded interactions. The benefit of this method lies in its depth and context-specific interpretations, as the expert can incorporate subtle behavioral cues and contextual factors into their assessment.

For example, a seasoned organizational psychologist might attend several executive team meetings, noting communication patterns, leadership behaviors, and group dynamics to determine the team's developmental stage.

However, this approach heavily depends on the subjective interpretation and expertise of a single evaluator, potentially introducing bias and variability in results. Consequently, outcomes may lack consistency, making replication or comparison across different evaluators challenging.

Assessment With Multiple Expert Raters

In contrast to relying on a single evaluator, this method employs multiple trained expert raters who independently evaluate qualitative data gathered through structured assessments, observational protocols, interviews, or group exercises. The collaboration of multiple experts significantly reduces individual biases and enhances the reliability and validity of the assessment outcomes.

For instance, three expert evaluators may each assess recorded interactions of an executive team independently, comparing their ratings afterward. The team then collaboratively resolves any differences, ensuring a more balanced, robust, and credible developmental assessment.

Although more resource-intensive due to the need for coordination among evaluators, this method offers greater objectivity and reliability compared to single-expert rater assessments. By triangulating results across multiple evaluators, this approach provides a more balanced, nuanced understanding of a group's collective developmental stage.

Assessment With Technology-Enhanced Instruments

Technological advancements, exemplified by the Vertical Mindset Indicator (VMI), utilize artificial intelligence (AI) to enhance accessibility and accuracy in vertical leadership assessment. AI algorithms trained on extensive developmental datasets from established development measures and automate initial scoring of assessments. Results generated by AI are subsequently reviewed and refined by human experts, combining technological efficiency with human interpretive insight.

Practically, this approach enables rapid and scalable assessments, providing immediate insights into leadership maturity across large, geographically dispersed teams. Very large companies can thus quickly identify developmental gaps and strategically plan tailored interventions based on reliable and objective data.

This hybrid approach offers substantial scalability, consistent reliability, and reduced subjective bias. Organizations benefit from rapid, standardized assessments that maintain human oversight for accuracy and interpretative depth.

Assessment by Examining Social Contexts

This innovative approach explicitly assesses collective phenomena within social contexts rather than relying solely on individual assessments or expert raters. It focuses directly on relational dynamics, communication patterns, decision-making processes, and other emergent systemic properties characteristic of group interactions. Grounded in systems theory, this method seeks to capture the authentic complexity of organizational behavior by analyzing how collective intelligence emerges through interactions.

Practically, this method could involve using real-time data analytics from digital collaboration platforms (e.g., Slack or Microsoft Teams) to analyze how communication patterns among team members influence decision-making, responsiveness, and problem-solving capabilities.

Supported increasingly by advanced analytics and technology-driven tools capable of real-time, data-rich analyses of group interactions, this method offers a sophisticated means to understand and foster collective vertical growth in organizations. It holds considerable promise for accurately capturing the intricate and evolving nature of collective developmental systems.

It's Not a Race, It's About Range

Vertical development growth is not about climbing to the latest stage as quickly as possible or achieving a permanent state of advanced leadership. Instead, it is about expanding your vertical range, the ability to draw from multiple stages of meaning-making and ways of leading, depending on what the moment calls for. This kind of development allows leaders to operate with greater nuance, presence, and adaptability. It's not about discarding earlier ways of thinking but about integrating them, so you can respond effectively across a variety of contexts and complexities. The real power of vertical development lies in the capacity to move fluidly between action, reflection, and deep sensemaking. Leaders with a broad vertical range are better equipped to engage with diverse perspectives, navigate ambiguity, and lead others through uncertainty with both clarity and care.

While vertical development assessment at the organizational level is relatively new and still developing, there is a clear need for methodologies that authentically capture both individual and collective complexities. Of course, making this a reality isn't without obstacles. In Chapter 5, we'll look at the heat experiences that invite vertical growth.

References

Emam, S. M., Fakhry, S. F., & Abdrabou, H. M. (2024). Leaders development program by 360 degree feedback: Reflection on head nurses' leadership practices. *BMC Nursing*, *23*(1), 772. https://doi.org/10.1186/s12912-024-02395-w

Garvey, B., Stokes, P., & Megginson, D. (2012). *Coaching and mentoring: Theory and practice* (4th ed.). SAGE Publications.

Geerts, J. M. (2024). Maximizing the impact and ROI of leadership development: a theory- and evidence-informed framework. *Behavioral Sciences (Basel, Switzerland)*, *14*(10), 955. https://doi.org/10.3390/bs14100955

Chapter 5

Turning Up the Temperature With Heat Experiences

What Are Heat Experiences?

Heat experiences are those pivotal developmental crucibles that push leaders beyond their comfort zones and habitual ways of thinking. In the journey of vertical leadership development—growing the capacity to think in more complex, systemic, and strategic ways—heat experiences act as powerful catalysts. Unlike routine challenges that we can handle with existing skills, true heat experiences disrupt our normal patterns and force us to confront the limitations of our existing approaches. They present us with situations where our tried-and-true strategies no longer suffice, creating pressure and uncertainty that demand new learning and perspective (Center for Creative Leadership, 2015).

Not all leadership challenges drive real growth. Heat experiences are high-stakes, stretch situations that push leaders beyond their comfort zones into new ways of thinking and operating. Unlike routine challenges that can be solved with existing skills, heat experiences disrupt and disorient habitual thinking, exposing gaps in our current mindset and compelling us to find new approaches. Simply put, heat experiences occur when what used to work no longer does, forcing adaptation and growth.

The Key Ingredients of a "Hot" Challenge

Not all challenges lead to profound growth. Some reinforce existing skills, while others serve as pivotal developmental crucibles that alter a leader's mindset. Heat experiences fall into the latter category, acting as powerful accelerators for vertical leadership growth by compelling individuals to think, act, and lead in fundamentally new ways.

What sets a heat experience apart from a routine challenge is its ability to create a meaningful rupture in a leader's familiar patterns by disrupting assumptions, demanding adaptive thinking, and placing them in situations where failure is a real possibility (Petrie, 2018). The intensity of these

DOI: 10.4324/9781003644941-5

experiences forces leaders out of their comfort zones and into the realm of transformative learning.

There are key features that define an authentic heat experience and characteristics that make a challenge more than just difficult but developmentally potent. Whether it's stepping into a high-stakes role, managing through crisis, or leading in unfamiliar territory, these experiences reshape how leaders perceive and approach complexity. Key features that define a heat experience the following:

- **Pushes You Beyond Comfort:** It creates real stretch, engaging you at the edge of your capability while challenging enough to demand growth but not so overwhelming that it leads to paralysis.
- **High Stakes and Visibility:** The outcome matters and is noticed, whether by senior leaders, stakeholders, or peers, adding pressure to adapt quickly.
- **No Ready-Made Solutions:** Past expertise isn't enough. New skills, perspectives, and improvisation are required to navigate complexity or ambiguity.
- **A Real Possibility of Failure:** Failure is likely, especially at first, but is rich with learning. Growth-oriented organizations view such failures as development opportunities rather than irreversible mistakes.

Examples of heat experiences include the following:

- **Managing a Larger Scope:** Moving from leading a small team to overseeing a full department.
- **Mission-Critical Turnaround:** Being tasked with rescuing a failing business unit.
- **Cross-Functional or Role Change:** Shifting from finance to operations, requiring new capabilities.
- **New Market or Innovation Challenge:** Opening a new international division or leading a project with no precedent.

These moments demand rapid adaptation and deep learning, ultimately shaping leaders into more capable, resilient, and strategic thinkers.

How Heat Experiences Spur Vertical Growth?

While everyday challenges hone skills, heat experiences transform mindsets. Routine challenges refine existing abilities, such as working late to meet a deadline or resolving a team conflict as they are tasks within one's comfort zone. Heat experiences, on the other hand, destabilize known patterns and demand significant shifts in thinking.

For instance, whereas a routine challenge might involve solving a problem using experience, a heat experience forces a leader to question assumptions, experiment with new approaches, and fundamentally change their perspective. This is why routine challenges refine skills, but heat experiences create breakthrough growth.

How heat experiences drive this shift:

- **Challenge to Current Mindset:** They reveal the limits of current ways of thinking and forcing leaders to recognize that their usual approaches are insufficient.
- **Positive Disequilibrium:** The tension of not knowing creates the urgency to learn. Without discomfort, there is no push for growth.
- **Lasting Mindset Shift:** After navigating a heat experience, leaders don't just get better at something; they see leadership differently.

Leaders later look back on their greatest growth periods and almost always cite their most intense heat experiences. Instead of something to avoid, heat becomes the catalyst for their transformation by accelerating their ability to lead in an increasingly complex world.

Heat Experiences at Each Stage

Each stage comes with its own strengths and blind spots, and naturally, each stage will find different situations "hot." A challenge that profoundly stretches an Opportunist leader might hardly faze a Transforming leader and vice versa because the heat is relative to one's current mindset.

In this section, we explore how different heat experiences apply at each of the seven stages, and how those experiences can catalyze movement to the next stage. You may recognize some of your own experiences or those of people you've worked with. Keep in mind that while the stages tend to progress sequentially, real life is messy so a single leader might exhibit behaviors of multiple stages depending on the context. However, the *stretch* experiences described are those particularly potent for helping a leader transition out of one dominant mindset stage and into the next.

Opportunist: From Crisis to Connection

Opportunists tend to see the world in terms of "me versus others" and often maintain an illusion of control by manipulating situations to their advantage. Rules are tools to use if they help or ignore if they don't. At their best, Opportunists are scrappy and reactive which are traits useful in actual emergency situations. At their worst, they can be seen as distrustful, egocentric, or even unethical, especially under pressure. They don't naturally ask for help or think in terms of group success.

Mindset Recap: The Opportunist mindset is self-oriented and survival-driven. At this earliest stage, a leader is focused on personal needs, winning, and immediate gains.

The Heat Experience

What kind of "fire" could possibly lead an Opportunist to grow beyond this self-centric view? Often it takes a hard collision with reality such as a crisis that even the most cunning or forceful individual cannot handle alone. In practice, many Opportunist-stage individuals only begin to shift when they hit bottom or come up against a situation such as major illness, job loss, or natural disaster, in which it is clear they cannot win or be safe unless they rely on or connect with others. In other words, the heat experience for an Opportunist is often a humbling failure or catastrophe that shatters the notion that "I can do this all myself" or "I'm invincible as long as I take what I want."

The Lone Wolf Learns to Ask for Help

Take the example of Daniel, a rising sales executive whose Opportunist tendencies had served him well in hitting aggressive targets. Daniel was known to bend rules and hog credit—as long as he was the top performer, he didn't mind ruffling feathers. This worked (sort of) until the year the market took a sudden downturn. Daniel's biggest client abruptly went bankrupt, and a few others cut their orders in half. His pipeline dried up. Desperate to still "win," Daniel doubled down on risky deals and overpromises. Nothing worked. By mid-year, he was at the bottom of the sales leaderboard for the first time in his life and in danger of being fired. To make things worse, a health scare a stress-induced minor heart attack—forced him to take a step back. This perfect storm was Daniel's crucible. In the hospital recovery room, he finally grasped that his usual tactic of working harder and pressuring clients had hit a wall. He *could not* turn this around alone. Swallowing his pride, Daniel reached out to a trusted colleague and admitted, "I'm in trouble. I can't figure this out." To his surprise, she rallied to help, along with several team members he'd never thought to lean on. Over the next months, Daniel learned to depend on others, accept their advice, and even let them lead in areas where they had more expertise. It was deeply uncomfortable—a direct affront to his lone-wolf identity—but also relieving. The experience of this near-career death and the support that saved him cracked Daniel's tough shell. He began to value trust and loyalty, discovering that there is indeed "safety in numbers and belonging," a realization that marks the opening to the Diplomat stage.

Growth to the Next Stage

For an Opportunist, the next stage is Diplomat, where one's identity broadens to include being part of a group. The heat experiences that catalyze this shift usually force the Opportunist to acknowledge the importance of allies, rules, or structure. In Daniel's case, the combination of personal failure and vulnerability (health crisis) was stark enough that he chose connection over pure self-reliance. Others might experience a similar shift through, say, a military boot camp, a team sport challenge, or a community disaster response or anything that makes it evident that "we" can survive or win where "I" alone cannot. Once an Opportunist starts to see the value of fitting into a group or system for mutual benefit, they begin shedding their zero-sum mindset. A formerly opportunistic leader might become an enthusiastic team player, trading some personal freedom for security and acceptance. In essence, the fire of crisis has melted their defensive individualism just enough to allow a new, more social perspective to solidify.

Diplomat: Stepping Out of the Comfort of Conformity

Diplomat leaders provide stability and loyalty, and these leaders excel at keeping the boat steady and executing established processes. However, the downside is that Diplomats can be overly deferential and fear standing out. They may operate from fear of not fitting in, conforming so much that they suppress their own ideas or ignore necessary changes. In environments where strict compliance is needed (e.g., regulatory or safety contexts), Diplomats shine. But in fast-changing environments requiring innovation, their reluctance to challenge norms can become a liability.

Mindset Recap: A leader in the Diplomat stage values cooperation, norms, and belonging. Having learned the power of group inclusion, Diplomats strive to follow the rules and make things work as part of the group.

The Heat Experience

To grow beyond the Diplomat stage, a leader must be shaken out of the comfort of consensus and into acting independently. In essence, the Diplomat needs to experience individual agency and independent thinking in a way that the group cannot immediately validate. A classic heat experience here is being thrust into a role that requires independent decision-making or innovation outside the established rules. One example: a Diplomat who takes a role or project that requires independent thinking outside the group. Suddenly, they cannot just defer to the usual way or wait for senior directives; they must step up and chart a course on their own. Another developmental stretch is exposure to diverse perspectives beyond their familiar circle—for instance, talking to people in different departments or industries to learn how they do things. This can plant seeds of curiosity and show the Diplomat that the group's way is not the only way. Essentially, the heat comes from situations where *conformity won't solve the problem*, forcing the Diplomat to risk the disapproval (real or imagined) of their group by trying something new.

The Rule Follower Finds Her Voice

Marisa had built her career as the reliable operations manager who never rocked the boat. She prided herself on knowing and enforcing her company's standard operating procedures. In fact, Marisa often said, "The rules are there for a reason—they've served us well" (a very Diplomat sentiment). When corporate HQ initiated a special task force to overhaul an outdated process, Marisa was selected precisely because of her deep knowledge of the rules. The task force's goal, however, was to *improve* those processes, even if it meant changing long-standing policies. At first, Marisa felt paralyzed. In meetings, she found herself defaulting to "But this is how we currently do it," until one day the task force leader responded, "We know, but that system isn't working anymore. What do you suggest we do instead?" No one had ever directly asked Marisa to devise a new way! She realized that if she kept quiet, the group might stagnate. So that night, she sketched out an idea—a new workflow that broke a couple of minor rules but could dramatically reduce turnaround time. Heart pounding, she presented her idea at the next meeting. To her shock, instead of disapproval, she was met with thoughtful consideration. In fact, a director in the room said, "That's an excellent suggestion. Can you and the team flesh that out?" This was a turning point. Marisa's small act of independent thinking, going against the established routine, was a heat experience for her. It felt risky and uncomfortable, but it revealed a new capacity within herself. Buoyed by this success, Marisa began regularly reaching beyond her usual circle for input, even *visiting other companies* to see how they tackled similar issues (something she'd never have done before). Through this project, she transformed from the quiet follower into someone who could challenge processes constructively and contribute original ideas.

Growth to the Next Stage

The stage after Diplomat is Expert, a mindset where one starts to develop confidence based on personal expertise and rationale rather than pure group consensus. Marisa's story shows the essence of this shift: *separating* a bit from the pack to cultivate her own knowledge and voice. The heat experience of the task force forced Marisa to prioritize solving the problem over pleasing her higher-ups, a key reorientation from external authority to an internal standard of competence. Similarly, a Diplomat leader who might take on an assignment in a different role or talk extensively with people outside her normal group is expanding her horizons and personal competence. In short, she learns to value being *capable* and *right* even if initially it means not everyone agrees. A successful outcome (or simply surviving the experience) provides positive reinforcement. The leader begins to think, "Perhaps I have insights and abilities that are valuable, even if they deviate from the norm." That budding sense of expertise and independent judgment is the hallmark of the Expert stage.

Expert: Broadening Beyond Expertise

Expert leaders take great pride in their craft or specialty. They often become the go-to person for technical problems and can produce high-quality individual results. In leadership, Experts set clear standards and procedures; they excel in roles like project management, engineering, finance, and any domain where expertise and analytical thinking rule. The limitations of the Expert mindset emerge in more complex team situations: Experts may struggle to delegate or collaborate, believing "I need to do it myself if I want it done right." They can also get defensive about their own views, privileging being right over being effective. Feedback from others might be dismissed if it contradicts their well-honed logic. Essentially, Experts trust their own knowledge above all and can become siloed.

> **Mindset Recap:** A leader at the Expert stage is all about personal competence, precision, and logic. This mindset is focused on what you know and do—mastering skills, perfecting techniques, and ensuring things are done the "right way."

The Heat Experience

The crucible for an Expert is often having to lead or succeed beyond the bounds of one's own expertise. A scenario that many Experts find intensely stretching is leading a team or project in which they are *not* the technical expert. Imagine a star software developer (Expert) promoted to lead a cross-functional product team with designers, marketers, and salespeople. Suddenly her coding brilliance isn't directly useful to decide a marketing strategy or a sales approach. If she tries to micromanage or solve everything herself, she fails there's simply too much outside her domain. This kind of assignment forces the Expert to develop new muscles: listening, influencing, and trusting others' expertise. It's a humbling experience to go from being the smartest specialist in the room to the least knowledgeable on many topics. Another heat experience for Experts is receiving hard feedback on their impact, for instance, learning that team members find them difficult to work with or that their perfectionism is slowing things down. Being asked to practice listening to learn rather than to fix, win, or compare can feel very awkward for an Expert used to always having an answer. In summary, any situation where being the technical whiz-kid isn't sufficient, and might even be counterproductive, will light a fire under an Expert to grow.

The Expert Becomes a Leader of People

Aisha was a brilliant data analyst in its analytics department. As an individual contributor, she won awards for her accuracy and problem-solving. Because of her track record, Aisha was promoted to Analytics Manager, now overseeing a team of six analysts. She thought, "Great, I'll show them exactly how to do the job right." In practice, she couldn't resist re-doing her junior analysts' work to match her standards. She set up strict protocols and expected the team to follow them exactly. Instead of improving results, this micromanaging stifled the team. Work started to bottleneck as everyone waited for Aisha's approval on every detail. One by one, her team members grew disengaged and some even left for other departments. Upper management noticed the rising turnover and issues in Aisha's group and sent an executive coach to work with her. The coach gathered anonymous feedback. Aisha was shocked (and hurt) to hear her team describe her as controlling, unsupportive, and oblivious to their ideas. This feedback hit her like a ton of bricks, an emotional heat experience that completely disoriented her self-image as an excellent leader. At first, she was defensive: "If they just listened to me, we'd have no problems!" But as her coach gently pointed out, *being right* was not yielding *good results*. If she continued this way, she'd lose her entire team and fail as a manager. In one pivotal coaching session, the coach asked Aisha, "Would you rather be right, or would you rather be effective?" That question hung in the air. Aisha realized that her obsession with correctness was undermining her effectiveness as a leader. It was time to try a different approach, one she wasn't initially comfortable with. Over the next months, as uncomfortable as it was, Aisha practiced letting go. She assigned one of her analysts to lead a project in an area where Aisha herself was not the expert and resisted the urge to intervene. She focused on listening to learn, biting her tongue when she noticed something she would have done differently. She also set up a system to actively ask for feedback from her team in biweekly check-ins, signaling she was open to change. The first few times she admitted, "I don't know the answer—what do you all think?" felt like freefalling without a parachute. But gradually, she noticed her team members growing more confident and proactive. They started solving problems without waiting for her, and results improved. Aisha's transformation from a laser-focused expert to a people-focused leader had begun.

Growth to the Next Stage

Through painful feedback and the experiment of leading in a new way, Aisha moved toward the Achiever stage of development. Achievers balance personal competence with the ability to achieve results through others—they value effectiveness over being right, and they orient to goals and outcomes more than processes. The heat experience for an Expert like Aisha, failing at leadership until she changed her approach, was crucial to jolt her out of the Expert silo. An Expert who experiences the limits of solo expertise will start to appreciate the importance of communication, teamwork, and shared goals. They realize that, to borrow the coach's phrasing, effectiveness in a larger sense (the team succeeding, the project advancing) is the real win, even if it means their own technical solution isn't the one used. This mindset shift is huge: it moves the leader from "my way is the right way" to "let's find *the best way together* and get results." The former Expert begins to develop skills in delegation, coaching others, and integrating feedback. In essence, the heat of leading beyond one's expertise melts the rigid "I" focus and forges a new "team/results" focus which is the hallmark of an Achiever.

Achiever: Embracing Ambiguity and Purpose

Achiever leaders combine the planning and analytical abilities of the Expert with a stronger awareness of organizational goals and the need to collaborate. Leaders at this stage set clear goals, organize people and resources to meet those goals, and can efficiently manage projects and teams. They typically value feedback if it helps achieve outcomes and are willing to work on interpersonal skills since they know it affects results. Many successful mid-level managers, directors, and executives operate at Achiever, and it's a very effective stage in a corporate context. However, Achievers can become over attached to goals and execution, sometimes at the expense of deeper questioning. Their identity may entwine with success ("I am my achievements"), and they can get caught in overwork or burnout by taking on too much responsibility. Achievers prefer predictability: if they encounter a barrier, their instinct is often, "Work harder or make a better plan." Highly ambiguous or values-driven dilemmas (where hard work alone doesn't solve it) can perplex an Achiever.

Mindset Recap: The Achiever mindset is the model of the effective, goal-oriented leader. Achievers are highly motivated, focused on results, and attuned to team performance.

The Heat Experience

To grow beyond Achiever, a leader often confronts complexity or value conflicts that pure goal-orientation cannot resolve. In other words, the next growth edge often involves ambiguity, change without clear-cut solutions, or a sense of emptiness even after achieving success. A few common heat experiences for Achievers are as follows:

- **Stretch Assignments in Complexity:** An Achiever might take on a developmental assignment that involves high uncertainty and ambiguity where you can't easily define the outcomes. Imagine an operations manager who is superb at executing plans being asked to create a strategy for a market that barely exists yet, and there is no clear end-state or metric for success. This forces the Achiever to operate without a checklist or past template, pushing them to adopt a more exploratory, learning mindset rather than a pure execution mindset.
- **Feedback That Prompts Self-Reflection:** Achievers are open to feedback but typically to improve performance. However, a different kind of feedback—say, someone asks them about their *purpose* or *fulfillment*—can spark new introspection. Alternatively, they might receive feedback that their strength (drive, efficiency) has a shadow side (e.g., "Your relentless focus on goals is burning out the team"). Such feedback invites the Achiever to look beyond the immediate task and consider the human or long-term aspects.
- **Burnout or Personal Transition:** Sometimes, the heat comes as a personal crisis. A hard-charging Achiever might hit a wall—perhaps a health breakdown, or they attain a big career goal only to find it hollow. That disappointment or burnout can become a heat experience that makes them ask, "What really matters to me? Is it just about the next goal?" Indeed, many Achievers start transitioning to the next stage when they realize achievement might not be the same thing as fulfillment, prompting them to seek deeper meaning.

Success Isn't Enough

Raj was known in his company as "Mr. Fix-It." If a project needed to hit an aggressive deadline, Raj was the leader for the job. He led multiple successful product launches, priding himself on working 12-hour days side by side with his team, rallying everyone toward clear targets. As an Achiever, Raj found validation in checking off goals and delivering results. After a decade of nonstop accomplishments, Raj was promoted to a senior role to develop an innovative new business line. This wasn't a straightforward project, and it was more like being asked to create a start-up within a larger company. There were no clear benchmarks, the technology was evolving, and success might mean many different things (market share? revenue? user engagement?). Raj approached it the only way he knew how: set bold objectives and hustle. Months went by, and despite his team's hard work, progress was murky. The usual metrics didn't fully apply, and Raj felt frustrated that he couldn't define the outcomes with clarity. Morale on his team started slipping—people were confused about priorities. Sensing trouble, Raj's boss assigned him an executive mentor, *Elena*, who had a reputation for guiding leaders through transformative projects. In one coaching conversation, Elena asked Raj a simple yet jarring question: "Why does this project matter to you personally?" Raj opened his mouth to spout the usual lines about targets and success but stopped. He realized he actually felt little personal connection to the project's deeper purpose; he was just chasing another win. That night, Raj confronted an unsettling feeling he'd been too busy to notice: *burnout*. For the first time in years, he wasn't excited by hitting the next milestone. He started to reflect on what truly energized him. He noticed that what had always lit him up was solving customer problems—yet he'd barely spoken to a customer in this new role, buried as he was in Gantt charts. The next week, Raj did something unusual: he set aside the rigid project plan and took his team on a field trip to visit several customers using competitor solutions. They spent two days listening and asking questions, without any predefined agenda. The insights were eye-opening. Raj returned to the office with a renewed sense of purpose, and he now had a *vision* for the business line that went beyond hitting a number; it was about fulfilling a real customer need. He communicated this vision to the team, acknowledging that success might not be linear and that was okay. He also began encouraging his team (and himself) to structure workdays with more balance, integrating breaks for reflection and making it "okay to be human" instead of running at 110% constantly. This was a significant mindset shift: Raj was allowing space for ambiguity, learning, and personal meaning, rather than just execution. It was uncomfortable at first—part of him felt like he was slacking by not pushing, pushing, pushing. But the result was a more engaged team and a more innovative approach. Eventually, the project found its footing in a creative pilot launch that didn't meet the original revenue target but generated invaluable learning and positioned the company as a pioneer in a new niche. Raj considered it one of the most fulfilling experiences of his career, despite it not being a clear "win" by his old definition.

Growth to the Next Stage

Through this journey, Raj began transitioning into the Redefining (or Individualist) stage. The hallmark of Redefining is a greater focus on purpose, meaning, and seeing things from multiple perspectives, rather than just executing a known playbook for success. The heat experiences that often propel an Achiever to Redefining involve doubts about the status quo definition of success. In Raj's case, the combination of an ambiguous project (where hard work didn't immediately equal success) and his own emerging burnout caused him to question, "What do I really want?" and "What truly matters here?" Those are Redefining-stage questions. Achievers stepping into Redefining may explore new perspectives (like Raj visiting customers, or an Achiever taking a sabbatical to travel or learn something new), and they become more open to values beyond achievement: fulfillment, creativity, making a broader impact. This can be a turbulent transition—Achievers often feel torn as their old drivers lose steam and new ones haven't fully formed. Raj, for example, had moments of guilt and confusion as he changed his work style. That turbulence is well documented: Redefining is described as a "particularly disruptive and turbulent" stage because it challenges long-held assumptions and habits. But with supportive experiences (like Raj's mentor and the experiential learning he undertook), Achievers gain the new perspective that success is not one-dimensional. They learn to navigate complexity and engage with a "greater purpose" beyond the immediate goals. In doing so, they begin to redefine success on their own terms, setting the stage for the Redefining mindset.

Redefining: Navigating the Turbulence of Transformation

Redefining leaders realize that the rules and goals of the game can be challenged and changed. Redefining leaders might ask "Why are we doing this at all?" even when everything seems to be going fine. They tend to be more aware of their own inner voice and values, which may or may not align with the organization's traditional metrics. This mindset often results in a post-heroic approach—it's less about the leader's personal success and more about what they empower and enable in others. Redefining leaders are willing to challenge the status quo and experiment with new ways of working, which can drive significant innovation. However, the Redefining stage comes with its challenges. Because everything is in flux, individuals can experience existential angst or confusion. The old ways don't hold the same meaning, but the new ways aren't yet clear. They may struggle with prioritizing since they see so many options and perspectives. In organizations, Redefining leaders can be seen as disruptors or "loose cannons" if not understood, since they might disregard traditional hierarchies or processes in pursuit of a bigger vision.

Mindset Recap: The Redefining stage is all about questioning, complexity, and authenticity. Leaders operating with a Redefining mindset start to see multiple perspectives and value purpose and people alongside performance.

The Heat Experience

Interestingly, simply *being* in the Redefining stage can feel like a continuous heat experience. This stage often starts because of prior heat experiences (like Raj's story of questioning fulfillment) that threw the leader into a period of searching and disruption. To continue developing within Redefining, leaders benefit from experiences that help them ground and integrate their many insights, as well as support through the turbulence. Key developmental experiences at this stage include the following:

- **Broadening Horizons Further:** Redefining thrives on exploration. A heat experience might be diving even deeper into difference—for example, taking an international assignment or cross-industry role that exposes the leader to radically different perspectives, truly challenging a familiar worldview. If they haven't done something like that already, it can accelerate the broadening of mind. Even if they have, each new context continues to stretch their thinking.
- **Polarity and Complexity Practices:** At Redefining, leaders see many sides of an issue and sometimes feel paralyzed by them. Learning tools for complexity can be a productive challenge. For instance, being tasked with a problem that has no clear right answer but requires balancing opposing priorities can be a heat experience that forces a Redefining leader to bring structure to chaos. Using techniques like polarity mapping to navigate competing issues is suggested as a stretch exercise for this mindset. It's hard work similar to mentally holding two fire-hot coals (opposite ideas) and not dropping either. But it teaches them to build both/and thinking, which is a critical skill to stabilize in this stage.
- **Personal Growth and Support:** Many leaders in Redefining seek out coaches, mentors, or even therapists as they wrestle with big questions. Engaging in deep coaching or mentorship is itself an experience that can further their growth, and it provides a safe space to sort through turmoil and can introduce higher-stage perspectives (if the coach is at a later stage). This is why one recommendation is to work with a coach or mentor to adapt new insights and get support for navigating the questions and disruption that often come with this stage. The heat here is less

about external pressure and more about the internal emotional work and confronting one's shadow, fears, or long-held beliefs.

In Redefining, a leader might consciously *seek* heat experiences as part of their quest for meaning. For example, some take a sabbatical to travel the world or volunteer in a completely different setting, deliberately putting themselves in novel, uncomfortable situations to spur growth. Others might initiate bold changes in their organizations, like starting a diversity and inclusion effort or a sustainability initiative—even if it's outside their formal role, because it resonates with their values. These can be risky moves that generate conflict (heat) but also deep learning.

The Maverick Finds Integration

Elena (the same mentor who helped Raj in our earlier story) has her own growth story. Earlier in her career, Elena was an accomplished marketing director (firmly Achiever) who began to feel that churning out marketing campaigns for consumer products was meaningless to her. After a personal epiphany during a volunteer trip building schools in rural areas, she entered a Redefining phase, returning to work with a storm of new ideas. She pushed her company to embrace social responsibility messaging, challenged the executive team on purpose beyond profit, and when met with resistance, she grew cynical. Feeling like the corporate world didn't get it, she left her job to pursue a master's degree in organizational development, hoping to bring change from a different angle. As a graduate student, Elena was swimming in perspectives—psychological theories, cultural studies, and systems thinking. Her mind was alive with possibilities but she also felt more confused than ever about what path to take. Recognizing she was in over her head, Elena got herself two mentors: a retired business leader known for transformative leadership (operating at a Transforming/Alchemical level) and a professor who was an expert in adult development. Through many late-night discussions (and a few tears), Elena learned to apply some structure to her exploration. One mentor taught her polarity mapping, which she used to reconcile her conflicting desires to change organizations *and* be accepted by them (a classic idealism vs. practicality polarity). The other mentor simply listened and occasionally posed grounding questions like, "What *values* would you hold to no matter what? What does that mean for how you engage?" These prompts acted like a mirror, helping Elena see through the chaos of her thoughts to the core principles she cared about, in her case, integrity and empowerment. Over time, Elena integrated her passion for purpose with a new strategy: she realized she could be more effective at working *with* organizations patiently rather than against them. She started consulting, framing her big ideas in ways business leaders could hear. For instance, instead of condemning her clients for not having a purpose, she'd ask, "What do you want your leadership legacy to be?" She learned to meet companies where they were, guiding them gradually to new insights. This both/and approach—honoring her vision *and* the reality of her clients' starting points—was hard-won through the heat of her Redefining journey.

Growth to the Next Stage

Elena's story illustrates movement toward the Transforming stage. Redefining can be a long, winding road; the heat is often self-induced by the desire to find one's authentic path and improve the world. The transition to Transforming happens as the leader starts to find calm and clarity amidst complexity, and commits to a clear, larger purpose. In Elena's case, the support and tools she engaged with were pivotal. They helped her turn the turbulent energy of Redefining into a focused dedication to change leadership (hence her eventual role as an executive mentor). A sign of moving into Transforming is when the leader gains an expanded capacity to relate to others who come at things from different mindsets, as well as an inner calm in what matters most. Elena exhibited this as she learned to speak the language of the very Achiever-type executives she used to criticize, thus bridging perspectives.

In general, the heat experiences for a Redefining leader—balancing polarities, surviving existential doubt, engaging in deep reflection—forge resilience and wisdom. They emerge with a more solid sense of self (having answered "Who am I, really, and what do I stand for?") and an ability to hold complexity without being overwhelmed. The exit from Redefining often comes with a sense of coming home to a deeper, more accepting sense of self and what matters most, creating a platform of clarity from which to operate. This platform is the launching pad for Transforming leadership, where one can truly focus on serving the broader system and vision.

Transforming: Integrating Systems and Inspiring Others

Transforming leaders often serve as bridge builders, bringing together opposing viewpoints and creating a middle path or collaborative solutions. They have a strong inner compass (established in the Redefining stage) and lead with empathy and vision. Transforming leaders are adept at creating conditions for success for others and acting like facilitators. They foster shared accountability and empowerment in their teams. They are keenly aware of their own shadows and limitations, and they strive to own and work with both their strengths and blind spots, showing vulnerability when appropriate. In essence, this stage produces authentic, visionary leaders capable of transformative change, not just incremental improvement.

Mindset Recap: The Transforming stage is characterized by a leader who can see across multiple systems and time horizons, integrating people, process, and purpose. A Transforming leader works comfortably in ambiguity and complexity, holding a big-picture perspective while also understanding the interdependence of all the moving parts.

Even at this high level of development, there are blind spots. Transforming leaders can become so enamored with their vision or complex thinking that they struggle to communicate simply to those at earlier mindsets. They might inadvertently come off as aloof or overly intellectual. Additionally, they may sometimes get stuck in analysis or complexity, seeking that "simplicity on the other side of complexity" but not always reaching it. Therefore, their growth edge often lies in translation and turning their advanced insights into actionable, relatable guidance for others, and in continually checking their ego (ensuring their confidence in seeing the big picture doesn't turn into a new form of arrogance).

The Heat Experience

For Transforming-stage leaders, heat experiences tend to revolve around testing their ability to catalyze change at the systemic level and truly empower others, as well as deepening their humility and empathy. Some potent challenges include the following:

- **Leading Major Culture Change:** A Transforming leader might take on the challenge of shifting an entire organizational culture or tackling a complex societal problem through a multi-stakeholder initiative. These are the kinds of tasks that require everything in their toolkit including strategy, empathy, conflict resolution, and long-term vision. Even for a skilled leader, this can be incredibly challenging because the *system* will push back. Success is not guaranteed, and they must learn to navigate resistance without losing faith.
- **Succession and Letting Go:** Another heat experience is preparing to hand over leadership or create other leaders. For someone used to being the visionary, stepping back to let others lead (perhaps mentoring a team of next-generation leaders) can feel like a loss of control. It's a test of how well they've truly internalized the idea of empowering others versus being at the center themselves. If they find they're reluctant to let go, that reveals remaining ego attachment to address.
- **Confronting Personal Vulnerabilities in Public:** Transforming leaders may need to model vulnerability as a strength. For instance, openly

acknowledging a personal failure or blind spot in front of their organization can be a heat experience, and it requires courage and trust in others. Yet doing so can dramatically increase their credibility and create a culture of psychological safety. An example exercise is to acknowledge when your shadow is operating and meet it with compassion and curiosity, perhaps even publicly. The "shadow" refers to those hidden fears or biases that accompany their strengths. By owning these, the leader demonstrates authenticity and continuous growth.

- **Simplifying the Complex**: Paradoxically, one of the toughest challenges is forcing oneself to distill a very complex idea into a simple message everyone can grasp. A suggestion for Transforming leaders is to drive for simplicity . . . so that it can be captured in a twitter-friendly message that all levels can relate to. This can feel like intellectual contortion for someone who revels in nuance, but it is a vital skill to truly enroll and inspire broad audiences. The heat here is the discipline of not hiding behind complexity and essentially; it's an exercise in extreme clarity and communication.

The Visionary Becomes a Teacher

Luis is a senior executive known for turning around organizations by inspiring profound cultural change. Operating from a Transforming mindset, he sees organizations as dynamic systems and intuitively grasps how altering one element will ripple through the whole. In his current role as CEO of a mid-sized tech company, he crafted a vision to shift from a product-centric culture to a customer-centric, agile culture. Rather than dictate the change, Luis set out to engage employees at all levels in co-creating this transformation. Early on, he hosted town halls where he spoke about the bigger picture purpose, not just beating competitors or making money but making our customers' lives easier and our employees' work more meaningful by being adaptable and innovative. People were energized; Luis had a knack for connecting hearts and minds to a vision. However, six months in, metrics were stagnating. Middle managers, in particular, struggled to translate the lofty vision into day-to-day actions. Through skip-level meetings and some blunt feedback, Luis discovered that while everyone respected his ideas, many found them too abstract. One manager confessed, "I love what you're saying, but I don't know what *you want me to do differently* on Monday." This was humbling. Luis realized that his ideas had to be made more concrete. He remembered a mentor's advice: *If you can't explain it simply, you don't fully get it yet.* So he treated this as a personal challenge and a bit of self-imposed heat. Luis worked with a communications coach to boil down his strategy into a one-page story that anyone from a new hire to a board member could understand. In it, he outlined three clear behaviors every team should adopt (e.g., start every project by interviewing three customers) and tangible actions tied to his vision. He tested this narrative in small group meetings, watching for reactions. The simplicity clicked; people began echoing the mantra and, more importantly, practicing the new behaviors. The culture shift gained traction. Along the way, Luis also shared some of his own "shadow." In one company all-hands, he admitted,

> As a leader, sometimes I get carried away with big ideas and I forget to check if I'm being clear. That's my growth edge, and I want you all to hold me accountable, ask me for clarity when I'm not making sense.

This candor made a strong impression. Employees remarked that it set a tone where it was okay to question and collaborate, rather than just quietly nod. Over the next year, Luis's company saw not only improved performance but a spike in engagement scores and people felt heard, inspired, and clear on how to contribute.

Growth to the Next Stage

Luis's journey, though already at a high level, shows a continued refinement of Transforming capacities. By facing the heat of having to simplify his complex vision and exposing his own vulnerability in communication, he became an even more effective Transforming leader. The next stage beyond Transforming is often dubbed Alchemical (or sometimes *Ironist* or *Unitive* in various theories). Reaching that stage is relatively rare and usually comes after sustained experience and often later in life. It involves an almost paradoxical, fluid way of viewing the world, deeply principled yet very flexible and detached from any one identity or frame work. For a Transforming leader like Luis, stepping toward Alchemical might involve even more profound shifts such as embracing the idea that *security is an illusion and everything is interconnected and impermanent.* It may entail mentoring and guiding on an even broader scale, perhaps influencing change across multiple organizations or societies, often behind the scenes with a quiet, wise presence. The kinds of heat experiences that spur a Transforming leader toward Alchemical are less about external assignments and more about internal transcendence, for example, a deep personal crisis that no external action can solve, only acceptance and wisdom; or experiences that blur the boundaries of self, such as spiritual retreats or profound service to others, leading to a shift in consciousness.

Alchemical: Wisdom, Fluidity, and Service Beyond Self

Alchemical leaders tend to prefer open, fluid conditions that allow them to embrace what shows up moment to moment, approaching situations with an almost fluid intelligence. Alchemical leaders often operate in the background, guiding transformations quietly. They have a profound sense of interconnectedness—seeing the unity behind apparent differences—and as such, they might appear spiritual or wise in their demeanor. They can adapt their style infinitely to meet the needs of the present moment, almost like shapeshifting: continually readjusting how they think, act, and present themselves to stay in the serenity that lies in the eye of the storm. This can make them seem enigmatic or "out there" to others. They also fully accept the impermanence of things (everything is constructed and liable to change), which gives them both humility and courage—nothing is too precious to change or let go, except perhaps a few core principles like compassion or truth.

> **Mindset Recap:** The Alchemical mindset represents the latest stage of vertical leadership maturity. Leaders at this stage embody a sense of balance, peace, and radical flexibility.

However, being at this stage can feel lonely. Few others truly understand their perspective, and their tendency to speak in terms of paradox or big picture can sound like "woo-woo" to more conventional ears. Alchemical leaders might struggle with functioning in traditional organizations for long, finding them constraining. The challenge for them is to stay connected and understood by the broader world. Their growth, to the extent we can talk about growing at this rarefied stage, often involves finding ways to express their wisdom in practical ways and to build bridges back to people at earlier stages, without losing the depth of their insight.

The Ongoing Heat (and Light) for Alchemical Leaders

By this point, heat experiences take on a somewhat different character. It's less about being challenged by external tasks (since Alchemical individuals have usually seen and done so much that they're not fazed by typical leadership challenges) and more about deepening and sustaining their enlightenment while functioning in the everyday world. Some developmental experiences or practices include the following:

- **Spiritual or Contemplative Practice:** Many Alchemical-minded leaders rely on practices like meditation, prayer, or time in nature to provide

support, grounding, and connection. Continuing to deepen these practices is both comforting and growth-inducing—it's like tending the fire that keeps their insight warm. For them, the "heat" might be the inner challenge of going further into self-awareness, even into the realm of the mystic, which can be a vast, sometimes unsettling journey.
- **Learning to Communicate Across Levels:** An Alchemical thinker might perceive truths that are hard to articulate. So a key challenge is learning the communication that works in their environment and working with others to communicate what they see in a way others can hear. For example, if an Alchemical leader has a gut sense about a strategic decision that defies conventional analysis, they need to translate that intuitive wisdom into a form that boards and teams can digest (perhaps by finding data that support it, or telling a compelling story). That translation is not easy, but it's crucial to their effectiveness and influence.
- **Seeking Fellowship and Wisdom Traditions:** Because of the potential loneliness, Alchemical leaders often find solace and growth by connecting with ancient wisdom traditions or diverse cultural perspectives. This might mean studying philosophy, scripture, or indigenous knowledge that resonates with their sense of the world's unity and relative nature. Such exploration can further enrich their perspective (imagine learning from sages across history) while also giving them a sense of community, albeit a community that might span time and space. It's suggested to explore ancient and different cultural wisdom traditions to connect with eternal teachings. This can validate and deepen their understanding, providing a broader context for their experiences.

Pragmatically, an Alchemical leader in an organization may use their stage to be a kind of *servant leader* extraordinaire or an organizational elder. They often mentor multiple people, catalyze change without claiming credit, and create pockets of transformation that persist even after they leave.

The Sage on the Sidelines

Consider Asha, a senior leader who has had a rich and varied career—from leading companies to working on humanitarian projects globally. In her later years, she stepped away from formal executive roles. She now works intermittently as an advisor during crises—the person you quietly bring in when things are on the brink and conventional wisdom has failed. During a national healthcare strike, Asha was asked to mediate. She spent the first week not in negotiation meetings, but sitting in hospitals and in workers' homes, simply observing and listening to everyone from patients to nurses to administrators. People were initially puzzled—why wasn't she diving into strategy? But Asha was absorbing the whole system. In a later debrief, she described it like being present with the pain of the whole, letting patterns and needs emerge in her awareness. When she finally convened the stakeholders, Asha had an uncanny ability to articulate each group's concerns better than they could themselves. She helped them see each other's humanity in a way that defused the animosity. Rather than pushing a specific deal, she guided the conversation to a point where the antagonists organically found common ground. Those in the room described the outcome as nearly miraculous; it was as if the solution unveiled itself. Asha hardly spoke in terms of demands—she asked a few powerful questions and occasionally reframed someone's angry outburst into a respectful insight. Following the resolution, people asked how she did it. She demurred, giving credit to everyone's willingness to listen. Truthfully, her "quiet wisdom . . . behind the scenes" was the catalyst. For Asha, this kind of intervention isn't a routine skill—it takes a tremendous amount of presence and compassion, and she admits it also takes a toll. After the healthcare strike, she retreated to a month-long meditation retreat to recharge her connection with the deeper currents. She finds that if she doesn't regularly ground herself, it's easy to feel disconnected or unseen, almost like an alien in fast-paced corporate environments. So her ongoing practice of reflection and spiritual study is not just personal but necessary to continue serving in her way.

Asha's story illustrates the Alchemical pattern: such leaders often come in and out of the spotlight, maintaining their equilibrium through a balance of engagement and retreat. Her heat experiences now are perhaps subtle—the internal challenge of holding the suffering of systems and staying compassionate and effective, and the discipline of resting in the moment and opening to what is emerging. There is no "next stage" after Alchemical that we can concretely describe (some theorists speculate, but it's largely uncharted). The journey here is about integration and service: continuing to refine one's ability to catalyze positive change with minimal ego and finding meaning in being part of something larger.

Having traversed these seven stages and their distinctive heat experiences, a few key themes emerge. First, the kinds of challenges that spur growth change as we grow—what is developmental at one stage may be just an average Tuesday at another. Second, support and reflection are crucial at every stage to turn heat into growth. Each leader we saw had some form of safety net or learning process (colleagues, mentors, coaches, personal reflection) that helped them process the heat. And third, embracing these experiences as *intentional* opportunities rather than dreaded ordeals makes a huge difference. In the next section, we'll explore how leaders and organizations can create conditions to harness the power of heat experiences deliberately, so that more people can grow vertically with a little less "accidental" suffering and a little more purposeful development.

Creating and Embracing Heat: How to Turn Up the Temperature—Intentionally

By now, it's clear that heat experiences are vital for vertical growth, but they often sound like things that "just happen" to leaders. Waiting around for a lucky (or unlucky) break to spur development isn't a very strategic talent development plan! The good news is that leaders and organizations can intentionally cultivate and navigate heat experiences. It's about creating the right conditions: enough heat to challenge, enough support to learn, and a culture that encourages stepping into the fire.

Designing Optimal Heat Experiences

Not all heat is good heat. Too little, and there's no growth; too much, and it can burn out a person rather than build them. The goal is optimal tension, sometimes called "productive disequilibrium." So how do we design or recognize optimal heat experiences? Here are some guidelines drawn from research and best practices:

Stretch, Don't Break: The experience should push a leader just beyond their current capacity, think of it like weightlifting, where you want to lift more than before but not so much that you injure yourself. Ensure the leader has or can develop *some* of the skills needed, even if they need to learn fast. If a task is wildly unrelated to anything they know (say, asking a finance expert to suddenly perform brain surgery), that's not developmental. But asking that finance expert to lead a sales team taps into related skills (analysis, strategy) while requiring new ones (relationship-building, influence). It's a significant stretch but doable with effort and learning.

Visible and Meaningful Stakes: Choose challenges that matter—to the individual and the organization. When a leader deeply cares about the outcome and knows others are watching, they're more likely to be fully engaged (and frankly, a bit scared in a good way). A project that has *real impact* if successful (or real consequences if not) naturally creates urgency. As one guide put it, the experiment should occur where others will notice the outcome. This isn't about public shaming; it's about motivating commitment. For example, giving an emerging leader the opportunity to present a new product idea to the board is hot, if it goes well, the company might invest, and if not, it's a missed opportunity everyone will see. That weight drives preparation and growth.

Supportive Failures (and Safe Zones): Plan for the possibility of failure and frame it as learning. Perhaps set up the heat experience in a way that if things go wrong, it won't be catastrophic to the business or the person's career. For instance, in a fail-safe assignment, there might be backup systems or mentors in place. When a company creates a culture of developmental risk-taking, it encourages people to attempt tough challenges and views failures as data, not death sentences. Leaders should explicitly communicate, "We're giving you this stretch role because we expect growth, not perfection. Mistakes are expected; learning from them is what counts." Then live up to that, and if the person stumbles, celebrate the lessons and help them course-correct, rather than punishing the risk taken.

Reflection and Sensemaking: A heat experience isn't truly developmental without time and tools to reflect on it. Whether it's through journaling, a coach, or guided after-action reviews, the leader should process questions like: *What assumptions of mine were challenged? What did I do when I didn't know what to do? How did I feel and why? What would I do differently if faced with a similar challenge?* Embedding these reflective checkpoints during and after the assignment helps turn experience into insight. This is essentially building the elevated sensemaking piece into the design. Some companies use formal processes like learning journals or cohort discussions for leaders in stretch roles to collectively reflect and support each other.

By attending to these elements, organizations can craft assignments or developmental experiences that maximize growth. Many progressive organizations already do this through rotational programs, action learning projects, hackathons, and more. For example, global companies might have a policy to send high-potentials on international rotations (heat experience) with a mentor assigned remotely (support) and a formal debrief when they return (sensemaking). The idea is to embed growth into the job—not as a one-off training event but as a series of stretch experiences woven into one's career.

Cultivating a Heat-Seeking Culture

Beyond individual experiences, the broader culture either amplifies or dampens the effect of heat. A culture that fears failure and clings to the status quo will smother the transformative power of heat experiences. In contrast, a "growth mindset" culture encourages smart risk-taking and views challenges as opportunities to evolve. Leaders play a huge role in setting this tone. Here are ways to cultivate an environment where heat experiences flourish:

- **Leaders Model Learning, Not Perfection:** When senior leaders share their own stories of past failures or stretches, it normalizes taking on tough challenges. Consider the impact of a respected executive telling a group of rising managers about their greatest "failures," what they learned, and how those failures ultimately helped them succeed. Rather than only parading success stories, celebrating *failure stories* (with lessons learned) is incredibly powerful. It sends the message: *We all start somewhere, we all screw up on the way to mastery—and that's okay.* Some organizations have even done failure forums where top leaders each recount a time they were in over their heads. This practice, as Nick Petrie notes (2018), can lead to huge breakthroughs in mindset. Suddenly, high-potentials realize that the leaders they admire were not always as capable as they are now; they grew through adversity. That frees them to step up and risk their own heat experiences without shame.

- **Align Rewards With Growth:** If every KPI and bonus is tied only to short-term results, no one will want to take a risk on a stretch project that might not pay off immediately. To counteract this, companies are starting to value learning metrics. For example, some firms include personal development goals in performance reviews or have promotion criteria that account for breadth of experience, not just narrow success. One tech company instituted an award for most innovative failure—given to a team that tried something bold that didn't pan out but yielded significant insight. When employees see that trying new things (responsibly) is praised, they are more likely to volunteer for heat experiences. Psychological safety, the feeling that you can fail or speak up without punishment, is the bedrock of a learning culture.
- **Provide Backup and Resources:** Encouraging heat experiences isn't the same as sink or swim in the deep end. Organizations should provide a metaphorical safety net: perhaps a coach on call, peer learning groups, or an open-door policy to discuss struggles. One approach is to pair people in stretch roles with late-stage mentors (leaders at Transforming/Alchemical stages) who can guide their sensemaking. Another is to use action learning teams or peer coaching circles so that individuals undergoing heat experiences can debrief with each other and trade perspectives. This brings the second condition, colliding perspectives (the who), into play alongside heat, and the third condition, sensemaking, through discussion—a powerful trio.
- **Tailor Challenges to Readiness:** A note of prudence: A culture of development meets people where they are. You wouldn't throw a new hire straight into negotiating a major acquisition—that may be too much heat too soon. Perhaps for a novice, a horizontal move or moderate increase in scope is the right amount of heat. Petrie (2018) reminds us that not everyone is ready for the same challenges at the same time. The best organizations calibrate—they plant seeds for vertical development early (like giving junior folks some cross-functional exposure), gradually increase the heat for those who show readiness, and always offer the right

support. It's a personalized journey. HR and talent professionals can use tools (like the VMI or other stage assessments) to understand a leader's current mindset, and then design appropriate next-step challenges. The aim is to have a pipeline of leaders, each getting the kinds of experiences that will help them move to their next level when they're ready.

In such an environment, employees come into their roles with different experiences, skills, perspectives, and stages of development and the organization intentionally meets them there. It's akin to personalized learning in schools—giving each student a bit of the struggle that will help them grow, but not the same test to everyone.

Practical Ways to Add Heat to Your Own Development

While organizations have a big role, individual leaders are not off the hook in owning their growth. You can cultivate a heat-seeking mindset in yourself—meaning, proactively seeking challenges that will force you to evolve. Here are some practical ways to incorporate heat experiences into your personal development plan:

- **Volunteer for Stretch Assignments:** Don't wait to be tapped on the shoulder. If you see an opportunity that scares you a little (or a lot)—a cross-department task force, a chance to lead a meeting, an expansion project—raise your hand. As one expert advised, create "heat-seeking" leaders by having them step up to challenges. Be that leader. You might even tell your boss, "I'm looking for a stretch opportunity; I want to grow." Managers often appreciate the initiative and can help find a suitable challenge.
- **Change Your Context:** If things have gotten too comfortable, shake up your environment. This could mean changing roles within your organization, moving to a new company or industry, or even an international assignment if life permits. A new context will inevitably test you in unforeseen ways—new culture, new jargon, new people. It's one reason job rotations are so effective for development. If an external move is too drastic, you can simulate this by taking on a temporary role—for example, shadow a senior leader for two weeks, or manage a short-term project in a different division.
- **Seek Cross-Perspective Interactions:** Remember the second condition for growth—colliding perspectives. Intentionally surround yourself with people who think differently. Join a mentorship group, attend conferences outside your domain, or simply befriend colleagues from other functions and really pick their brains. Their challenges and approaches will present you with viewpoints that may collide with your own, which

is good. It prevents tunnel vision and stimulates vertical growth by broadening how you see problems.

- **Create Learning Goals, Not Just Performance Goals:** When setting your quarterly or annual goals, include at least one goal that is about learning something new or improving a capacity, even if it's not tied to an immediate result. For instance, "Lead a team brainstorm using methods I've never tried before," or "Incorporate design thinking into at least one project." These goals inherently carry a bit of heat because they require you to step into the unfamiliar and maybe fail initially. Track progress on them like you would a sales or cost goal. This keeps you accountable for staying in the growth zone.
- **Mentors and Coaches:** Leverage wise guides. You can even form a personal "board of advisors" for your career—people you check in with for perspective after handling a tough situation. They can help you extract the lesson (sensemaking) and encourage you to go further. Sometimes just knowing you have someone to discuss things with makes you braver to jump into a challenge. If a formal coach is available (through work or hiring one), that's an excellent asset during heat experiences—coaches often help leaders reframe failures as growth, maintain confidence amidst stress, and ensure the experience actually translates into vertical development, not just survival.
- **Reflect in Real Time:** During a heat experience, it's not comfortable to reflect—you're busy, maybe stressed. But even journaling one line a day about what you're feeling or learning can make a difference. When possible, hit the pause button: step back and ask, "What is this situation asking of me that's new?" and "What's going on inside me right now?" (those questions from the Redefining stretch list apply at any stage). These reflections in the moment will enrich the learning later and might even yield immediate insight that helps you perform better under pressure.

The Heat Experience Playbook for Organizations

For organizations aiming to systematically use heat experiences to grow leaders, here's a mini playbook combining many of the ideas above:

- **Identify Growth Edge for Each Leader:** Use assessments or manager feedback to determine what vertical stage a leader is at and what the next stage might be. What kind of challenge would most help them develop capacities of that next stage?
- **Match to Stretch Assignments:** Maintain a list of key projects, assignments, or rotations that could serve as developmental crucibles. During talent reviews, for each high-potential or emerging leader, discuss which

stretch experience would benefit them and make a plan to provide it. Make sure these assignments have buy-in from senior leadership as legit opportunities, not just "side tasks."

- **Equip With Support:** Before the leader jumps in, brief them on why you believe this assignment will help their development (transparency helps them approach it as a learner). Assign a mentor or coach and set up regular reflection sessions (even a monthly one-hour chat to debrief is great). Ensure their previous responsibilities are adjusted so they aren't overwhelmed—development is part of work, but it needs space.
- **Normalize Struggle:** Through training and culture, let people know that it's okay to feel uncomfortable in a new role—that doesn't mean they're failing, it means they're growing. Teach managers to check in and ask, "What are you finding challenging? What are you learning?" rather than "Are you hitting all your targets right away?" in the first few weeks of a stretch role.
- **Rotate Perspectives:** Where possible, incorporate cross-functional exposure or peer learning alongside the heat experience. Maybe two leaders swap roles or co-lead a project precisely because each will bring a different perspective to the other (e.g., a marketing head and an engineering head tandem on a new initiative).
- **Capture Lessons Learned:** After the heat experience, conduct an after-action review with the leader (and team if applicable). Ask: *What were the key learnings? How has your approach or thinking changed?* Link it back to the competencies of the next developmental stage: *Do you feel you've grown in your ability to . . . (e.g., take others' perspectives, manage ambiguity, etc.)?* This helps consolidate the vertical growth and also signals to the leader that growth was indeed the goal. It also provides the organization with success stories and case studies to further reinforce a development culture.
- **Repeat and Progressively Layer:** Vertical development is a journey, not a one-time. After one heat experience, plan the next. As Nick Petrie observed, learning-agile leaders often seek heat every few years—they go through a cycle of challenge, mastery, boredom, and then seek challenge again. Organizations can mirror this by moving leaders through diverse experiences deliberately. This not only develops the individual but also creates leaders with broad perspective for the company—a win-win.

By turning the ad-hoc occurrences of heat into an intentional development strategy, companies future-proof their leadership. They build a bench of resilient, adaptive leaders who not are just skilled in today's competencies but have the capacity to handle tomorrow's complexity.

Reflection and Practices: Turning Your Heat Into Growth

Having explored the concept and seen it in action, it's time to turn the lens to you, the reader. How can you personally make the most of heat experiences—past, present, and future—to fuel your own vertical development? This section offers some exercises and reflection prompts to integrate these ideas. Consider it a mini-workshop to ensure that reading this chapter leads to real insight and action for you.

Reflect on Past Heat Experiences

One of the richest sources of learning is your own history. Begin by mining your past for heat. Think about the most challenging experiences of your leadership career (or life in general):

- **Identify 2–3 Pivotal Experiences:** These could be crises (a project failure, a personal hardship while in a leadership role), big promotions or role changes, conflicts, or even positive successes that were stretching. Jot down what they were and roughly when.
- **What Made Them Heat?** For each, ask: What about this experience disrupted my usual way of doing things? Did I feel in over my head? Why? Perhaps it was the scale, the uncertainty, the novelty, the people dynamics, or something else. By articulating this, you're identifying the conditions that most challenge you (your "heat signature," so to speak).
- **Lessons Learned:** Now consider, what did you take away from that event? How did you change afterward? Sometimes we don't consciously claim our learnings. Maybe you became more confident in speaking up after surviving a confrontational meeting, or you learned to ask for help after a health scare, or you discovered a new perspective on what success means. If it's hard to find a lesson, ask what *someone else* might say you learned ("My mentor at the time noted that I became more X after that experience").
- **Share Your Story:** If you have peers or a team you trust, consider sharing one of these stories in a deep storytelling session. As we saw with the Experience Explorer at CCL, telling our stories and hearing others can unlock new realizations. You might find that in explaining it to someone, you articulate an insight you hadn't before. Moreover, you contribute to a culture of openness and learning by doing so.

Through this reflection, you may come to a completely new understanding of how to develop yourself. You might notice, for example, that every time you grew significantly, it involved taking on a tough interpersonal challenge—a clue that maybe your next growth step lies in that realm. Or you might realize you've been avoiding a kind of challenge that in the past actually helped you. Patterns and insights will emerge.

Self-Assessment: Where Are You Now?

Next, take stock of your current mindset stage and growth edge:

- **Current Mindset Home:** Think about the seven stages (Opportunist, Diplomat, Expert, Achiever, Redefining, Transforming, Alchemical). Without judgment, which stage's description is most true for you, most of the time? Where do you feel most at home? For many professionals, it might be Achiever or perhaps Expert or Redefining. The goal isn't to inflate or deflate your ego but to orient yourself. If you're unsure, reflect on how you respond to complexity and change. Do you prefer clear goals and plans (Achiever), or do you often question them to seek more meaning (Redefining), or do you mainly stick to proven methods and expertise (Expert)?
- **Benefits and Limits:** What are the benefits of operating from this mindset stage for you, given your current situation? Every stage has strengths. Write down what your stage helps you accomplish or how it serves you and your organization. Then ask, "How might this mindset limit what is possible . . . for you at this time?" For instance, if you identify as Expert stage, a benefit might be high quality and technical excellence; limit might be not empowering your team or missing bigger strategic moves. This honest appraisal sets the stage for why you might want to grow. If the benefits outweigh limits in your context, fine—but often, as life conditions change, the limits start to pinch more, signaling a need to expand.
- **Next Stage to Stretch Toward:** Based on the above, what is the next stage that feels like a meaningful step for you? Not a leap to the top, just the next rung. If you're Diplomat, maybe aiming for Expert's independent thinking. If Achiever, maybe Redefining's purpose-driven experimentation. Also consider: who do you know that operates at that next stage? Observing or talking to them can give insight (e.g., "How does my mentor handle things with such calm and system-level thinking? What can I learn from that?").

Plan a Heat Experiment

Now design a small experiment for yourself. What is one small experiment or practice you might try to stretch your mindset capacity? This should align with the next stage you identified:

- Choose something actionable in the next few weeks. It could be drawn from the stretch suggestions given in this chapter. For example:

- If you want to move toward Diplomat → Expert: You might volunteer to lead a meeting or make a decision without deferring to higher-ups, essentially practicing independent thinking.
- Expert → Achiever: Deliberately delegate a task you usually do yourself to a team member and support them instead of taking over. Or ask for feedback on your communication.
- Achiever → Redefining: Block an afternoon to map out a vision or strategy that isn't directly tied to current KPIs, practicing stepping back for bigger questions. Or engage someone very different from you in a conversation to broaden your perspective.
- Redefining → Transforming: Facilitate a dialogue between two departments with very different viewpoints (practice integrative leadership), or simplify a complex idea into a story and share it for feedback.
- Transforming → Alchemical: Try a week of a new mindfulness practice, or mentor someone purely by asking questions and reflecting back (minimize giving any advice) to hone your servant leadership and deep listening.

- **Set Up Conditions to Enable It**: What would need to shift to enable you to step into that practice or experiment? What will it take? Who or what will support you? What might you need to let go of or accept? This is crucial. If your experiment is to delegate more, you might need to let go of some perfectionism (what to let go), accept that the result might not be exactly as you'd do it (accept uncertainty), and maybe inform your team member "I'm doing this to grow us both, so let's debrief after" (enlisting support and understanding). If your experiment is having a tough conversation, you might need to shift your schedule to give it time (resource), ask a colleague to be present as a support, and let go of the fear that conflict will damage the relationship. Accept that constructive conflict can improve it. Write these enablers down and address them one by one.
- **Reminders of Why**: Before you embark, clarify what makes this development worth doing for you. Is it to be a better leader for your team? To reduce stress on yourself? To reach a career goal? To live more aligned with your values? When the heat turns up and you feel discomfort, remembering your motivation will keep you in it. You might even jot a sticky note with a phrase like "Why: to grow into a more visionary leader" or "so I don't burn out again," whatever resonates, and keep it where you'll see it.
- **Execute and Reflect**: Do the experiment. Treat it with curiosity, as if you're a researcher exploring your own leadership. Immediately after, or at least that day, note what happened, how you felt, and anything learned. If it went poorly, it kindly: What might you try next time? If it

went well, what does that open up for you? Decide if you need to repeat the experiment (often one try is not enough to fully internalize a new capacity and you might delegate on one project, then try it on a bigger one next).

- **Get Feedback:** If possible, tell a trusted colleague or friend about your experiment *before* and ask them to debrief *after*. Outside perspective can illuminate things you miss. Maybe they noticed you seemed calmer, even if you felt anxious which may indicate growth in your presence. Or they might gently point out where you reverted to old habits, which is normal and helpful to know.

Continual Practices for Harnessing Heat

Finally, adopt some ongoing practices that will help you integrate heat experiences into your leadership development perpetually:

- **Periodic Self-Check-Ins:** Schedule a quiet hour perhaps every quarter to review your development. Ask yourself: *What's the most significant challenge I faced this past quarter? What did I learn? Am I avoiding any challenges? What might be a good stretch for next quarter?* Putting this on the calendar ensures you don't go on autopilot. Vertical growth is a deliberate journey.
- **Learning Journal:** Keep a section in your journal or digital notes specifically for "Leadership learnings." Whenever you have a tough day or a big win, note what you learned about yourself or leadership. Over months, you'll see progress and patterns. It becomes evidence of your evolution, which builds confidence to take on more heat. It's also a great way to gather examples if you ever do a 360 review or coaching—you have concrete instances of how you've grown.
- **Mindset Reminders:** It's easy to slip back into old mindsets under stress. Develop a personal cue to remind you of the mindset you aspire to. Some people choose a word or mantra. For example, if you're moving from Expert to Achiever, when facing a problem you might pause and think: Enable others, to counteract the instinct to solve it all yourself. If moving to Redefining, your reminder might be "What truly matters here?" to look beyond immediate results. These little questions or cues, used consistently, will nudge you to practice your new capacities especially when the pressure mounts (which is exactly when you most need them).
- **Celebrate Growth:** Don't forget to acknowledge when you've handled a heat situation better than you would have a year ago. Maybe you remained calm during a conflict, or you successfully led a project in a new domain. That's worth celebrating! It reinforces the mindset that you *can*

grow and you are not fixed at one stage. Some leaders keep a "wins" list and include development wins on there, not just business outcomes. This positive reinforcement makes you more likely to embrace the next challenge rather than dread it.

As you go forward, remember that vertical development is a continuous journey. Just like a seasoned rock climber always looks for the next handhold up the cliff, a seasoned leader looks for the next growth challenge. There's always another level of capacity to build, especially as the world keeps changing around us. The key is to approach each heat experience—whether chosen or unexpected—with the attitude of a learner. In doing so, you transform what could be merely stressful events into crucibles that shape you into a more complex, adaptive, and empathetic leader.

Embracing Heat for Ongoing Growth

Leadership is not a static state of being but an evolving process of becoming. The journey up the vertical development ladder is not achieved by avoiding difficulties but by engaging with them fully. Heat experiences are the forge in which higher leadership capacities are formed—the intense fires that can melt down our old beliefs and reshape us with stronger, more expansive understanding. As we've seen, from the emergent Opportunist learning to trust others, to the seasoned Transforming leader learning to simplify and let go, at every stage the pattern holds: meaningful growth demands stepping into uncertainty and challenge.

No leader grows vertically by staying comfortable. In the words of one vertical development principle, "Growth demands a temporary surrender of security" and a willingness to let go of the safe and familiar, to reach a new level of capability. Heat experiences provide that exact mix of insecurity and possibility. They upset our equilibrium just enough to make us reach for a new balance at a higher level. Rather than seeing challenges as threats or inconveniences, transformative leaders come to see them as *gifts* that are sometimes painful or wrapped in problems but gifts nonetheless. They understand that heat isn't the enemy; it's the accelerant for their development.

For organizations, deliberately harnessing heat experiences is a way to future-proof leadership. In a world where the only constant is disruption, leaders who have been forged and tempered by prior challenges are the ones who can handle whatever comes next. A company culture that says "It's okay to not know all the answers—let's learn together through this tough problem" is a culture that will innovate and adapt. By intentionally creating those high-heat, high-support growth opportunities, organizations ignite the vertical growth of their people and, by extension, their collective capacity.

For you personally, embracing heat experiences means shifting your mindset from *fear* to *curiosity* when you encounter the edge of your comfort zone. Instead of asking, "Can I handle this?" you learn to ask, "What can I *learn* from this?" It means remembering, when you feel the heat of a challenge, that this is exactly how you expand. You are like steel being tempered—each time, you emerge a bit stronger and more flexible. Over a career, those moments of heat become the proud stories you tell of how you became the leader you are.

As we close this chapter, consider one final reflection: What is one upcoming or current challenge in your work or life that might be a heat experience in disguise? How will you approach it now, armed with the insights from this chapter? Perhaps you will seek out a mentor for it, or reframe it as an experiment, or be more mindful during it to capture the lessons. By doing so, you transform from a passive recipient of heat to an active "heat-seeker," someone who doesn't shy away from the hard stuff but carefully uses it to grow.

In summary, heat experiences are the catalysts that can propel you through the vertical stages of leadership growth. They are intense and sometimes daunting but ultimately invaluable. With the right mindset and support, each heat experience can become a breakthrough on your journey. So, step into the challenge. Trust that through the fires of experience, you are being refined into a more capable, wise, and impactful leader. Embrace the heat and continue your ascent.

References

Center for Creative Leadership. (2015). *The how-to of Vertical Leadership Development: Part 2–30 experts, 3 conditions, and 15 approaches.* Center for Creative Leadership.

Petrie, N. (2018). *Lessons in vertical leadership development.* https://dragonfly-recorder-nty9.squarespace.com/s/Lessons-in-Vertical-Leadership-Development_Nick-Petrie.pdf

Chapter 6

Colliding Perspectives—Expanding Worldviews for Vertical Growth

The Power of Diverse Perspectives in Development

Leaders develop most when their current ways of thinking are challenged by colliding perspectives—encounters with vastly different opinions, backgrounds, or worldviews. Research on vertical leadership development finds that exposing leaders to diverse perspectives breaks them out of echo chambers and static thinking. In fact, *30 leadership experts* identified "colliding perspectives" as one of three essential conditions for growth, alongside challenging *heat experiences* and guided sensemaking. Without fresh perspectives, leaders tend to reinforce what they already know, remaining in comfortable routines. Our brains naturally seek confirming information, creating self-reinforcing loops (a cognitive echo chamber). Thus, deliberate exposure to contrasting viewpoints is needed to unsettle assumptions and spark development.

Colliding perspectives work by increasing the number of mental lenses through which a leader sees the world (Wilber, 2000). This expansion is directly linked to more complex thinking and better decision-making. While simplistic thinkers view problems from a single angle, more complex thinkers can examine a situation from multiple angles. The ability to "hold more perspectives" correlates with higher adaptability in today's uncertain, volatile environments. Crucially, perspective-taking also nurtures empathy: when leaders deeply listen to others' experiences and values, they begin to feel those perspectives. Exercises like deep listening force leaders to shift from advocating their own view to genuinely understanding others, which is a "radical shift" that builds empathy and trust. As leaders practice seeing through others' eyes, they develop the capacity to relate and collaborate across differences—an emotional intelligence boost that technical training alone cannot provide.

Colliding perspectives often create cognitive dissonance which is the uncomfortable clash between new information and existing beliefs. This tension, rather than being harmful, actually *fuels* growth and adaptation.

DOI: 10.4324/9781003644941-6

Nick Petrie of Center for Creative Leadership (2015) describes how a disrupting event or idea disorients the leader's habitual way of thinking, making them realize their current mindset is inadequate. This dissonance or disequilibrium destabilizes old mental models and opens the mind to new ways of sensemaking. In other words, a bit of mental turmoil is the catalyst for vertical development. Leaders who never experience such discomfort may remain static; those who do, and are supported in processing it, can advance to more complex mindsets. Studies show that when leaders face novel perspectives and then integrate them (with coaching or reflection), they emerge with a larger, more advanced worldview that "with time, stabilizes" at a higher developmental stage. Simply put, exposure to new perspectives shifts leadership mindsets by expanding what leaders deem possible and important (Adeption, 2021). This chapter explores how colliding perspectives promote vertical growth at each stage of a leader's development and how organizations can harness this powerful mechanism.

Colliding Perspectives at Each Stage

Opportunist Stage (Power-Oriented, Self-Protective)

Mindset Recap: The Opportunist mindset is self-oriented and survival-driven. At this earliest stage, a leader is focused on personal needs, winning, and immediate gains.

Colliding Perspective Experience for Growth

Opportunists, who thrive on personal wins and self-interest, need to experience a direct challenge to their lone-wolf mentality. This often comes in the form of an ethical mentor or a trusted colleague who refuses to engage in manipulation or power plays. They might also face a crisis where their usual tactics fail, forcing them to recognize that trust, loyalty, and collaboration create more sustainable success than self-serving strategies.

Colliding Perspective Example

After his near-collapse in sales and health, Daniel had begun to rely more on team collaboration, reluctantly acknowledging that success wasn't just about individual wins. But his next challenge would push him even further—forcing him to redefine success itself. His company assigned him to mentor a new, rising sales star—Ava. She was ambitious but operated differently than Daniel had at her peak. She focused on building long-term client relationships rather than chasing quick wins. Daniel, still wired to maximize short-term gains, watched in frustration as she spent extra time nurturing lower-value clients instead of closing high-revenue deals.

One afternoon, Daniel bluntly confronted her: "Why waste so much time on small accounts? You should be focusing on the biggest fish." Ava didn't back down. "Because loyalty compounds," she countered. "The small clients I invest in now will remember me when they scale. Relationships, not just numbers, build lasting success." Daniel scoffed at first—his old mindset resisted the idea that patience could outplay aggression. But as he watched Ava's steady success, a realization dawned: his most reliable clients—the ones who stuck with him even in the downturn—were the ones he had treated well, not just the biggest ones he had closed quickly. For the first time, Daniel saw the value of trust and reciprocity over sheer dominance.

Leaning into this new perspective, he experimented with Ava's approach, focusing on cultivating partnerships instead of just securing deals. The results surprised him: his pipeline stabilized, and his stress levels dropped. Daniel had crossed the threshold into the Diplomat stage, shifting from "I must win" to "We succeed together." What once seemed like wasted time—building relationships, investing in others—became the foundation of sustainable leadership.

Diplomat Stage (Seeks Harmony, Avoids Challenging Norms)

> **Mindset Recap:** A leader in the Diplomat stage values cooperation, norms, and belonging. Having learned the power of group inclusion, Diplomats strive to follow the rules and make things work as part of the group.

Colliding Perspective Experience for Growth

Diplomats, who prioritize group harmony and conformity, need exposure to diverse viewpoints that challenge the status quo. This might come from leading a team with differing cultural or generational expectations, or working in an environment where blind adherence to tradition causes inefficiency. The discomfort of navigating conflicting opinions helps them realize that independent thinking and expertise are just as valuable as fitting in.

Colliding Perspective Example

After successfully navigating her heat experience on the process improvement task force, Marisa had gained confidence in her ability to think independently and challenge norms when necessary. But her next leadership challenge would push her growth even further—forcing her to confront the tension between harmony and constructive conflict.

Now managing a newly diverse team, Marisa found herself in a collision of perspectives that she could no longer avoid. The team brought together employees from different departments, backgrounds, and generations, each with vastly different ways of working and expectations for leadership. For years, Marisa had kept teams aligned by avoiding confrontation—defaulting to "Let's not make waves" whenever disagreements surfaced. But in this new environment, conflict was unavoidable. One day, during a policy review meeting, a junior analyst spoke up: "This policy is outdated—it unintentionally excludes younger employees who need more flexibility. Why haven't we changed it?"

The room fell silent. Marisa's instinct was to smooth things over. "This policy has been in place for a reason," she began, but she saw frustration in some team members' faces. Another employee added, "Just because it's the way we've always done it doesn't mean it still works."

Marisa felt the pull of her old mindset—keeping the peace, maintaining order—but she also recognized something new: silencing conflict wouldn't serve the team's progress. Instead of deflecting, she leaned in. "Tell me more," she said. What followed was an open, sometimes tense conversation that surfaced real concerns about outdated norms and the need for change. Instead of seeing disagreement as a threat to harmony, Marisa realized it was a catalyst for innovation and inclusion.

Over time, she practiced engaging in difficult discussions, learning to facilitate dialogue rather than suppress it. She sought input from employees across levels, ensuring new policies balanced fairness with business needs. By embracing constructive dissent, Marisa fully transitioned into the Expert stage—no longer just maintaining group cohesion, but actively shaping better ways of working through informed, independent thinking. Growth is marked by a shift from "I must fit in at all costs" to "I can constructively challenge norms for the greater good."

Expert Stage (Technical Authority, Struggles With Feedback)

> **Mindset Recap:** A leader at the Expert stage is all about personal competence, precision, and logic. This mindset is focused on what you know and do—mastering skills, perfecting techniques, and ensuring things are done the "right way."

Colliding Perspective Experience for Growth

Experts, who define success by technical mastery, need collisions with nontechnical perspectives that challenge their rigid approach. This could mean collaborating with marketing, HR, or leadership teams that prioritize strategy, customer needs, or people dynamics over pure logic and precision. Learning that being right isn't always effective pushes them to embrace teamwork, delegation, and broader business acumen.

Colliding Perspective Example

Aisha had spent months adjusting to her new role as Analytics Manager, wrestling with the discomfort of letting go of control. She had made progress—delegating more, seeking team input—but her biggest collision of perspectives was yet to come. Her company launched a major cross-functional initiative, and Aisha was tapped to lead the data strategy for a new product launch. She welcomed the challenge, confident her analytical rigor would ensure success. But this time, she wasn't just working with other data experts—she had to collaborate with marketing, sales, and HR leaders, each bringing perspectives that didn't fit neatly into her technical framework.

In early meetings, Aisha outlined a highly detailed, data-driven roadmap, explaining how predictive models would optimize product performance. She expected appreciation. Instead, the marketing director raised a hand: "How do we know customers actually care about these features?" Then, the HR leader added:

"We need adoption metrics that include behavioral insights, not just efficiency. How will this impact team workflows?" Aisha felt frustration creeping in. These concerns weren't grounded in raw data—they were subjective, messy, human-centered questions. Her instinct was to push back with logic, to prove why her model was correct. But she caught herself.

Instead, she paused and genuinely listened. Over the following weeks, she met one-on-one with stakeholders, seeking to understand how they defined success. She realized that pure technical accuracy wasn't enough—if no one could act on the insights, they were meaningless. Through this collision of perspectives, Aisha learned that effective leadership wasn't just about being right—it was about ensuring alignment, communication, and shared ownership. She refined her approach, balancing analytics with narrative storytelling, making insights actionable for nontechnical teams.

By the project's launch, Aisha had not only delivered a successful strategy but transformed her leadership mindset. No longer just a brilliant analyst, she had become a bridge between data and decision-making, between precision and people—signaling her true shift from Expert to Achiever.

Achiever Stage (Results-Driven, Task-Focused)

> **Mindset Recap:** The Achiever mindset is the model of the effective, goal-oriented leader. Achievers are highly motivated, focused on results, and attuned to team performance.

Colliding Perspective Experience for Growth

Achievers, who equate success with goal completion and efficiency, need experiences that redefine success beyond metrics and productivity. This often happens through working in new cultural contexts where relationship-building matters as much as results, or through engaging with purpose-driven leaders who prioritize social impact or long-term sustainability over short-term gains. Such experiences force Achievers to expand their definition of success to include meaning, adaptability, and holistic impact.

Colliding Perspective Example

After years of equating achievement with success, Raj's transition into the Redefining stage was met with a profound collision of perspectives—one that challenged his deeply ingrained belief that hard work and efficiency were the ultimate measures of success. Following his company's expansion into new international markets, Raj was tasked with leading regional teams across diverse cultures. He approached the challenge with his usual goal-oriented mindset, setting aggressive targets and driving teams toward strict deadlines. However, what had always worked for him in high-performance corporate environments failed to yield the same results in these new settings.

In one region, he faced resistance from local partners who prioritized relationship-building over rapid execution. Deals stalled because his insistence on efficiency was perceived as dismissive and transactional. In another market, his team measured success not just in revenue growth but in community impact and employee well-being—metrics Raj had never considered essential.

At first, Raj resisted. "If we hit our numbers, everything else will fall into place," he argued. But the more he engaged with his teams, the clearer it became: his definition of success was too narrow. Through deep conversations with regional leaders and firsthand exposure to different success paradigms, Raj began to see success as multidimensional. He adjusted his leadership approach—balancing efficiency with empathy, targets with long-term trust, and performance with purpose.

This shift was uncomfortable but transformative. Raj no longer measured success solely in numbers—he embraced a broader perspective that valued sustainable growth, cultural alignment, and impact beyond profit. This marked his true entry into the Redefining stage, where purpose and adaptability became as important as results.

Redefining Stage (Identity Shift, Integrating Opposing Views)

Mindset Recap: The Redefining stage is all about questioning, complexity, and authenticity. Leaders operating with a Redefining mindset start to see multiple perspectives and value purpose and people alongside performance.

Colliding Perspective Experience for Growth

Redefining leaders, who are questioning traditional success models and seeking deeper purpose, need exposure to complex, systemic challenges where multiple truths coexist. This might involve leading cross-sector initiatives, managing conflicting stakeholder interests, or working on global-scale issues where no single perspective is sufficient. These encounters develop their ability to synthesize competing viewpoints, integrate paradoxes, and lead in high-ambiguity environments.

Colliding Perspective Example

After years of redefining her leadership around purpose-driven work, Elena faced a moment where two seemingly opposing perspectives collided, forcing her to reconcile the idealism she had embraced with the pragmatism she once resisted. Now working as a consultant, Elena had gained a reputation for helping companies integrate sustainability and social impact into their business strategies. But her latest client—a fast-growing tech firm looking to rebrand as a sustainability leader—challenged her assumptions in ways she didn't expect.

The company's CEO was eager to embed sustainability into their business model but had no intention of compromising profitability or shareholder returns. In meetings, executives praised Elena's ideas but repeatedly asked, "How does this align with our bottom line?" To some, this was a reasonable business concern; to Elena, it felt like a dilution of true purpose.

Her frustration grew until a conversation with a frontline employee shifted her perspective. The worker, an engineer passionate about renewable energy, told her: "I love working here, but if we don't show how sustainability drives value, leadership won't invest in it long-term." That moment reframed Elena's approach. She had been viewing profit and purpose as competing forces, when in reality, the challenge was integrating them in a way that sustained both.

Instead of pushing for an overhaul of the company's strategy, Elena worked with leadership to align sustainability with business growth, demonstrating how ethical supply chains, renewable energy investments, and responsible AI practices could drive both brand loyalty and financial returns. She introduced metrics that measured impact alongside profit, creating a framework where both could reinforce each other rather than compete.

The experience solidified Elena's evolution as a Redefining leader. She no longer saw corporate structures as barriers to purpose but as systems that, with the right framing, could evolve toward meaningful change. Through colliding perspectives, she refined her ability to meet organizations where they were, integrating ideals with reality—not by choosing one over the other but by weaving them together.

Transforming Stage (Leading Systemic Change)

> **Mindset Recap:** The Transforming stage is characterized by a leader who can see across multiple systems and time horizons, integrating people, process, and purpose. A Transforming leader works comfortably in ambiguity and complexity, holding a big-picture perspective while also understanding the interdependence of all the moving parts.

Colliding Perspective Experience for Growth

Transforming leaders, who already operate with a broad, integrative worldview, need perspectives that challenge even their most expansive assumptions. This could come from engaging with radically different philosophical, spiritual, or existential viewpoints, or from navigating moral dilemmas where every choice has profound implications. These experiences help them refine wisdom, detachment, and the ability to guide others through uncertainty without rigid attachments to any single ideology.

Colliding Perspective Example

After leading his company's cultural transformation toward agility and customer-centricity, Luis found himself facing an unexpected collision of perspectives—one that tested his ability to bridge opposing viewpoints without compromising core values.

His company had recently secured a major investment from shareholders eager for faster returns on innovation. The board pressured leadership to prioritize efficiency and profitability, emphasizing short-term gains. At the same time, Luis's employees, who had embraced the company's vision of adaptive innovation and meaningful work, were resisting these shifts. Middle managers feared sacrificing long-term growth and employee well-being in favor of quarterly results.

Tensions escalated during an executive meeting when a senior investor bluntly stated, "If we don't hit these margins now, there won't be a future to build." A product lead countered, "If we rush every decision, we'll break what's actually working and drive people away." Luis could see the truth in both arguments, yet neither side recognized the full picture.

Instead of choosing a side, Luis held the tension. He spent the next few weeks in deep discussions, gathering insights from both stakeholders and employees. He acknowledged that financial health and a strong culture weren't competing needs but interconnected necessities.

Rather than forcing a compromise, Luis reframed the debate:

> What if our greatest competitive advantage is balancing speed with sustainability?

He proposed a dual-speed strategy—certain product lines would fast-track development to meet investor expectations, while others would prioritize long-term innovation. He also introduced a transparent decision-making model, giving employees visibility into how financial and cultural priorities aligned.

The outcome wasn't a perfect resolution but a new way of thinking—one that integrated multiple perspectives into a cohesive strategy. By refusing to see the problem as a binary choice, Luis reinforced the essence of Transforming leadership: creating solutions where none previously existed by bridging seemingly contradictory truths.

Alchemical Stage (Integrating the Global and the Personal)

> **Mindset Recap:** The Alchemical mindset represents the latest stage of vertical leadership maturity. Leaders at this stage embody a sense of balance, peace, and radical flexibility.

Colliding Perspective Experience for Growth

Alchemical leaders, who exist at the highest levels of integrative leadership, need perspectives that test their ability to translate deep insight into practical, tangible change. This often involves mentoring or coaching leaders at earlier stages, helping them bridge their own colliding perspectives. By continuously engaging with those who see the world differently, Alchemical leaders ensure their wisdom remains grounded, relevant, and actionable.

Colliding Perspective Example

After years of navigating crises with a quiet, profound presence, Asha found herself at an unexpected crossroads—this time, not in the heat of an immediate conflict but in the slow, grinding tension between two opposing worldviews. A global development organization sought her guidance on an emerging dispute: local communities, whose lands were earmarked for an ambitious sustainability initiative, were resisting the very interventions designed to protect their future.

The project—a reforestation and conservation effort spanning multiple nations—was hailed as a breakthrough in corporate-environmental partnerships. Funded by multinational companies eager to offset their carbon footprints, it aimed to restore ecosystems while creating new jobs. On paper, it was a win-win. But on the ground, the local farmers and indigenous leaders saw it differently. To them, this was yet another top-down "solution" that disregarded their livelihoods, traditions, and autonomy.

Asha spent weeks moving between worlds, sitting in corporate boardrooms where executives discussed long-term climate targets, and then traveling to remote villages where farmers spoke of generational survival. The collision of perspectives was stark. The corporate backers, operating on a 50-year vision for sustainability, saw the initiative as a necessity for planetary health. The local farmers, facing immediate economic instability, saw it as a threat to their way of life.

Both sides were right—and both were incomplete.

Rather than imposing a middle-ground compromise, Asha immersed herself in their realities, listening deeply until the true fractures emerged.

The corporations were disconnected from the lived experiences of the people their project impacted, while the local leaders, wary of external control, struggled to see how global shifts were already shaping their future. Neither group saw the full system.

In a pivotal meeting, Asha posed a question that neither side had asked:

> What if the success of this project wasn't measured in trees planted or land conserved, but in the strength of the communities that steward them?

This reframing sparked an unexpected shift. It was no longer a battle between economic survival and environmental protection, but an invitation to co-create a solution that honored both. Over time, the initiative transformed—not into a perfect solution but into a dynamic partnership where local farmers became stakeholders, reforestation plans were adjusted to accommodate traditional agriculture, and corporations invested in long-term local economic resilience alongside conservation.

Through this experience, Asha once again embodied the Alchemical leader's role: holding seemingly opposing truths in tension until a larger, more integrative perspective emerged. She did not push for a singular outcome but created the conditions for a deeper synthesis of perspectives—where neither side "won," yet both expanded their understanding of what was possible.

This, she knew, was the paradox of true leadership: the more deeply one engages with opposing realities, the clearer the interdependencies become.

Creating and Embracing Colliding Perspectives: How to Expand Worldviews for Growth

By now, it's clear that colliding perspectives are essential for vertical growth, but they often seem like experiences that happen spontaneously. Waiting for an accidental perspective shift isn't a reliable growth strategy! The good news is that leaders and organizations can intentionally create and navigate these experiences, ensuring that exposure to diverse viewpoints leads to deep learning and transformation. The key is finding the right balance—enough contrast to challenge assumptions but enough support to integrate new perspectives effectively.

Designing Optimal Perspective Collisions

Not all perspective clashes are productive. Some simply reinforce biases, while others may be overwhelming rather than developmental. The goal is to create "productive dissonance"—a level of cognitive discomfort that sparks growth without causing shutdown or resistance. Here are some principles for designing or recognizing optimal collisions of perspective.

Expose Yourself to Radical Differences

To truly break out of an echo chamber, leaders must intentionally seek out perspectives that contrast with their own. This might involve working with people from different industries, cultures, or disciplines. For example, a finance leader accustomed to quantitative metrics might work closely with a creative marketing team that prioritizes storytelling and brand identity. These interactions force leaders to reconsider their assumptions and adopt a broader lens.

Engage in High-Stakes, Cross-Functional Collaboration

Perspective collisions are most powerful when the stakes are real. Working on a critical project with people who hold diverse viewpoints and expertise ensures that perspectives aren't just exchanged but must be reconciled to achieve meaningful results. Consider assigning leaders to initiatives that require balancing business strategy with human-centered design, or merging technological innovation with ethical considerations. The tension between these priorities creates space for higher-level thinking.

Turn Resistance Into Inquiry

When confronted with a perspective that challenges your deeply held beliefs, the natural instinct is to defend, dismiss, or debate. Instead, leaders should lean into the discomfort with curiosity. A practical method is to pause and ask clarifying questions rather than making immediate counterarguments. Questions like "What led you to that conclusion?" or "How would success look from your viewpoint?" create space for mutual understanding and deeper insight.

Encourage Psychological Safety for Disruptive Ideas

Colliding perspectives only lead to growth if people feel safe to express disagreement. Organizations that foster open debate, idea-sharing, and constructive conflict create a culture where leaders continuously refine their thinking. One strategy is to normalize dissent by assigning a "Devil's Advocate" in meetings or inviting external critics to challenge company strategies. By making opposition a healthy part of decision-making, leaders become more adept at holding multiple perspectives.

Cultivating a Perspective-Seeking Culture

Beyond individual experiences, organizational culture determines whether diverse viewpoints are embraced or resisted. In cultures that value alignment over debate, perspective collisions are rare, and growth stagnates. In contrast, cultures that celebrate intellectual diversity, challenge assumptions, and prioritize learning create more adaptive, innovative leaders. Here's how to build a culture that thrives on diverse perspectives:

- **Leaders Model Learning Over Certainty:** Senior leaders should demonstrate openness to new perspectives by sharing how their views have changed over time. When executives openly admit to past blind spots or describe how a dissenting voice improved a decision, it sets the tone for intellectual humility and flexibility.
- **Diverse Representation in Decision-Making:** Leaders should intentionally include stakeholders with different viewpoints in key discussions. A common mistake is only consulting those who already agree or share the same background. Bringing in cross-functional teams, global perspectives, and nontraditional voices expands the range of insights considered.
- **Normalize Discomfort in Leadership Development:** Many organizations shy away from discomfort, yet it is the key to transformation. Growth-oriented companies encourage leaders to seek out challenges that make them rethink assumptions. Whether through structured mentoring with someone from a different discipline or reverse-mentorship programs where junior employees provide insights to senior executives, perspective collisions should be an expected part of leadership growth.
- **Encourage Critical Thinking, Not Compliance:** Organizations that overvalue agreement and efficiency can stifle critical thinking. Instead of seeing dissent as inefficiency, leaders should reward constructive debate. Practices like "pre-mortems" (considering what could go wrong before finalizing a decision), polarity mapping, and scenario planning all help leaders actively work with multiple perspectives rather than rejecting them outright.

Practical Ways to Integrate Colliding Perspectives Into Your Leadership Growth

While organizations play a role, individual leaders must take responsibility for broadening their perspectives. You can cultivate a "perspective-seeking mindset"—a deliberate approach to engaging with different viewpoints to sharpen your thinking and expand your leadership capacity.

1. Seek Out Conversations That Challenge Your Views

Don't just surround yourself with like-minded colleagues. Make it a habit to talk to people who see the world differently. This might mean engaging in discussions with

- A peer from another function who approaches problems from a completely different framework.
- A mentor or coach who deliberately pushes you outside your comfort zone.
- Industry outsiders who can offer fresh insights on entrenched challenges in your sector.

2. Immerse Yourself in a Different Work Context

Nothing forces perspective shifts like being thrown into an unfamiliar work environment. If possible, take on a temporary role outside your usual domain, or shadow a team in a completely different function. Experiencing the challenges and mindset of another field creates empathy and new ways of thinking.

3. Engage With Different Cultural Perspectives

Culture profoundly shapes worldviews. Spending time in different cultural or international settings can challenge assumptions about decision-making, leadership, and success. Even if you can't travel, try

- Reading memoirs or business books from different global perspectives.
- Attending international industry events or cross-cultural leadership forums.
- Watching documentaries or interviews featuring leaders with different lived experiences.

4. Run an Experiment That Forces a New Approach

Pick an aspect of your leadership style that feels deeply ingrained and experiment with doing the opposite.

- If you tend to make decisions quickly, slow down and seek multiple perspectives.
- If you typically focus on data, challenge yourself to consider intuition or qualitative insights.
- If you avoid conflict, initiate a candid conversation where disagreement is welcomed.

By deliberately shifting perspectives, you'll develop greater flexibility, adaptability, and awareness of blind spots.

Embracing Perspective Collisions as a Growth Engine

Colliding perspectives may feel uncomfortable, but they are the key to deeper leadership growth. Without exposure to contrasting viewpoints, leaders risk becoming rigid, narrow in vision, and resistant to change. By continuously seeking out and engaging with diverse perspectives, leaders develop greater complexity in their thinking, stronger emotional intelligence, and the adaptability needed for today's dynamic world.

As you reflect on this chapter, consider the following:

- What is one perspective you've recently encountered that challenged your assumptions?
- How did you initially react, and how did it change your thinking?
- What intentional steps will you take to expand your perspectives moving forward?

Growth happens at the edges of our understanding. By embracing perspective collisions, you expand your worldview, strengthen your leadership, and prepare yourself to navigate an increasingly complex, interconnected world.

References

Adeption. (2021). *A leader's guide to vertical development.* Adeption.

Center for Creative Leadership. (2015). *The how-to of vertical leadership development–part 2.* Center for Creative Leadership.

Petrie, N. (2015). *Vertical leadership development: Developing leaders for a complex world.* Center for Creative Leadership.

Wilber, K. (2000). *Integral psychology: Consciousness, spirit, psychology, therapy.* Shambhala Publications.

Chapter 7

Elevated Sensemaking

Making Sense for Growth

In a turbulent world of rapid change and ambiguity, effective leadership requires more than just technical skills, and it demands a higher-order capacity to interpret and learn from complex experiences. Elevated sensemaking refers to a leader's ability to thoughtfully integrate diverse information, experiences, and perspectives into a coherent understanding, enabling wiser action in complexity. This is not just about solving one problem at a time but about developing richer "mental maps" of reality that allow leaders to navigate uncertainty and change with insight. Elevated sensemaking sits at the heart of vertical leadership development, the process by which adults expand their mindsets to handle greater complexity.

To appreciate the importance of elevated sensemaking, imagine a leader suddenly facing a novel crisis with no clear precedent—perhaps a disruptive new competitor or a global pandemic. A traditional leader might react by applying familiar formulas or doubling down on past expertise. In contrast, a leader skilled in elevated sensemaking will pause to interpret what is really happening: questioning assumptions, seeking out multiple viewpoints, and reflecting on what new response the situation demands. This reflective meaning-making process helps the leader avoid knee-jerk reactions and instead craft a more adaptive strategy. In today's environment, where "disruption is a feature, not a bug" of work and life, such sensemaking is crucial. It enables leaders to deal with *ambiguous, uncertain, and complex challenges* by continually evolving their mindsets rather than relying on static knowledge (Rybeck, 2021). In fact, research suggests that vertical development—growing one's mindset capacity—is what allows leaders to meet opportunities with a greater range of mindsets and behaviors.

Elevated sensemaking is the third primary conditions that fuel vertical growth, alongside heat experiences (Chapter 5) and colliding perspectives (Chapter 6). Heat experiences provide the raw material for growth

DOI: 10.4324/9781003644941-7

by pushing leaders out of their comfort zones, and colliding perspectives expand their view of the world. Elevated sensemaking (The How) is the integrative process that ties it all together—it's *how* a leader digests those challenging experiences and perspectives to form a larger, more advanced worldview. Without adequate sensemaking, developmental events may remain fragmented or overwhelming. The Center for Creative Leadership found that when programs provide new challenges and perspectives but *no support for sensemaking*, leaders "lack time and support to integrate these perspectives into a larger worldview," and thus little change happens beyond finding the experience "interesting." In other words, elevated sensemaking is the key that turns developmental stimuli into lasting development. Nelson Mandela, for example, famously spent years in prison reflecting on his experiences—an extreme case of sensemaking that helped him emerge as a transformational leader.

Key Characteristics of Elevated Sensemaking

At its core, elevated sensemaking is about how a leader interprets and learns from complexity rather than just how they react to it. This capacity has several distinct characteristics that set it apart from basic problem-solving:

- **Integrative Meaning-Making:** Elevated sensemaking involves making meaning from a tangle of disparate inputs—it is a reflective process of connecting the dots. Instead of tackling one problem in isolation (as in basic problem-solving), the leader steps back to see the bigger picture and relationships between issues. They reflect deeply on experiences to "extract insights, integrate new understandings, and develop more sophisticated mental models." This means lessons learned in one context are carried into a broader framework of understanding. A basic problem-solver might fix an immediate issue and move on; an elevated sensemaker considers what that issue signifies in a wider context (e.g., a customer complaint might reveal a systemic process flaw or a shifting market expectation).
- **Multiple Perspectives and Flexibility:** Basic problem-solving often assumes that the problem is straightforward and has a right answer known in advance. Elevated sensemaking, by contrast, assumes complex challenges benefit from multiple perspectives and creative thinking. Leaders strong in sensemaking intentionally seek out diverse viewpoints and even contradictory ideas to inform their understanding. They can hold opposing ideas and work toward *both/and* solutions rather than purely *either/or*. This flexibility is critical in complexity. As one leadership expert notes, sensemaking leaders "approach challenges with flexibility and creativity" instead of relying solely on established procedures. In

practice, this might look like bringing together cross-functional teams to discuss a problem or considering technical data alongside employee sentiment and stakeholder values before deciding a course of action. Elevated sensemaking thus expands the solution space beyond the obvious, whereas basic problem-solving might stick to tried-and-true methods.

- **Depth of Reflection and Time Horizon:** Elevated sensemaking is a more proactive and strategic approach, whereas basic problem-solving tends to be reactive and short term. A problem-solving mindset often jumps straight into tackling symptoms ("How do we fix this glitch now?"). In contrast, an elevated sensemaking mindset pauses to reflect on underlying causes, patterns, and longer-term implications ("Why did this situation arise? What does it mean for our strategy going forward?"). This often requires carving out time for reflection, which is easy to neglect in busy organizations. Experts recommend making reflection a significant part of any leadership development process. For instance, Nick Petrie suggests that about *one-third* of a leader's development work should be devoted to structured reflection and sensemaking. Without this deliberate pause, leaders remain in firefighting mode. Elevated sensemaking stretches the time horizon—leaders think about not only immediate wins but also how today's challenges connect to future opportunities or risks.
- **Meta-Cognition and Self-Awareness:** Another hallmark of elevated sensemaking is awareness of one's own thinking. Leaders engaging in sensemaking don't just gather external data but also examine their own mental models, biases, and assumptions. In fact, a key part of the sensemaking process is to surface and question the beliefs that may be limiting how a leader sees the situation. A basic problem-solver might rarely question their own approach if it has worked before; a sensemaking leader is more likely to ask, "How am I thinking about this problem? Is my viewpoint too narrow? What am I not seeing?" This self-reflection enables continuous learning. Over time, leaders who practice elevated sensemaking become more comfortable saying "I was wrong" or changing their approach when new insights emerge, which is vital for adapting in a changing environment. They effectively become students of their own thinking—a level of meta-cognition that basic problem-solving doesn't typically require.
- **From Reactive to Generative:** Ultimately, elevated sensemaking turns leadership into a more generative, creative act rather than a reactive one. Instead of merely reacting to problems as they come (which is often how basic problem-solving is practiced), leaders using elevated sensemaking generate new possibilities and proactively shape the situation. They use sensemaking to inform strategic planning, not just fix issues. It shifts leadership from "putting out fires" to building fire-resistant systems or even envisioning a completely new future. As one analysis put it, integrating disparate insights "shifts leadership from reactive problem-solving

to proactive, strategic planning." In other words, elevated sensemaking enables leaders to anticipate and influence change, because they've synthesized a wide array of inputs into a guiding vision or understanding.

In summary, elevated sensemaking is distinguished by its breadth (embracing multiple perspectives), depth (reflection and self-awareness), and height (a higher-level view of patterns and strategy). It is the "how" of vertical development—the sophisticated way of thinking that allows leaders to turn complex challenges into growth.

Sensemaking Across Vertical Development Stages

To truly grasp how this capability unfolds, let's explore how leaders at different developmental stages make sense of the world. Each stage of vertical development brings a larger mindset "container" for sensemaking. Through a narrative lens, we'll see how an individual might evolve from basic sensemaking at early stages to elevated sensemaking at later stages, illustrating the growing capacity to interpret complexity.

Opportunist: "What's in It for Me Right Now?"

Worldview: The Opportunist stage is the most self-focused and short term in perspective. Leaders at this stage make sense of situations primarily through the lens of personal advantage, survival, and immediate gratification. In other words, "winning isn't everything, it's the only thing," as the Opportunist's motto goes. Their sensemaking revolves around "one's personal needs, self-protection, and working the environment so they come out on top." If information or advice doesn't serve their immediate goals, they tend to dismiss it. This mindset often maintains an *illusion of control*—believing they can bend rules or manipulate situations to secure safety or victory.

> **Mindset Recap:** The Opportunist mindset is self-oriented and survival-driven. At this earliest stage, a leader is focused on personal needs, winning, and immediate gains.

Example

Consider Daniel, a sales manager early in his career, who operates at the Opportunist stage. When a new complex project is announced, Daniel's immediate thought is how he can use it to make himself look good. The project involves multiple departments, but Daniel sees it as a zero-sum game for budget and credit. In meetings, he interprets colleagues' comments as attempts to either support or thwart his personal agenda. When a problem arises—say, a supply chain hiccup—Daniel's "sensemaking" is basically asking, "How do I fix this fast so I don't get blamed and maybe even come out a hero?" He might shortcut a proper fix in order to achieve a quick win that makes him look successful. For instance, he might pressure a vendor aggressively to cover the delay, without considering the longer-term relationship damage. If someone suggests a more collaborative approach, Daniel feels they're just not as tough or savvy; in his mind, every situation is a competition to be won.

Sensemaking Capacities and Limits

At the Opportunist stage, Daniel's capacity for sensemaking is rudimentary. He notices mainly the pieces of information that relate to his own success or security; everything else is noise. Complex challenges often get reduced to simple binaries: win or lose, friend or foe. While this opportunistic logic can sometimes produce quick results in crisis or highly competitive scenarios, it severely limits elevated sensemaking. Daniel rarely reflects on *why* a problem occurred or *how* different factors interconnect—he only cares about the immediate fix and personal impact. He also doesn't truly seek multiple perspectives (except perhaps to figure out others' weaknesses to exploit). In fact, Opportunists often distrust others' input and may ignore rules or data that constrain their freedom. The result is a very narrow meaning-making process: if the answer isn't obvious to *him*, he assumes others are wrong, and he charges ahead with his own approach.

Crossing the Edge to the Next Stage

For an Opportunist like Daniel to grow, something usually has to crack his self-focused worldview. Often it's a "hit bottom" experience or a stark failure that shows him he can't succeed alone. In Daniel's case, imagine his quick fixes backfire—the vendor he bullied cancels their contract, causing a bigger crisis that Daniel cannot solve by himself. He realizes that in a complex organization, sometimes "they cannot win or be safe unless they rely on or connect with others."

This painful lesson is a heat experience that can spur development. Daniel might also meet a mentor or coach who helps him distinguish between real threats and the "perceived" threats he's been reacting to. With support, Daniel starts to see that there is safety (and success) in numbers and belonging to a team. This insight marks the beginning of transition to the next stage. He might begin asking a new kind of question when making sense of a situation: "How can we win together?" That question signals a shift to a broader, more social frame of reference—the hallmark of the Diplomat stage.

Diplomat "Follow the Rules and Fit In"

Worldview: At the Diplomat stage, a leader's sensemaking broadens slightly from pure self-interest to include the norms and expectations of a group. Diplomats view the world in terms of affiliation: maintaining harmony, following rules, and adhering to authority are paramount. They make sense of situations by asking, essentially, "What do the rules (or our group) say about this?" The Diplomat mindset "relies on clear rules and norms and expects others to fall in line." There is comfort in the familiar structure; a Diplomat leader believes that if everyone just does what's expected and keeps conflict to a minimum, things will work out. In practice, this can look like a "command and control" approach when in authority, or strict obedience to a leader or policy when not in charge. The emphasis is on *belonging*: fitting in with the group and not challenging the status quo. Diplomats find meaning through group identity and loyalty.

> **Mindset Recap:** A leader in the Diplomat mindset values cooperation, norms, and belonging. Having learned the power of group inclusion, Diplomats strive to follow the rules and make things work as part of the group.

Example

After learning some hard lessons as an Opportunist, Marisa evolves into a Diplomat-minded leader. Now suppose Marisa is promoted to lead a small team. She becomes very concerned with doing things "the right way" as laid out by company policy and her own boss's directives. When a complex problem emerges—say the team's product fails a quality test—Marisa's instinct is to look up the standard operating procedures and ensure everyone follows them to a tee. In meetings, she defers to whatever consensus is emerging, even if he has private doubts. For instance, if most team members blame the manufacturing department for the quality issue, Marisa will also align with that view publicly to maintain unity, even if evidence suggests it's a design flaw on his team's side. Her sensemaking filters out discordant information that might cause conflict. If an engineer on Her team voices a different interpretation ("I think the flaw might be in our design"),

Marisa might gently shut it down to preserve harmony, saying, "Let's not point fingers internally—we know manufacturing had issues, so let's stick to that narrative." In Marisa's mind, following the established rule (in this case, an unwritten rule of avoiding internal conflict and siding with the majority) keeps the group safe and functional. She values being seen as a loyal company person and a good team player above all.

Sensemaking Capacities and Limits

At the Diplomat stage, sensemaking is still relatively constrained, but it's oriented toward *social* cues rather than purely personal ones. Marisa now considers other people's opinions—but mainly those in her immediate group or authority hierarchy. She has grown from "me" to "we," which is progress. Diplomat sensemaking excels at stability: it interprets events in ways that uphold group cohesion. For straightforward environments with clear rules (think of a military unit or a high-compliance industry), this mindset can actually be effective in enforcing standards and order. Marisa, for example, ensures that his team rigorously follows the company's quality checklist (adherence that an Opportunist might scoff at). However, the Diplomat's weakness in sensemaking is a lack of independent critical thinking. Because Marisa defers to group consensus and fears standing out, she's prone to groupthink. She seldom asks if the prevailing rules or assumptions are actually valid; she assumes they are, because challenging them feels unsafe. As a result, novel or complex problems can stump him. If the situation doesn't fit the old rules, a Diplomat may try to force it to fit or else feel paralyzed. In Marisa's case, if neither the team nor the rulebook has an answer to the product quality issue, she might freeze, hoping higher-ups will tell her what to do. Also, Diplomats avoid conflict and nuance—they prefer "simple and superficial solutions" that won't rock the boat. Thus, elevated sensemaking—which often requires digging into complexity and embracing dissenting views—is limited at this stage. Marisa's understanding of the quality problem remains shallow (blaming the other department) because he avoided exploring the uncomfortable possibility of his team's fault.

Crossing the Edge to the Next Stage

Transition from Diplomat to the next stage (Expert) usually involves gaining the confidence to think for oneself. For Marisa, this might happen when she encounters a scenario where slavishly following the rules fails. Imagine a situation where her team faces a technical crisis that the standard procedures can't address. Marisa's manager might say, "We need *your* analysis on why this is happening," pushing her to step up independently. Or Marisa might start feeling stifled—perhaps he notices that always deferring to the group is holding back her personal growth or the team's innovation. The stretch exercises for a Diplomat mindset include "taking a role that requires independent thinking outside the group" and talking to people in different roles to broaden his perspective. If Marisa takes on a special project where success depends on his expertise rather than consensus, she'll have to rely on her own judgment. Maybe she's asked to liaise with an R&D group that has a very different culture, forcing him out of his comfortable compliance role. Over time, Marisa begins to pay attention to her own interests and ideas (e.g., discovering she actually loves problem-solving in engineering), not just what the group expects. A subtle but important shift occurs in his sensemaking: she starts asking "What do *I* think about this problem?" rather than "What *should* I think (per the rules)?" That heralds the emergence of the Expert mindset, where competence and independent logic take center stage.

Expert: "I Know What's Right—Leave It to Me"

Worldview: The Expert stage is characterized by a focus on personal expertise, logic, and correctness. Leaders at this stage make sense of the world through the lens of technical mastery and rational analysis. They trust their own ability to figure things out through hard data, deep knowledge, and experience in a given domain. The Expert mindset "focuses on what you know and do," emphasizing *competence* and methodical, linear thinking with clear right-or-wrong answers. In contrast to the Diplomat's deference to the group, the Expert asserts their own perspective as *the* correct one—often with the attitude, "If I want it done right, I have to do it myself." They pride themselves on being the authority in their area. This mindset is highly valuable for problem-solving in specialized domains: Experts excel at diagnosing and fixing technical issues, optimizing processes, and applying best practices. Their sensemaking style is analytical and detail-oriented, but it can also be rigid—they may struggle with perspectives outside their expertise or problems that don't have a clear technical solution.

> **Mindset Recap:** A leader at the Expert mindset is all about personal competence, precision, and logic. This mindset is focused on what you know and do—mastering skills, perfecting techniques, and ensuring things are done the "right way."

Example

Now in her career, Aisha has grown confident in her own skills and has perhaps specialized in a field (say, project management or engineering).

As an Expert-stage leader, Aisha tackles complex challenges by diving into the technical details. If her team's project is behind schedule, he immediately scrutinizes the project plan, identifies task dependencies, and finds the bottleneck—perhaps a particular component design. She then personally works overtime to redesign that component, convinced that her hands-on expertise is what's needed. When colleagues from other departments offer input (e.g., marketing suggesting a simpler feature to meet the deadline), Aisha may dismiss those ideas because they come from "non-experts." In meetings, she often finds herself explaining (or defending) the one "correct" approach in her view, and she gets impatient when others don't get it. For example, if the team brainstorms about the project delay, Aisha zeros in on a technical glitch as the root cause and might ignore a teammate's comment that communication issues are to blame. Her internal narrative: "People just need to follow the plan and use the tools correctly—the data shows where the problem is, and I've solved it." She feels a sense of pride in being the go-to problem-solver. However, the project continues to struggle, perhaps because morale is low (an issue outside Aisha's technical focus). Aisha's sensemaking filter—which values technical truth over "soft" factors—leads her to see the situation in terms of flawed processes rather than human dynamics.

Sensemaking Capacities and Limits

At the Expert stage, Aisha's ability to make sense of problems has grown more sophisticated in an analytical way. Compared to Diplomat, she's now willing to challenge others' ideas and assert her own—meaning he can cut through groupthink and introduce logical analysis. She no longer blindly follows the old rules; instead, she follows evidence and her own reasoned conclusions. This is a major step toward independent thinking. Expert leaders are often excellent at problem-solving within a defined system—they will ferret out errors, improve efficiency, and implement solutions in their realm of expertise. Aisha's careful project plan analysis and technical fix exemplify this strength. In many organizations, this mindset is rewarded because it produces tangible improvements and shows strong individual contribution. However, the Expert stage also has notable limitations for elevated sensemaking. Narrow perspective is one: Experts can become siloed, seeing the world chiefly through their specialty. Aisha, for one, dismisses the marketing perspective and team dynamics, which are actually crucial to the project's success. This stage's mantra "being right is what matters" hints at a blind spot: Experts often conflate *their* truth with *the* truth. Thus, they may resist input that doesn't align with their analysis, undermining collaboration. They also tend to solve the problem that's in front of them (the technical issue) but might miss the bigger picture (the project context or strategic goal). In complex, multifaceted challenges, a pure Expert approach can lead to partial solutions. Additionally, Experts often struggle with ambiguity—they believe "there is a clear solution to every problem," so when faced with a truly ambiguous situation, they may double down on analysis paralysis or overconfidence.

Aisha's sensemaking at this stage is detail-rich but context-light. She's asking, "How do we technically fix this issue?" but not yet "Why does this issue matter and who does it affect?" For elevated sensemaking to develop, leaders must eventually transcend the limits of their own expertise and integrate other viewpoints.

Crossing the Edge to the Next Stage

The shift from Expert to Achiever (the next stage) often comes when leaders recognize that personal expertise alone is not sufficient to reach larger goals. For Aisha, this realization might dawn when she notices that despite her technical fixes, the project is still failing due to team coordination problems or unmet customer needs. Perhaps for the first time, Aisha can't solve a key problem by herself—it requires cooperation and a broader outlook. She might also feel the desire to have a bigger impact than just her technical domain; maybe she aspires to a higher leadership role, which demands engaging and leading others effectively. A key insight that propels Experts forward is that it's "not enough to be right, smart, or perfect. You also need to be effective and bring others along." Aisha begins to see that even if she is right about the technical fix, it doesn't matter if the team as a whole fails or if the solution doesn't address the client's real concern. This dawning awareness—that success requires *communication, influence, and teamwork* in addition to technical acumen—is huge.

Some developmental experiences that facilitate this shift include leading a cross-functional project (forcing Aisha to speak the language of others, not just engineering), receiving feedback about her teamwork or communication, or perhaps failing at something because he didn't consider nontechnical factors. In Aisha's company, maybe she is put in charge of launching a new product, which means he must coordinate R&D, marketing, and operations. At first, he approaches it as an Expert—focusing on the Gantt chart and technical specs. But he soon finds that the real challenges are rallying the team around a shared goal and adapting to market feedback, things her technical plan didn't cover. Guided by a mentor or coach, Aisha works on skills like vision setting, influencing conversations, and conflict resolution—hallmarks of the next stage. She practices listening to his teammates' concerns (even if they're not technical) and learns to adjust his plans based on input. Over time, she starts to take pride not just in being right but in being effective through others. When Aisha begins asking herself, "How can we achieve this goal together? How do I ensure everyone is on board and understood?"—she is thinking like an Achiever, the stage where both people and outcomes become central.

Achiever: "Let's Plan and Get Results—Together"

Worldview: The Achiever stage marks a shift to a strategic and outcome-oriented mindset that also values collaboration. Leaders at this stage see the world as a place where vision, planning, and teamwork can shape the future. They define success by setting clear goals and achieving them, often through organized effort with others. The Achiever mindset "comes across as highly motivated, attentive to team effectiveness, and focused on results." Achievers broaden their sensemaking to balance multiple elements: both people and process are valued, insofar as they serve the defined goals and outcomes. In other words, Achievers care about relationships and team morale, but largely because they know those are crucial to executing plans successfully. They are willing to embrace complexity more than Experts do—they'll consider different facets of a problem (market trends, team input, technical details, timelines)—but they tend to structure that complexity into plans, strategies, and metrics. This stage is often associated with the effective mid-level to senior managers who drive projects to completion, lead teams, and deliver results. Achievers are also typically aware of the need for adaptability: if working harder doesn't solve a problem, they'll try working smarter or reworking the plan. However, they may still equate their identity with success ("I am my achievements") and can get uncomfortable when success is not clearly defined.

> **Mindset Recap:** The Achiever mindset is the model of the effective, goal-oriented leader. Achievers are highly motivated, focused on results, and attuned to team performance.

Example

Raj, now an experienced manager, has grown into an Achiever-stage leader. He is responsible for an entire department with multiple project teams. When faced with a complex challenge—for example, a new product launch in a highly competitive market—Raj's approach is to set a bold objective ("Launch by Q4 with 20% market share in the first year") and then rally his teams around this goal. He organizes planning sessions to map out work streams, assigns clear roles and responsibilities, and establishes KPIs (key performance indicators) to track progress. Raj actively communicates a vision for the launch, emphasizing how each team's work contributes to a successful outcome. He holds regular team check-ins to ensure alignment and encourages cross-functional problem-solving when issues arise. If the R&D team hits a snag, Raj brings in marketing and customer service to help, recognizing that feedback from all sides might spark a solution. He's pragmatic—if an initial plan isn't yielding results, he's willing to adjust timelines or redefine features (unlike the more rigid Expert he once was). For instance, if early customer testing reveals a need for a change, Raj weighs the trade-offs and might pivot the strategy to meet customer needs while still keeping the end goal in sight. He is also open to feedback on his leadership; if team members say they are burning out, he takes it seriously and looks for ways to redistribute work or clarify priorities. Essentially, Raj's sensemaking now involves juggling the who (people), how (process), and what (results)—integrating them into a plan of action. His narrative might be, "We need a clear plan and everyone rowing in the same direction. If we communicate well and stay focused, we will succeed together."

Sensemaking Capacities and Limits

At the Achiever stage, a leader's sensemaking capacity has expanded significantly. Raj has moved beyond relying only on himself—he actively involves others and values their contributions. He interprets events with an eye toward goals and outcomes: everything is evaluated by, "Does this help us reach the goal, or not?" Achievers tend to be excellent at medium-term planning and execution. They can manage complexity by breaking it into projects and tasks. Importantly, Achievers can handle conflicting priorities better than earlier stages—Raj can balance quality, speed, and cost, for example, whereas an Expert might have obsessed over quality only. Achievers also understand organizational dynamics; Raj realizes he must manage up (keeping his boss informed) and manage down (motivating his team), using emotional intelligence in service of results. His sensemaking now incorporates *others' perspectives and needs* more genuinely—not just as rules to follow but as factors to consider for success. This makes him more empathetic and motivational. He has learned that "to be effective you need to bring others along." Thus, Achievers often develop good communication and influence skills, something Raj demonstrates in his cross-team collaboration.

The Achiever stage is often considered the pinnacle of the conventional mindset in organizations—many leaders operate here effectively. Yet it has its limits, especially as complexity continues to increase. One limit is scope of purpose: Achievers are great at reaching defined goals, but they may not question whether the goals themselves are the *right* or most meaningful ones. Raj, for instance, is focused on hitting market share targets (a conventional success measure). He might not deeply consider broader questions like "Are we solving the right problem for society?" or "What's a truly fulfilling outcome for me and the team?" His worldview still largely equates success with *external achievement*—promotions, metrics, accolades. This can lead to overwork or burnout, as Raj may shoulder a lot of responsibility to ensure success. Another limitation is that Achievers prefer problems where success criteria are clear. They handle complicated projects well, but in truly chaotic or value-conflicted situations, they may struggle. They might default to what has worked in the past ("work harder or smarter") even when facing a novel type of challenge, risking diminishing returns. Achievers can also inadvertently become trapped by their success—proud of their checklist of accomplishments, they may ignore deeper personal development. Raj might start to feel a nagging emptiness even after big wins, wondering why the fulfillment doesn't last. In terms of sensemaking, Achievers may not fully grapple with paradox or subjective values yet; they typically assume with enough effort and planning, and any goal is attainable and the best path will reveal itself.

Crossing the Edge to the Next Stage

The transition from Achiever to Redefining (also known as Individualist in some models) is often spurred by a search for deeper meaning and flexibility beyond the success = efficiency equation. For Raj, this transition might begin when he achieves a major career goal (say the product launch is a success) yet feels oddly unfulfilled. He has proven he can be effective and "make a mark," but now he starts to question, "Is this all there is? What truly matters to me?" It's common at this stage for people to hit what seems like the pinnacle of conventional success—a big promotion, a completed mission—only to find that achievement is not the same as fulfillment. Raj might also encounter situations that challenge his neatly organized worldview. Perhaps his company faces an ethical dilemma, or a personal life event (like a health scare or family change) shifts his perspective on what's important. The Achiever's focus on goals can begin to feel hollow or too narrow when life presents messy trade-offs and value conflicts.

A classic developmental catalyst is being thrust into a context with more ambiguity and diversity of perspectives than ever before. For example, Raj might take an international assignment or move into a role that involves integrating very different functions (imagine going from a product-focused role to a strategy or innovation role that has to question fundamental assumptions). According to one leadership guide, entering Redefining often comes with experiences like "an overseas detail, a move to a more ambiguous and complex role, or a life-altering experience" that shakes an Achiever's familiar worldview. Raj could be asked to lead a change initiative that doesn't have clear-cut metrics and provokes pushback on multiple fronts. Suddenly, his usual playbook doesn't guarantee success. He's confronted with questions of purpose, values, and identity—realms he hadn't paid much attention to before. With some coaching or reflection, Raj begins to explore these questions: "What *does* fulfill me deeply? What's the larger purpose of our work? Are there other ways to define success beyond the quarterly targets?"

This is typically a challenging transition because it involves a kind of unraveling. Achievers often have to let go of the certainty and comfort of their previous effectiveness and allow themselves to not know, to question, and to experiment with new ways of thinking. Raj might start reading up on new leadership paradigms, or seek out mentors who seem to "see the world differently." He may even become a bit critical or cynical about the old metrics of success, feeling that they miss the point. The stage is set for Raj to redefine himself and his approach to leadership—to become a Redefining/Individualist leader who is focused on authenticity, purpose, and integrating multiple systems of thought.

Redefining: "Why Are We Doing This? What Really Matters?"

Worldview: The Redefining stage marks a profound shift in sensemaking from the conventional to the post-conventional. Leaders at this stage start to question the assumptions and definitions of success that they took for granted before. The focus moves to authenticity, purpose, and plurality of perspectives. A Redefining leader looks beyond the organization's immediate goals or their own success, asking larger questions about meaning and impact. Their sensemaking becomes much more contextual and systemic—they consider not just *how* to achieve something but *whether* it should be done, and *what* the endeavor means in a broader context. The Redefining mindset is described as "characterized by a focus on both people and purpose." Leaders at this stage often strive to align their work with their deeply held values and what "deeply resonates" with them. They are no longer satisfied with traditional definitions of success; they seek *authentic fulfillment.* This often leads them to empower others and question hierarchical or one-dimensional thinking. In fact, the Redefining action logic is sometimes called "post-heroic," meaning it's less about the leader's heroics and more about what they *enable in others* and in the larger system. Redefining leaders embrace complexity not just to tame it (as Achievers do) but to explore and learn from it. They are willing to sit with paradoxes and competing values, trying to find a deeper integration (or at least balance) between them.

> **Mindset Recap:** The Redefining mindset is all about questioning, complexity, and authenticity. Leaders operating with a Redefining mindset start to see multiple perspectives and value purpose and people alongside performance.

Example

Elena has now stepped back from the relentless pursuit of conventional success after her big project and life experiences prompted soul-searching. Imagine Elena in a scenario where she is leading a division of the company that is tasked with creating a long-term sustainability strategy. She approaches this task very differently than she would have at Achiever stage. Instead of immediately setting numeric targets, Elena convenes diverse groups—employees from all levels, community representatives, and even critics of the company—to hear their perspectives on what sustainability means. She might say, "We need to understand what really matters to all stakeholders before we decide what to do." Elena actively explores questions like "What is our larger purpose here? How do our products affect society and the environment?" She encourages open dialogues that might have made his old Achiever-self uncomfortable—for instance, allowing employees to vent about company practices that feel misaligned with their personal values. Elena takes these perspectives seriously, even if they challenge the company's traditional strategy.

In meetings, Elena often plays devil's advocate to spark fresh thinking: "We've always defined success as growth and profit. But what if success also meant community well-being or employee happiness? How would our decisions change?" Her team sometimes finds him puzzling—he seems less decisive, more experimental. For example, instead of handing down a concrete plan, Elena initiates a pilot program for a radically different business model that prioritizes social impact over immediate profit. She's essentially testing new hypotheses about what could work, rather than executing a known plan. Some colleagues worry that Elena is "overcomplicating things" by considering too many variables. There are moments she herself feels confused or torn—should they stick with the core business model or pivot to something that feels more meaningful but risky? This internal conflict is common at Redefining; Elena is juggling multiple value systems. She finds herself mediating between opposing viewpoints and values: the finance department's focus on quarterly returns and the innovation team's passion for green technology that might pay off only in the long term. Elena tries to find a path that honors both, perhaps by redefining the company's mission to include sustainable innovation as a goal alongside profitability.

Sensemaking Capacities and Limits

Elena's sensemaking now is far more expansive and inclusive. At the Redefining stage, she actively seeks out and values diverse opinions, perspectives, and styles—including examining her own blind spots. This is a huge leap from his earlier mindsets. She's no longer content to operate within one system or one set of metrics; he instead navigates multiple systems of thought. Redefining leaders excel at seeing the bigger picture—not necessarily in a simplistic "one big picture" way but in seeing how things connect across different domains. Elena sees the interplay between business results and social values, between personal fulfillment and professional achievement. This often makes them systems thinkers and change agents who push their organizations to evolve. They are also typically innovators; because they question status quo assumptions, they can come up with out-of-the-box strategies. Elena's willingness to pilot a new business model for sustainability reflects that innovative streak.

Another strength at this stage is a heightened empathy and people focus. Redefining leaders truly listen. Elena takes time to include others in decisions and change processes, knowing it enriches the outcome. She might mentor others on finding their own purpose, not just their productivity. The team likely feels more seen and heard by her than ever before. And importantly, Elena starts to decouple his identity from just his role or achievements—she's exploring who he is and what he really stands for beyond external validation. This can make her more resilient in the face of setbacks, since her ego is less tied to any single success or failure.

However, the Redefining stage can be as challenging as it is liberating. One common watch-out is that in embracing many perspectives, leaders can struggle to make decisions or appear indecisive. Elena sometimes gets caught in analysis paralysis, considering every angle endlessly. Her team might feel a lack of clear direction at times. This stage can also breed a bit of cynicism or conflict with the establishment—Redefining leaders might become *cynical about traditional business practices* or frustrated with those still playing by old rules. Elena has to be careful not to come off as self-righteous or dismissive of colleagues who are content with Achiever-style goals. Another challenge: Redefining individuals often experience a kind of identity upheaval—confronting big questions like "Who am I now?"—which can be disorienting. Elena may feel a sense of existential angst as she navigates new territory, which can sometimes seep into a feeling of being lost or not fully confident. In sensemaking terms, he doesn't have a single guiding star like he used to (for Achiever Elena it was hitting the plan); now she's exploring constellation of possibilities. That exploration, while rich, can slow down execution and even cause friction with those expecting quicker, more concrete results.

Crossing the Edge to the Next Stage

The Redefining stage is a fertile ground for personal growth, but to move to the next level—Transforming—a leader typically must find ways to reintroduce coherence and commitment after the period of exploration. For Elena, having opened herself to many perspectives and experimented with new ideas, the challenge becomes integrating these into a new, stable form of leadership. In practical terms, this might mean Elena refines her sense of purpose and starts to clearly articulate a *new vision* that synthesizes the multiple agendas she's considered. Perhaps through reflection or coaching, she identifies a core principle that can guide him through complexity—a "north star" such as a dedication to both big-picture purpose and tangible results.

A hallmark of moving toward Transforming is developing the ability to handle paradox by creating transformational solutions that satisfy multiple needs. Elena might stumble upon approaches that don't force a trade-off between profit and sustainability but find innovative ways to achieve both—discovering a "middle path" or a higher-order solution. For instance, maybe her pilot project reveals a business model that is both profitable and eco-friendly when scaled appropriately. This success could strengthen his inner confidence that embracing complexity works. Elena also likely deepens her self-acceptance; she becomes more comfortable with who she is, paradoxes and all, which results in a steadier presence. The Redefining stage's turbulence settles as she starts to answer, "Who am I now?" with a new, more secure identity.

To aid this transition, Elena might pair with mentors or coaches who operate at later stages, who model how to bring together the *inner* growth and *outer* effectiveness. She might also benefit from frameworks and tools that help integrate thinking (e.g., learning about polarity mapping to balance competing priorities, or systemic mapping tools to see patterns). If Elena can consolidate the lessons of the Redefining stage—the importance of purpose, the value of multiple perspectives, the humility of knowing one's limits—and combine them with the decisiveness and focus of earlier stages, she begins to embody the Transforming mindset. The key insight here is often that systems can be transformed not just understood. Elena starts to see herself as a transformer of the larger system not just an observer or a critic. With that, she moves into the Transforming stage, capable of truly high-level leadership that can reconcile and synergize diverse elements of an organization or even society.

Transforming: "I Can See How It All Fits Together—Let's Transform It"

Worldview: The Transforming stage (often called *Strategist* in some models) represents a powerful integration of insight, scope, and effectiveness. Leaders at this stage make sense of the world through a systems thinking lens, seeing multiple perspectives, dynamics, and time horizons all at once. They are attentive to everything from the *internal* (their own and others' emotions and values) to the *external* (market trends, societal needs), from the *personal* to the *collective*, from the *immediate* to the *long term*.

This expansive awareness allows them to address complexity with confidence and creativity. The hallmark of Transforming leaders is that they seek transformational change rather than just incremental improvements or one-off solutions. They're often the visionaries who can not only imagine bold new possibilities but also bring people together to achieve them. A key capability here is to hold and resolve paradox—"bring together opposing viewpoints and create a middle path or collaborative solutions." Transforming leaders don't get stuck in "either/or"—they find the "both/and" or a higher synthesis. They maintain focus on a big-picture purpose while also empathizing with individuals and understanding what it takes to get there on the ground.

> **Mindset Recap:** The Transforming mindset is characterized by a leader who can see across multiple systems and time horizons, integrating people, process, and purpose. A Transforming leader works comfortably in ambiguity and complexity, holding a big-picture perspective while also understanding the interdependence of all the moving parts.

In terms of identity, a Transforming leader often has not only a strong sense of true self (they know their values, strengths, and shadows) but also a lightness of ego—they can put the mission and the collective interest above their own need for credit. They take stands based on principle and long-term vision, even if unpopular, yet are adept at engaging others in those visions. People at this stage are often described as strategic change agents, able to reinvent organizations or lead major societal initiatives. They create environments where others can thrive and contribute (coaching and developing others is second nature to them). In short, their sensemaking is integrative at a grand scale: they integrate head and heart, vision and execution, self and system.

Example

Luis has evolved into a Transforming-stage leader after refining his purpose at Redefining. Imagine Luis now as a senior executive, perhaps a COO or CEO, tasked with turning around a struggling company in an industry facing disruption. His approach reflects his broadened perspective. Luis starts with the big picture: he works with his leadership team to craft a vision that addresses not just the company's profits but its role in the industry and community. For example, he articulates a purpose like, "We will transform our industry to be sustainable and inclusive, while delivering innovative products"—a vision that speaks to multiple stakeholders and timelines. Luis identifies that success will require changes in organizational culture, not just strategy. So he sets about fostering a culture of learning and innovation. He might implement cross-functional "innovation hubs" where employees from different departments and levels collaborate on strategic challenges. In one scenario, Luis leads a session on a thorny problem—say, the company's supply chain is efficient but not resilient to global shocks. In that session, he invites opposing viewpoints: one group argues for cost-saving (short-term efficiency), another for re-localizing suppliers (long-term resilience). Instead of choosing one, Luis guides the group to design a supply chain model that uses technology to gain both efficiency and resilience, perhaps by creating a dynamic supply network that can switch modes depending on conditions. He helps them see the interconnectedness of the system ("the systems, functions, and people dynamics are all interconnected") and find a solution that serves the overarching purpose.

Luis also demonstrates personal agility. If mid-course he realizes a strategy is not working, he's quick to pivot and communicate the reasons transparently, using it as a learning moment rather than a failure. He might say to the organization, "We tried X, learned Y, and now we'll integrate that learning and adjust course." His authenticity and openness build trust. People see him as someone who "translates complexity in ways others can relate to"—for instance, he can take a very complex plan and distill it into a clear story or metaphor that everyone from the board to the frontline understands. Luis also pays attention to his team's development: he often coaches his direct reports, encouraging them to own both their strengths and shadow sides. When one of his leaders has a blind spot (say, a tendency to micromanage), Luis might share observations about it and provide support to grow beyond it, creating a ripple of vertical development in the organization. His meetings are inclusive and forward-looking; he doesn't dominate but rather facilitates dialogue among diverse voices to co-create solutions (this is that post-heroic leadership fully realized—success is "ours" not just his).

Sensemaking Capacities and Limits

Luis's sensemaking as a Transforming leader is highly elevated. He's essentially doing real-time synthesis of vast amounts of information and aligning it with core principles. Several capacities stand out:

- **Strategic Systems Thinking:** He sees patterns among what might seem like unrelated elements. Luis perceives how a decision in R&D could affect customer perception, which affects brand value, which ties to long-term survival—a whole web of connections. This lets him anticipate second- and third-order effects of decisions, a key to navigating complex change.

- **Integrating Polarities:** Transforming leaders do not get flustered by contradictions; they expect them and skillfully manage them. Luis, for instance, balances short term versus long term, centralized versus decentralized, stability versus change—often by creating solutions that leverage the best of both poles. This "polarity thinking" is a sophisticated sensemaking tool that earlier stages lack. Where an Achiever might pick one side and a Redefining might oscillate or feel torn, a Transforming leader finds a way to honor both.
- **Empowering and Developing Others:** Luis knows that transforming a system requires many leaders, not just one. He therefore focuses on building *capacity in others*. His sensemaking includes reading people and their development needs. He likely creates programs or uses coaching questions that help others see from a higher perspective. For example, he might ask his managers not just to meet their targets but also to consider how their work contributes to the greater mission or how they can grow through the challenges—thereby instilling sensemaking in them too. In a way, a Transforming leader is a *leader of leaders*.
- **Calm Amid Complexity:** Because they have worked through personal purpose and ego issues in the previous stage, Transforming leaders like Luis often exhibit a calm confidence even in chaos. They've internalized that change is constant and manageable. Luis can be a steadying presence—the "eye of the storm"—which reassures those around him. He stays focused on what matters most (purpose, values) and is less rattled by the unexpected.

Even at this high level, there are potential limitations or pitfalls (though minor in comparison to earlier stages). One is that Transforming leaders can sometimes appear aloof or too cerebral to others. Because Luis thinks so broadly, he might inadvertently talk in abstract terms or focus on big visions that some practical-minded folks struggle to connect with. Not everyone can immediately follow his leaps in understanding, so he must continuously practice translating his insights to meet others where they are. Another challenge: in being very future-oriented and complex, they might overlook some immediate simple fixes or underestimate how much hand-holding people at earlier mindsets need. If Luis moves too fast with a grand transformation, parts of the organization might resist or not catch up. However, truly effective Transforming leaders learn to mitigate this by flexing their style—they can dial back to an Achiever mode temporarily to set short-term goals or give step-by-step guidance if that's what's needed to bring people along. They essentially can operate on multiple altitudes of development as situation demands (this ability to "toggle" is a known strength of later-stage leaders).

Crossing the Edge to the Next Stage

The later stage in this journey is Alchemical (also known as Alchemist). Not all leaders reach this rare stage—it often involves a profound transformation of consciousness and is less common. If Luis were to move toward Alchemical, it would involve an even larger expansion of perspective, one that might transcend the organization entirely and encompass a more global or spiritual view. Typically, moving beyond Transforming requires an embrace of the idea that everything is connected and in flux at an existential level, and a comfort with deep change and uncertainty that might unsettle even Transforming leaders. Luis would be looking at not just transforming systems but transforming consciousness and seeing hidden potentials in situations that others might consider hopeless. Often, this stage is marked by an extraordinary capacity to renew or reinvent not just organizations but entire social systems, and to do so with compassion and systemic wisdom.

For Luis, experiences that could spark this shift might be confronting profound uncertainty or encountering leaders who operate at a seemingly "wise" level that inspires him further. Perhaps he mentors under someone known for their enlightened leadership approach, or he engages in intensive personal development practices (like meditation, spiritual retreats, or deep immersion in radically different cultures) that alter how he experiences reality. He might start perceiving patterns in a more intuitive way or develop a desire to contribute to humanity at large, not just his enterprise. As Luis's journey has shown, each stage has built on the previous; moving to Alchemical would be the ultimate integration—combining action and insight to an almost artful degree, effectively becoming a catalyst for change at a grand scale.

Alchemical: "Everything Is Connected—I Am Here to Catalyze Positive Change"

Worldview: The Alchemical stage is so named because leaders at this level can seem almost magical in their ability to facilitate transformation. This stage is extremely rare and represents the pinnacle of vertical development as understood in most models (sometimes loosely mapped to visionary or servant leadership on steroids). Leaders operating with an Alchemical mindset perceive reality as interwoven, dynamic, and fundamentally fluid. They often understand that what we consider "reality"—organizations, strategies, even social norms—are human constructions that can be changed. As one description puts it: these individuals "see how security is an illusion and everything is constructed and therefore liable to change." This realization, which might be "freeing and terrifying at the same time," allows Alchemical leaders to approach change without the usual fear or attachment. They are fully comfortable with paradox, uncertainty, and the unknown.

Mindset Recap: The Alchemical mindset represents the latest stage of vertical leadership maturity. Leaders at this stage embody a sense of balance, peace, and radical flexibility.

Alchemical leaders tend to prefer open, fluid conditions where they can respond in the moment to what arises. They have a strong presence, often a *quiet wisdom* that can ground and inspire others around them. Interestingly, they might work behind the scenes rather than seek the spotlight, influencing through personal charisma, profound questions, and creating spaces for transformation. Their sensemaking is deeply intuitive as well as rational—they might "sense" what's trying to emerge in a system and help midwife it into existence. These are the leaders who sometimes seem a bit enigmatic or unconventional but have a remarkable impact. They can instill calm in chaos ("the serenity in the eye of the storm") by their mere presence. They often focus on ethics, spirit, and global/historical perspective—not just "our company's survival" but "the evolution of our society or humanity" is on their mind.

Alchemical leaders also recognize the importance of developing others who can carry on transformation. They seek to pass on wisdom and create other change agents, often through storytelling, mentoring, or role modeling a new way of being. At this stage, leadership becomes truly about *service* to something larger than oneself, combined with an uncanny ability to manifest change.

Example

If Asha were to reach an Alchemical stage, her leadership might transcend his formal role. Perhaps he has become a renowned leader known for guiding organizations through massive change in a humane and visionary way. Picture Asha now as an advisor to multiple companies or even governments, called upon in times of extreme challenge. In one scenario, a community is facing a major crisis—say an economic collapse due to industry changes. Asha convenes a meeting of business leaders, government officials, and community representatives. Instead of presenting a plan or even facilitating a structured discussion, she begins by sharing a story—maybe about a historical transformation or a personal anecdote—that helps everyone step back and see the situation from a fresh perspective. In the discussion that follows, Asha doesn't direct it forcefully; she listens deeply, occasionally asking a piercing question like, "What opportunity might be hidden in this crisis that could benefit everyone?" She encourages participants to drop their usual defensiveness and speak from the heart. Under her guidance, what starts as a tense, fearful gathering turns into a collaborative brainstorming about completely new approaches for the community—perhaps retraining workers for different industries, or forming an alliance to attract new forms of commerce that also address social needs. People leave the meeting feeling surprisingly hopeful and energized, not entirely sure how it happened—only that Asha's presence made it feel safe to envision a bold future together.

Back in her own organization, Asha operates in a very fluid way. She might not stick to a rigid schedule; instead, he moves to where energy is needed. One day she spends hours walking around talking individually to frontline employees, gleaning their honest feelings and quietly coaching them. Another day she might retreat and meditate on a tough dilemma, emerging with an insight that solves a problem in minutes that others had struggled with for months. For example, if two departments have been at odds and even the Transforming-level plans haven't fully resolved it, Asha might conceive a new structural change or a symbolic act that dissolves the tension entirely (akin to how an alchemist might add a catalyst to clear a murky solution).

SENSEMAKING CAPACITIES AND LIMITS

Alchemical sensemaking is holistic and transformational to the extreme. Leaders like Asha at this stage integrate across all levels—they see the material, mental, emotional, and even spiritual dimensions of situations. Some capacities of Alchemical leaders include the following:

- **Profound Systemic Insight:** They don't just see the system; they *feel* it and can intuit leverage points for change that others overlook. Asha, for instance, intuitively understands that healing a rift between departments might require not another strategy meeting but perhaps a shared meaningful experience (like a volunteer day or an offsite retreat where people connect as humans). She perceives subtle dynamics (trust, fear, aspiration) that underlie business issues.
- **Adaptive Identity and Role:** Alchemical leaders can wear different identities fluidly to suit the situation—almost like shapeshifting. Asha might be a mentor, a follower, a challenger, or a visionary at different times.

She has "the ability to continually readjust how they think, act, and present themselves to stay in the serenity at the eye of the storm." This adaptability means his sensemaking is not bound by ego or title—he can learn from a janitor and debate a head of state on the same day, extracting wisdom from both.

- **Presence and Serenity:** Perhaps one of the most commented qualities of such leaders is their presence—a combination of mindfulness, compassion, and confidence. They remain calm amidst chaos and thus help others remain calm. Asha's sensemaking benefits from this serenity because it allows him to observe and think clearly when everyone else is panicking. People often say about such a leader, "When they are here, things just feel more possible."
- **Bridging Reality and Vision:** Alchemical leaders can inspire with lofty visions while also grounding them in practical steps via others. Asha might talk about an almost utopian goal but then empower teams to figure out the implementation, stepping in only to keep things aligned with the high-level vision or values. She doesn't impose control; she sets direction at a principle level and trusts the flow of the system to self-organize toward it, intervening only to remove barriers or infuse insight.

If we look for limitations at this stage, it's less about the leader's capacity (which is quite high) and more about the context. One challenge is operating in conventional environments—an Alchemical leader might be so far ahead in thinking that others can't relate. Traditional organizations might resist their approaches or label their behavior as impractical or strange. Asha sometimes finds she must "dial down" her style to meet people where they are, or else he risks being isolated. Additionally, because so few people operate at this level, Alchemical leaders can feel lonely or misunderstood. They see connections and potential others don't, which can be frustrating. But typically, part of their journey is coming to peace with that solitude (hence the mention of a mix of despair and enlightenment). They often cultivate relationships with peers outside their organization or find solace in philosophy, art, or spirituality where their views are reflected by great minds of the past or present.

In essence, at the Alchemical stage, elevated sensemaking reaches a pinnacle: it becomes almost transcendent sensemaking—the leader perceives the interconnectedness of all things and uses that awareness to catalyze positive change well beyond themselves. A leader like Asha, at this stage, serves as a kind of human catalyst: turning collective lead into gold, so to speak, by helping groups find wisdom and possibility in the most challenging circumstances (Torbert & Rooke, 2005).

Having painted this journey from Opportunist all the way to Alchemical, it's clear that as leaders grow vertically, their sensemaking transforms from simple and self-centric to profoundly complex and altruistic. Each stage builds on the prior, adding new dimensions to how a leader interprets events and navigates problems. With this understanding of the stages, we now turn to how we can *develop* elevated sensemaking. What practical methods can organizations and coaches use to help leaders grow their sensemaking capability, no matter their starting stage? The next section offers tools and strategies for fostering this kind of vertical growth.

Practical Tools and Strategies for Fostering Sensemaking

Elevated sensemaking can be cultivated—it's not a mysterious talent reserved for the few. By intentionally creating the right conditions and supports, organizations can help their leaders gradually expand their sensemaking capacities. Here, we outline several practical methods, exercises, and reflections that have proven effective in leadership development programs aiming to boost sensemaking. These tools correspond to the developmental needs we've discussed: they encourage reflection, broaden perspectives, and guide leaders through making meaning of complex experiences.

Structured Reflection and Journaling: One of the simplest yet most powerful tools for sensemaking is regular reflection. Leaders need *time and space* to process their experiences and extract lessons. Encourage a habit of journaling—writing down thoughts about the day's challenges, decisions, and feelings. Providing prompts can help focus this practice (e.g., "What assumptions of mine were challenged today?" or "How did I handle uncertainty this week and what did I learn?"). Some leadership programs build in reflective pauses: for instance, 15 minutes of writing at the end of each day of a training workshop. Over time, journaling becomes a mirror through which leaders can observe their own evolving thinking. It externalizes their thought processes and reveals patterns. Group reflection sessions can complement solitary journaling. In these facilitated debriefs, peers share their recent challenges and insights. Hearing others' reflections not only introduces new perspectives (helping with the "colliding perspectives" aspect of growth) but also normalizes the struggles of sensemaking—leaders realize others too wrestle with ambiguity and can learn from how they frame it. Organizations can leverage digital tools for this, using online journaling platforms or forums where leaders post short weekly reflections and comment on each other's posts. This builds a reflective learning community (more on that later). The key is consistency: making reflection a routine. As one expert insightfully said, "Structured reflection is the bedrock of elevated sensemaking"—without it, the insights from challenging experiences remain fragmented. Leaders should be encouraged to treat reflection not as a luxury but as part of their job. In fact, many high-caliber organizations now schedule regular "pause and learn" intervals for their managers.

Developmental Maps and Stage Assessments: Another useful strategy is to give leaders a map of vertical development—a framework (like the stages we discussed) that helps them locate their current mindset and see what growth might look like. Research has found that when adults understand the roadmap of adult development, they can navigate their growth more effectively. In practice, this means educating leaders about stages (in an accessible way, not to put them in a box but to spark curiosity). Workshops can introduce the seven stages with examples, and leaders might self-assess where they think they predominantly operate. Even more powerful is using vertical development assessments—tools like the Vertical Mindset Indicator (VMI) or sentence completion tests that provide feedback on one's center of gravity stage. When leaders receive a stage assessment report, it often is eye-opening. For example, someone might realize, "I'm making meaning like an Expert/Achiever, but the challenges I face may need a Redefining perspective." This creates a developmental tension—a positive motivation to grow. One effective approach noted by Bill Joiner (author of *Leadership Agility*) is to have leaders read stories of someone at their stage and one stage above. The differences become tangible, and they can ask, "How might my current leadership challenge be approached from that higher-stage view?" This question directly stimulates elevated sensemaking by pushing them to try on a more complex perspective.

Developmental maps also reinforce patience—they show that growth is sequential and that each stage has value. This can reduce frustration; leaders see that it's normal to struggle at the edge of their current mindset and that it's not about "good/bad" but about *expanding capacity*. Incorporating stage concepts should be done with care (to avoid misuse like labeling). But when done well, it becomes a powerful tool for self-awareness. Leaders begin to notice, for instance, "Oh, I'm in my Expert mindset when I insist on being right. Maybe I need to lean into Achiever behaviors, like inviting others in." Organizations can integrate these assessments into their leadership programs and follow up with personalized coaching using the results. Essentially, stage knowledge provides a language for sensemaking about one's own development.

Vertical Coaching and Mentoring: Personalized guidance is extremely beneficial for developing sensemaking. Vertical coaching means coaching with an awareness of the leader's current developmental stage and their next growth edge. Coaches or mentors who understand adult development can tailor their questions and challenges accordingly. For example, with an Achiever-stage client, a coach might gently challenge their definitions of success and prompt exploration of personal values (nudging toward Redefining). The coach acts as a "guide" who knows the territory ahead, akin to a Sherpa guiding a climber to the next camp. Research by Nick Petrie emphasizes three ingredients organizations should provide: Time, Map, and Guide. We've covered time (reflection) and map (developmental framework); the guide is this coaching element. Mentors who operate at later stages themselves are especially valuable. Pairing a high-potential leader with a late-stage mentor creates rich sensemaking opportunities. As Petrie notes, when you spend time with a mentor from a later stage, "you can't help but notice they ask different questions . . . their perspectives don't mesh with the way you see the world." While this can be disorienting, it's also enlightening. If trust is built, those "peek experiences" into a higher-stage worldview can powerfully pull a leader upward. For instance, a Transforming-minded mentor might regularly ask an Expert-minded mentee things like, "What are we not seeing in this situation? Who else's perspective should we include?" Over time, the mentee internalizes these broader questions in their own thinking.

Implementation Tip: Train internal coaches in vertical development theory. A coach with a vertical lens will meet the leader where they are and also push them gently to their growing edge. They might use techniques like Socratic questioning or immunity-to-change maps (Kegan's method) to help leaders surface hidden assumptions. Additionally, encourage mentoring across levels—not just higher executives mentoring juniors on skills but explicitly on how to think about problems. Even peer coaching circles can be effective: peers can share how they each would tackle an issue and thereby expose each other to different mindsets.

Integrative Feedback and Dialogue: Feedback loops are critical for sensemaking because they provide the leader with external mirrors for their behavior and thinking. Tools like 360-degree feedback, which includes perspectives from bosses, peers, and subordinates, can highlight discrepancies that spark reflection (e.g., "I see myself as collaborative, but my peers score me low on listening—why is that?"). Ensure that feedback is not framed as judgment but as data for learning. After major projects or "heat experiences," conduct after-action reviews that focus on not just what happened but *how people interpreted* what happened. For example, ask team members in a post-mortem, "How did we each view the challenge initially, and how did our thinking evolve?" This kind of discussion brings sensemaking to the surface and allows collective learning. It also helps leaders practice *open dialogue*, adjusting their mental models when presented with others' perceptions.

Another strategy is to establish reflective learning communities or forums (sometimes called peer councils or communities of practice). In these groups, leaders regularly come together to discuss their ongoing challenges in a reflective, no-blame setting. They share stories of success and failure in making sense of issues, and they help each other reframe problems. For instance, one leader might present a dilemma and explain their thinking;

peers can then gently offer how they see it differently. These sessions pool diverse insights and promote *collaborative sensemaking*, which often yields a richer understanding than any one leader could achieve alone. It also builds a culture where reflection is valued, not seen as a sign of weakness. Over time, such communities can increase psychological safety in an organization—people feel more open to express uncertainties or wild ideas, which is fertile ground for learning and innovation (Amy Edmondson's work on psychological safety is relevant here).

Additionally, consider bringing in external perspectives for dialogue: invite customers, partners, or even thinkers (academics, futurists) to sessions with leaders. Their outside view can jolt leaders out of habitual interpretations and spark new sensemaking. Some companies do "reverse mentoring" where a young tech-savvy employee mentors an older executive on digital trends—effectively colliding perspectives in a constructive way. All these interactions, if done in a spirit of curiosity, expand the frames of reference leaders use.

Mindfulness and Somatic Practices: Sensemaking isn't purely intellectual; it's also about emotional regulation and intuition. Practices like mindfulness meditation, yoga, or breath work can enhance a leader's ability to stay present and calm amid complexity. Google and other forward-thinking companies have introduced mindfulness training to leaders to improve focus and openness. By quieting the constant reactive chatter of the mind, mindfulness helps leaders observe situations (and their own thoughts) more objectively. This can lead to those "aha" moments where a new understanding emerges. Somatic practices (attention to bodily sensations and responses) also build self-awareness—leaders learn to notice when they're feeling defensive or anxious, which is often a sign their current mindset is being challenged. Instead of impulsively reacting, a mindful leader can pause, breathe, and choose to explore the discomfort ("What is this frustration telling me about how I'm viewing this issue?"). Over time, such practices increase a leader's capacity to handle complexity without overwhelm, essentially enlarging their inner sensemaking space.

Furthermore, encourage leaders to engage in multiple modes of knowing: not just analysis but also listening to their gut feelings and emotions, and even using visualization or storytelling to understand issues differently. An exercise sometimes used is guided reflection where leaders visualize a challenge from a third-person perspective or imagine explaining it to their future self—this often reveals new angles. These techniques might seem "soft," but they can powerfully complement the hard analytics, leading to more integrative solutions.

Developmental Assignments and Polarity Challenges: To foster growth, you have to walk the talk—give leaders experiences that *require* elevated sensemaking. One approach is to design stretch assignments deliberately aimed at their developmental edge. For an Expert-stage leader, that might be leading a project that demands cross-functional collaboration and has ambiguous success criteria (forcing them to rely on others and consider nontechnical aspects). For an Achiever-stage leader like old Asha, it might be an assignment where the outcome is not easily defined or there is no clear "right answer," as was suggested: "a developmental assignment involving uncertainty and ambiguity where you can't easily define the outcomes." This pushes Achievers to develop comfort with emergent goals and multiple pathways. For Redefining-stage folks, assignments that involve managing competing priorities or polarity mapping exercises can be useful—for example, leading an initiative that must balance innovation and efficiency (a polarity), which forces them to practice both/and thinking.

Another tactic is to implement job rotations or role swaps that expose leaders to entirely different perspectives—for example, putting a technical leader into a customer-facing role for a while. This "Frame-breaking experience" is akin to Petrie's suggestion: "spend a day in your customer's rice paddy" (meaning, go immerse in the end-user's world). Such firsthand encounters with different realities challenge leaders' existing mental models and enrich their sensemaking palette. The key is to follow up these experiences with reflection and coaching, as mentioned earlier; otherwise, the insights can fade. But with guidance, leaders will integrate the lessons (e.g., our technical lead might realize the customer cares about simplicity over fancy features, shifting how he makes decisions later).

Immunity-to-Change maps (by Kegan and Lahey) are another practical exercise: leaders identify a change goal, and then uncover hidden commitments and beliefs preventing it. This is a structured way to force sensemaking about one's own contradictions. By surfacing these competing commitments, a leader might have an epiphany about why a recurring problem (like delegating more) has been hard—revealing an underlying mindset issue (like "If I don't do it, I'm not valuable" belief). Confronting and updating that belief is vertical growth.

Embedding Sensemaking in Culture: Finally, the tools above are most effective when supported by a culture that values learning. Leaders, especially senior ones, should model elevated sensemaking by visibly engaging in it. This means leaders publicly sharing not just decisions but the thought process and the lessons from when things went wrong. When an executive says, "Here's how I reframed our failure and what I learned," it sends a powerful message that sensemaking is part of success. Organizations might incorporate short reflection sessions into regular meetings (e.g., start staff meetings with a quick check-in: "What's a lesson or insight you've had this month?"). Celebrate not just wins but learning breakthroughs—for example, highlight a team that changed course because they gleaned a new insight about customer needs. By doing so, you reward elevated sensemaking in action.

Another cultural element is psychological safety—people must feel safe to speak up with new perspectives or to admit confusion. Leaders can foster this by how they respond to bad news or dissenting opinions (thanking people for the input rather than shooting the messenger). Encouraging questions like "What are we missing?" or "Is there another way to see this?" in every major discussion keeps multiple viewpoints in play.

In summary, fostering elevated sensemaking is about creating a continuous developmental ecosystem: experiences that challenge (heat), exposure that expands (colliding perspectives), and reflection that integrates (sensemaking). The strategies above—from journaling and dialogue to coaching and strategic assignments—all serve to keep leaders in that growth zone where they are slightly uncomfortable, openly curious, and richly supported. Over time, these practices help leaders move from simply accumulating knowledge (horizontal development) to truly transforming their mindset (vertical development), which is what today's complex world demands.

Elevated sensemaking is not just a leadership add-on but the very process that allows leaders to convert complexity into clarity and insight. In an era where change is relentless and problems have no easy answers, leaders who cultivate this capacity have a distinct advantage. They become adept navigators of uncertainty—able to find meaning where others see chaos, and thereby chart effective paths forward. Throughout this chapter, we saw that as leaders grow through vertical development stages, their sensemaking abilities expand dramatically. Early-stage leaders interpret events through narrow lenses of self-interest or rule-bound thinking, limiting their ability to deal with novelty. But with each progressive stage, a leader gains a wider lens: from the tactical expertise of Experts to the strategic collaboration of Achievers, and further into the purpose-driven, systemic thinking of Redefining and Transforming leaders, and even the holistic vision of the rare Alchemical leader. This journey underscores a vital point: elevated sensemaking is the culmination of the vertical development process—it is the integrative act of synthesizing diverse experiences into a coherent worldview. It's what turns trials and exposure into genuine growth.

Why is elevated sensemaking so essential today? Because the challenges we face—whether in business, government, or society—are complex, ambiguous, and multi-stakeholder. Technical know-how or charisma alone won't solve climate change, navigate global market disruptions, or heal a broken organizational culture. We need leaders who can do what elevated sensemakers do: embrace multiple perspectives, reflect deeply, and adapt their mental models to emerging reality. Such leaders don't get stuck in old paradigms; they evolve and in doing so, help their organizations evolve. Elevated sensemaking is what enables a leader to transform a "win–lose" standoff into a creative win-win solution, or to discern a trend beyond the data that everyone else is missing. It's the difference between merely reacting to the last problem and proactively preparing for the next opportunity.

Moreover, elevated sensemaking builds resilience and agility. Leaders who practice it develop an inner confidence born not of having all the answers but of knowing how to learn whatever they need to learn. They become, in essence, *chief meaning-makers*—providing context and direction when things are uncertain. This has a powerful effect on those they lead. In turbulent times, teams and organizations look to leaders for sensemaking. When a leader can say, "Here's how we might understand what's happening and here's our path forward," and that understanding rings true (incorporating data, people's concerns, and a vision), it galvanizes collective action. Elevated sensemaking thus underpins a leader's ability to inspire and guide others effectively.

In the leadership development field, there's growing recognition that mindset growth is the key to sustained improvement. Skills and competencies (the horizontal aspect) still matter, but without an elevated mindset to orchestrate them, leaders hit a ceiling in complexity. By focusing on sensemaking in development programs—using the tools and strategies we discussed—organizations can accelerate the vertical growth of their talent. This means deliberately moving the needle on things like reflection, perspective-taking, and cognitive agility. The payoff is substantial: leaders who can handle bigger challenges, knit together diverse teams, and innovate in the face of constraints.

At a practical level, developing elevated sensemaking helps ensure that the time and money spent on "heat experiences" (stretch roles, challenging projects) and "perspective broadening" (diversity, rotations, training) actually translate into *lasting growth*. Without sensemaking, those experiences might remain isolated events; with sensemaking, they become integrated into a leader's new way of thinking. As noted earlier, many leadership programs fail not due to lack of content but due to lack of integration—leaders are exposed to new ideas but not supported in making meaning of them. By correcting this, organizations unleash the full developmental power of their programs. Leaders begin to connect the dots between various lessons and apply them in concert, which is when development truly "sticks" back on the job.

The Journey of Sensemaking

In conclusion, elevated sensemaking is both a personal journey and an organizational imperative. For the individual leader, it represents the growth of wisdom—an evolution from reacting with instinctual or learned responses to responding with insight and foresight. It's about becoming the kind of leader who can walk into a fog of uncertainty and illuminate a path because they've trained themselves to see what others do not and to remain open to continuous learning.

By committing to practices that develop sensemaking—from reflection circles to mentoring to embracing stage frameworks—we effectively create a pipeline of such leaders. It ensures that as the world changes, our leaders have the mental elasticity to change with it, and even to shape the change proactively. In the end, elevated sensemaking is essential because it enables adaptive leadership: the capacity to not only solve today's problems but also build the collective understanding needed to tackle tomorrow's dilemmas. It is the engine that drives vertical growth, turning experiences into evolution. Leaders who master this art will find themselves better equipped, more fulfilled, and more capable of leading effectively in today's world—and tomorrow's.

References

Rybeck, J. (2021). *A leader's guide to vertical development*. Adeption.

Torbert, W. R., & Rooke, D. (2005). Seven transformations of leadership. *Harvard Business Review*, *83*(4), 66–76.

Chapter 8

Overcoming the Challenges and Criticisms of Vertical Development

Vertical Leadership Development (VLD) offers transformative potential for leaders and organizations alike by fostering deeper, more reflective, and adaptive mindsets. However, as with any significant change in leadership philosophy, the path to vertical development is not without its challenges and criticisms. In this chapter, we explore the common obstacles—ranging from individual resistance and organizational inertia to widespread misconceptions about the process—and provide evidence-based strategies for overcoming these hurdles. Our goal is to equip leaders, human resources professionals, and organizational change agents with practical insights and actionable steps to address resistance, dispel misunderstandings, and successfully implement vertical development initiatives.

While earlier chapters have laid the groundwork by introducing the core concepts, theoretical underpinnings, developmental stages, practical tools, and cultural supports for VLD, here we turn our focus to what stands in the way of realizing its full potential. We will examine the nature of resistance to change, the specific misconceptions that can derail progress, and the pragmatic hurdles that organizations must overcome to integrate vertical development into their leadership practices. In addition to these practical challenges, it's important to address critiques from thought leaders in the field. One such critique comes from Dave Snowden, which we examine next.

Snowden's Critiques and the Vertical Development Community's Response

Dave Snowden, widely known for his work on complexity and the Cynefin framework (discussed in Chapter 1), has offered several critiques of vertical development theory. His primary concerns center around what he views as the oversimplification inherent in stage-based models. Snowden argues that vertical development approaches, by presenting growth as linear or sequential, risk oversimplifying the inherently complex, contextual,

DOI: 10.4324/9781003644941-8

and dynamic nature of human and leadership development. He contends that human growth cannot be neatly captured by universal developmental stages because real-world contexts are far too nuanced and varied. Snowden also expresses concern over the perceived elitism embedded in vertical stage models, noting that they can inadvertently imply that later stages are intrinsically superior, potentially creating hierarchical biases. Such biases may unintentionally marginalize the valuable contributions of individuals whose mindset or approach aligns with earlier stages.

Advocates and scholars within vertical development have responded thoughtfully to these critiques, recognizing their importance while offering clarifications and counterpoints. First, prominent theorists such as Jennifer Garvey Berger, Susanne Cook-Greuter, Nick Petrie, and Bill Torbert explicitly acknowledge that developmental progression is neither rigid nor strictly linear. They emphasize that vertical development models function primarily as frameworks or heuristics rather than absolute truths. These scholars highlight that individuals frequently fluctuate across developmental stages depending on life circumstances, contexts, and challenges, thus accommodating the complexity Snowden emphasizes.

Second, vertical development theorists address the critique of elitism by clarifying the intent behind stage or hierarchical models. Robert Kegan, for instance, has consistently underscored that advanced stages do not represent intrinsic moral or personal superiority; rather, they indicate an expanded capacity for perspective-taking and the ability to manage complexity and ambiguity. Susanne Cook-Greuter similarly reinforces that each developmental stage, including earlier ones, holds unique strengths and value depending on context. Thus, vertical models are positioned as descriptive of different capacities rather than prescriptive measures of personal worth or achievement.

Third, in response to Snowden's emphasis on contextual sensitivity, vertical development practitioners increasingly highlight context-dependent approaches within their assessments and methodologies. Tools such as the Shifting Horizons assessment and context-specific scenario-based assessments reflect deliberate efforts to incorporate situational awareness. Scholars like Jennifer Garvey Berger advocate for flexible developmental coaching that adapts insights from vertical models to specific leadership scenarios, ensuring that vertical frameworks maintain relevance within varied organizational contexts.

Finally, regarding concerns over empirical rigor and reliability, vertical development researchers acknowledge the ongoing need for methodological improvements. Researchers such as Otto Laske, Theo Dawson (Lectica), and Susanne Cook-Greuter have continued refining assessments through rigorous psychometric validation and integrating technological innovations like digital delivery platforms and AI-assisted scoring. These ongoing developments aim to bolster the objectivity, validity, and reliability of vertical development assessments, directly addressing Snowden's concerns around measurement challenges.

Overall, Snowden's critiques have encouraged valuable introspection and continuous improvement within the vertical development field, prompting scholars and practitioners to deepen their commitment to nuance, flexibility, context sensitivity, and empirical rigor. In addition to these theoretical considerations, leaders and organizations also face very practical, human challenges when attempting VLD.

Individual Resistance: The Fear of Change and Vulnerability

One of the most frequently encountered barriers to adopting VLD is individual resistance. At its core, vertical development challenges leaders to move beyond familiar cognitive frameworks and to question deeply held beliefs and assumptions. This process can be both intimidating and unsettling. For many, the idea of reexamining one's worldview evokes a fear of vulnerability and a reluctance to confront personal limitations.

Leaders who have achieved success through traditional methods may worry that shifting to a more reflective and transformative mode of thinking could undermine their established competencies. This resistance is often rooted in the comfort of existing mental models and the fear that change might expose areas of weakness or inexperience. Research in adult learning consistently shows that individuals may cling to known methods even when presented with evidence that alternative approaches could lead to higher performance and innovation (Kegan, 1994).

Furthermore, research on immunity-to-change theory (Kegan & Lahey, 2009) highlights that many individuals unconsciously resist transformation because it threatens deeply held assumptions that are central to their sense of identity. This fear of vulnerability echoes what we noted in Chapter 5: without "heat experiences" to push them, leaders often retreat to familiar mindsets. This can manifest in reluctance to engage in reflection exercises, avoidance of feedback, or passive participation in development initiatives. Overcoming this resistance requires structured support, including psychological safety, coaching, and gradual exposure to developmental challenges that encourage growth without triggering overwhelming anxiety.

Organizational Inertia and Cultural Barriers

Beyond individual fears, organizations themselves can be significant sources of resistance. Many companies operate within entrenched structures and cultures that value short-term results, standardized procedures, and risk aversion. In such environments, vertical development—often perceived as a long-term, introspective, and sometimes abstract investment—can be seen as a distraction from day-to-day operational demands. Without a culture of learning and psychological safety, vertical growth can be dismissed as "soft."

Cultural inertia in organizations often manifests as a reluctance to deviate from the status quo. For example, a company heavily focused on quarterly sales targets might cut reflection sessions or coaching programs first when time is tight, signaling that such developmental activities are not truly valued. This resistance can be further compounded by existing performance metrics that prioritize measurable outputs over transformative thinking. Research on organizational learning suggests that performance-based cultures often resist developmental initiatives that do not yield immediate, quantifiable results. When vertical development is introduced without sufficient alignment with an organization's current culture and systems, it can be dismissed as "touchy-feely" management that does not contribute directly to the bottom line. Thus, even if individual leaders are willing, an unsupportive organizational culture can stall vertical growth before it starts. Overcoming cultural barriers requires aligning vertical development with existing business priorities and demonstrating its value—approaches we will explore later in the chapter.

Misconceptions About Vertical Development

Confusion With Horizontal Development

A recurring criticism is the misconception that VLD is merely an extension of traditional (horizontal) training. Many skeptics argue that vertical development simply adds another layer of seminars, workshops, and online modules to the already crowded landscape of leadership training. Some critics misinterpret VLD as just more skill training (horizontal development), but as established in Chapter 1, it is a fundamentally different, deeper growth. This misconception overlooks the core idea that VLD changes how leaders think, not just what they know. Organizations that misunderstand this distinction risk implementing development programs that reinforce existing mindsets rather than expanding leaders' ability to navigate complexity.

Perception of Abstraction and Impracticality

Another common critique is that vertical development is too abstract to be practical. Critics contend that while the concept of "shifting mindsets" is appealing in theory, it lacks concrete, measurable outcomes. They worry that efforts to foster self-awareness, adaptive thinking, and systemic perspective may not translate into clear business metrics or immediate improvements in performance. This skepticism is particularly strong in organizations that are highly results-driven, where investments are typically evaluated against short-term, quantifiable outcomes.

However, emerging research contradicts this perception. Chapters 2 and 3 highlight that leaders who engage in vertical development exhibit greater strategic foresight, improved decision-making under uncertainty, and enhanced team collaboration. Organizations that invest in vertical development often report increased adaptability, higher employee engagement, and greater resilience in the face of disruption.

To address the "intangible" critique, some organizations have adopted new measurement frameworks that capture qualitative shifts in leadership effectiveness. 360-degree feedback, longitudinal assessments, and behavioral indicators have been used to track leaders' progression and developmental of greater vertical range, providing evidence of growth in complexity-handling capacity and relational intelligence.

Resource Intensity and Implementation Concerns

Vertical development is also criticized for being resource-intensive. Many organizations worry that the time, effort, and financial investment required to support deep developmental processes will divert resources away from more tangible, operational priorities. This criticism often emerges from a misunderstanding of the long-term returns on investment associated with vertical development.

While the process does require commitment and persistence, organizations that successfully implement vertical development programs enjoy benefits such as

- Increased adaptability in navigating change
- Enhanced strategic insight and decision-making
- Improved leadership resilience and reduced executive burnout

By aligning vertical development initiatives with existing leadership programs and integrating mentorship, coaching, and developmental assignments into day-to-day work, organizations can create scalable, cost-effective solutions that do not require excessive new investments.

Resistance and skepticism are natural responses to any transformative change, and vertical development is no exception. Whether the hesitation stems from individual fear of vulnerability, organizational inertia, or misconceptions about its practicality, these challenges must be addressed with strategic, research-backed approaches.

In the next section, we will explore practical strategies for overcoming resistance and integrating vertical development into organizations in a way that is sustainable, measurable, and aligned with business objectives.

Practical Strategies for Overcoming Resistance and Misconceptions

As organizations increasingly recognize the value of Vertical Leadership Development (VLD) in fostering adaptive, strategic, and resilient leaders, many still struggle with resistance to change and widespread misconceptions about the process. Next, we will review actionable steps to address resistance at individual, organizational, and cultural levels to ensure sustainable vertical development integration.

Building Leadership Buy-In: Addressing Resistance at the Top

Role Modeling by Senior Leaders

One of the most effective ways to reduce resistance to vertical development is securing buy-in from senior leadership. Leaders who actively engage in development initiatives set the tone for the rest of the organization, influencing cultural norms and employee perceptions of growth efforts. If senior leaders demonstrate curiosity, adaptability, and openness to developmental experiences, middle managers and frontline employees are more likely to follow suit.

Best Practices for Leadership Engagement

- Publicly endorse vertical development: Senior executives should actively speak about the benefits of vertical growth in company-wide meetings and strategy sessions.
- Lead by example: Top leaders should participate in developmental coaching, reflective practices, and feedback loops to model desired behaviors.
- Share personal growth experiences: When leaders openly discuss their own learning journey, challenges, and mindset shifts, they normalize vulnerability and the developmental process for others.

Storytelling and Sharing Successes

A powerful strategy for overcoming skepticism at all levels of the organization is storytelling, which helps employees relate to the development process in tangible ways. Studies in leadership development suggest that real-life stories of transformation increase buy-in by making abstract concepts more accessible and personally meaningful (Brown et al., 2020).

Organizations that document successful cases of vertical development—through videos, articles, or in-person testimonials—can use these narratives to inspire participation. Consider an automotive company implementing VLD: one department head initially resistant to the approach later became an advocate after experiencing a mindset shift during a high-stakes project. By capturing and sharing his journey, the company created a ripple effect, motivating other employees to engage in the program.

TACTICS FOR STORYTELLING SUCCESS

- Develop "Leader Growth Spotlights" showcasing leaders who have benefited from vertical development.
- Encourage peer-led discussions where employees can hear from colleagues about their growth experiences.
- Use before-and-after reflections to highlight the long-term impact of vertical development.

By humanizing vertical development through success stories, organizations pave the way for broader acceptance. Next, it's also important to eliminate confusion about what vertical development truly means.

Clarifying the Concept: Addressing Cognitive Barriers to Adoption

Defining Vertical Versus Horizontal Development

As mentioned earlier in this chapter, one of the major barriers to the successful adoption of vertical development within organizations is the confusion between horizontal and vertical development. These two concepts are often misunderstood and frequently conflated, leading to a lack of clarity around their value and application. Table 8.1 provides a side-by-side comparison. The distinction is often lost, resulting in resistance or skepticism when employees fail to see how vertical development can tangibly enhance their leadership abilities. To address this, organizations must educate stakeholders by clearly differentiating the two.

For organizations to successfully implement vertical development, it's critical to clearly define these concepts, ensuring that all stakeholders—leaders, HR teams, and employees—understand the difference between the two and how each contributes to leadership growth. Horizontal development may

Table 8.1 Clarifying Horizontal and Vertical Development

Horizontal Development	*Vertical Development*
Adds new skills and competencies	Expands cognitive and emotional complexity
Training-based and transactional	Transformational and iterative
Primarily content-driven	Experience-driven (e.g., heat experiences, colliding perspectives)
Can be completed in a set timeframe	Requires ongoing practice and reflection

be valuable for building specific skills, but vertical development is what drives strategic thinking, resilience, and adaptability—all essential traits for leaders in today's complex, ever-changing business environments.

ACTION STEP: INTEGRATING VERTICAL AND HORIZONTAL DEVELOPMENT LANGUAGE INTO THE ORGANIZATIONAL CULTURE

To avoid the confusion between horizontal and vertical development, organizations should make a concerted effort to embed clear language that distinguishes the two concepts throughout the leadership development narrative. This can be done by the following:

1. Using consistent terminology in leadership development discussions, ensuring that leaders and employees understand the value of both horizontal and vertical development, and how they complement each other.
2. Incorporating both horizontal and vertical growth into the organization's leadership training programs, making sure that each is given appropriate focus. For example, horizontal development might be emphasized in technical skills workshops, while vertical development is integrated into leadership coaching, mentoring, and experiential learning programs.
3. Creating visual tools (like roadmaps or frameworks) that clearly illustrate the distinct yet complementary roles of both types of development. A visual representation of how a leader moves through different developmental stages, develops vertical range, and how vertical development enhances their strategic thinking and adaptability will help demystify the concept.

By addressing the abstract critique head-on, organizations can make the case for vertical development's practical, real-world applications, showing how it directly enhances leadership capabilities that are crucial for thriving in a complex, fast-paced world.

Incremental Implementation and Piloting: Reducing Perceived Risk

Starting Small to Mitigate Resistance

Many organizations face hesitation when considering the implementation of vertical development programs, fearing that such initiatives may disrupt productivity or require a significant investment of resources. These concerns are valid, especially when there is uncertainty about how the new approach will align with the organization's culture and goals. One effective way to address these concerns and mitigate resistance is by starting small, with a pilot program. This approach allows organizations to experiment with vertical development on a more manageable scale before committing to a broader rollout, thus minimizing the perceived risk and demonstrating the value of the program in real-world settings.

Pilot programs offer organizations the opportunity to test vertical development in a controlled environment. By selecting a small group of high-impact leaders to participate in the pilot, organizations can focus on those individuals who are likely to have the greatest influence on the broader leadership culture. This strategic selection not only ensures that the pilot program has a measurable impact but also creates champions who can advocate for the program once it's proven successful. The participants in the pilot are typically chosen based on their potential to drive change and influence others, making them the ideal group to test the approach and provide valuable insights for refinement.

To measure the effectiveness of the pilot, organizations should use pre- and post-program assessments to track shifts in the participants' complexity-handling capacity—an essential metric in vertical development. These assessments help gauge how participants' abilities to navigate complex, uncertain situations evolve as they progress through the program. Additionally, gathering feedback from participants through surveys and focus groups offers another layer of valuable insight. These feedback mechanisms help refine the approach, identifying strengths and areas for improvement before the program is scaled to a larger group. This iterative process ensures that the program is fine-tuned to meet the unique needs of the organization and its leaders.

By starting small with a well-designed pilot program, organizations can gradually introduce vertical development while reducing the risk of disruption. This approach not only addresses concerns about resource allocation and productivity but also builds a foundation of support and confidence that will be critical when expanding the program to a broader audience. As the pilot demonstrates its effectiveness, organizations can move forward with the knowledge and experience necessary to fully integrate vertical development into their leadership frameworks. This approach of starting small also directly addresses the earlier concern that vertical development might be too disruptive or costly—it allows proof of concept with minimal disturbance. With evidence and support gathered from a successful pilot, organizations can then move to integrate vertical development more deeply into their leadership culture.

Embedding Vertical Development Into Organizational Culture

Integrating Vertical Growth Into Leadership Programs

To ensure long-term success, vertical development must be woven into existing leadership frameworks, rather than positioned as a separate initiative. Research suggests that embedding developmental experiences into leadership pipelines enhances retention and engagement.

Best Practices for Seamless Integration

- Incorporate vertical development principles into succession planning and leadership competency models.
- Align performance reviews with vertical development metrics, recognizing adaptive thinking and complexity-handling skills (e.g., ability to navigate complex, uncertain situations).
- Train internal coaches in vertical development methodologies to provide ongoing support.

Measuring and Communicating Progress

One of the most effective ways to sustain engagement is to track and communicate developmental progress. Organizations that use 360-degree feedback, developmental assessments, and behavioral indicators can create a compelling case for continued investment in VLD.

TRACKING GROWTH EFFECTIVELY

- Use both qualitative and quantitative metrics such as evidence of increased cognitive flexibility, improved cross-team collaboration, and greater resilience under stress.

- Publish annual vertical development internal impact reports to reinforce credibility.
- Reward leaders who actively engage in developmental coaching and self-reflection.

Overcoming resistance to VLD requires a multilayered strategy involving leadership role modeling, education, incremental adoption, and cultural integration. Organizations that effectively clarify the concept, provide structured frameworks, and embed vertical growth into leadership programs can significantly enhance adaptive capacity, strategic decision-making, and resilience. However, even with these internal efforts, organizations often find that external support can accelerate and strengthen vertical development. In the next sections, we explore the role of external facilitators and partnerships in sustaining this transformation.

The Role of External Facilitators and Partnerships

While Vertical Leadership Development (VLD) has demonstrated its effectiveness in fostering leaders who can handle complexity, ambiguity, and adaptive challenges, organizations often struggle to implement it effectively on their own. Internal resistance, cultural inertia, and a lack of developmental expertise can make it difficult to sustain meaningful change.

To address these barriers, many organizations turn to external facilitators and partnerships to enhance their vertical development efforts. This section explores how external coaches, consulting firms, academic institutions, and peer learning networks contribute to overcoming resistance and accelerating transformation. We also examine best practices for integrating external expertise, balancing it with internal capabilities, and ensuring long-term sustainability.

Leveraging External Expertise for Vertical Development

The Role of External Coaches in Vertical Growth

Executive and leadership coaching has become a key lever in vertical development, as it provides leaders with structured support in navigating complexity and deepening self-awareness. Research by McCauley and Palus (2021) highlights that leaders engaged in developmental coaching demonstrate greater shifts in cognitive complexity and adaptability than those who rely solely on traditional training. While internal mentoring and coaching programs exist, external professional coaches often bring neutrality and specialized expertise, which can accelerate vertical growth.

How External Coaches Drive Vertical Growth

1. **Facilitating Self-Discovery:** Unlike conventional training programs, vertical development requires deep self-reflection and exploration of mental models. Coaches trained in constructive-developmental frameworks help leaders uncover unexamined assumptions and shift from reactive to adaptive mindsets (Kegan & Lahey, 2009).
2. **Providing Psychological Safety:** Many leaders resist vertical development because it involves uncertainty, discomfort, and self-examination. Research suggests that external coaches provide a neutral space where leaders feel safe to explore vulnerabilities and engage in transformational learning.
3. **Encouraging Iterative Growth:** Vertical development is not a one-time intervention but a continuous sensemaking process. External coaches guide leaders through cycles of experimentation, feedback, and reflection, reinforcing developmental progress over time (Day et al., 2014).

Best Practices for Integrating Coaching Into Vertical Development

- Structure coaching engagements for long enough durations (e.g., 6–12 months) to support sustained mindset shifts. Not only avoid overly short or one-off coaching interventions but also set clear time frames (instead of open-ended engagements) so progress can be assessed.
- Align coaching with organizational goals, ensuring that developmental shifts contribute to business strategy and leadership culture.
- Pair leaders with coaches who understand adult development theory (e.g., Immunity-to-Change, Action Logics, or Subject-Object Theory).

By offering a confidential space and expert support, external coaches directly address individual leaders' fear of change and vulnerability discussed earlier. In addition to individual coaching, organizations can also partner with specialized leadership development firms to drive vertical growth on a larger scale.

Engaging Leadership Development Firms for Strategic Transformation

For many organizations, the internal expertise required to drive VLD may not always be readily available. In these cases, partnering with specialized leadership development firms becomes an invaluable strategy to access structured programs, facilitation expertise, and validated assessment tools. These firms are skilled in crafting and delivering vertical development initiatives that are rooted in evidence-based practices and designed to meet the evolving needs of modern leaders.

By engaging external partners, organizations can overcome common challenges such as limited internal capacity, lack of developmental psychology expertise, or difficulty measuring long-term growth. These firms often have a profound impact: companies that collaborate with them report higher engagement in leadership programs. External facilitators bring fresh perspectives and objective insights, which inspire leaders to fully commit to the development process. Additionally, they see more measurable improvements in leaders' complexity-handling capabilities, equipping leaders to navigate increasingly intricate and interconnected challenges in the business world. Perhaps most importantly, these partnerships help organizations achieve greater success in embedding vertical development into their corporate leadership frameworks, making it an integral part of the organizational culture and ensuring that it drives sustainable growth.

Common Services Offered by Leadership Development Firms

Leadership development firms offer a range of services that can address the various needs of an organization striving to foster vertical growth. One of the most powerful tools provided by these firms is developmental assessments and indicators. These assessments, such as the Leadership Maturity Framework (LMF), the Global Leadership Profile (GLP), the Adeption VMI assessment, and the Action Logics Inventory, provide a structured roadmap for tracking a leader's vertical development. These tools enable organizations to pinpoint specific areas where leaders need to grow, whether in cognitive complexity, emotional intelligence, or relational awareness. They create a personalized developmental path for each leader, offering a clear understanding of their starting point and the steps needed to progress to higher stages of leadership maturity.

In addition to assessments, leadership development firms often design and facilitate immersive vertical development programs. These programs are not just workshops or seminars but are transformative experiences that combine peer learning, leadership coaching, and reflective exercises to help leaders advance through developmental stages. By participating in these programs, leaders engage in deep learning experiences that challenge their thinking, broaden their perspectives, and ultimately help them operate at a higher level of cognitive and relational complexity. These programs are carefully crafted to address the real-world demands of leadership, ensuring that leaders gain the skills and insights they need to navigate the complexities of modern organizational environments.

Another critical service offered by leadership development firms is customized organizational integration. This service ensures that vertical development isn't just a standalone initiative; it becomes embedded within the organization's talent strategies, performance reviews, and succession planning. Aligning vertical growth with performance management and succession planning ensures that the transformation extends beyond individuals—ultimately fostering a systemic shift in culture where vertical development is recognized as essential for long-term success. Given these valuable services, choosing the right development partner is crucial.

Selecting the Right Development Partner

Choosing the right leadership development partner is crucial to the success of any vertical development initiative. Organizations must begin by evaluating whether a potential partner aligns with their organizational needs. Does the firm specialize in cognitive and emotional complexity building, or is its focus primarily on horizontal skills training that addresses specific tasks or short-term outcomes? Vertical development is about expanding leadership capabilities to handle complexity and uncertainty, and it requires a partner who understands the depth and breadth of this transformation.

It is also essential that the coaches and facilitators provided by the development firm are trained in vertical development frameworks—such as those pioneered by Kegan, Torbert, and Cook-Greuter. These frameworks are based on developmental psychology research and offer a sophisticated understanding of how leadership evolves over time. Facilitators who are knowledgeable about these frameworks can guide leaders through the stages of vertical development, helping them grow in ways that align with the latest psychological theories and best practices.

Organizations should look for firms that use evidence based methodologies. This ensures that the programs offered are grounded in solid research and are not just based on popular trends or untested ideas. Evidence-based methods are crucial because they provide measurable results that organizations can track over time. The firm's track record of empirical success in vertical development ensures that the methodologies they use have been rigorously tested and validated in real-world settings, offering the organization a high return on investment. Also consider the partner's ability to customize their approach to your industry and culture—a one-size-fits-all solution may not address your unique context. Another source of external expertise comes from the realm of research and education. Collaborating with academic institutions can bring cutting-edge insights to your vertical development efforts.

Collaborating With Academic Institutions for Research-Driven Growth

The Value of University Partnerships in Vertical Leadership Research

An additional way to overcome resistance is through working with higher education institutions. Higher education institutions can be pivotal partners in advancing VLD. They offer empirical validation of frameworks and access to the latest adult learning and leadership maturity research, thus bridging the gap between academia and practice. This partnership helps bridge the gap between academic research and practical application, creating robust programs for sustainable leadership growth.

Research by Iordanoglou (2018) highlights how university-affiliated vertical development programs result in deeper shifts in cognitive flexibility, systemic thinking, and ethical decision-making. This research contrasts the impact of university-based programs with corporate-run programs, revealing that leaders who engage with academic-driven initiatives experience more profound and lasting developmental outcomes. The academic rigor behind these programs helps mitigate the common barriers to success in leadership development, such as superficial engagement or short-term results, by ensuring that development is grounded in evidence-based practices.

Collaborating with universities offers several concrete benefits.

Access to Evidence-Based Models: Universities conduct longitudinal studies on leadership maturity, complexity handling, and transformation. These studies provide data-driven insights that support the continuous evolution of corporate leadership programs. By incorporating these models, organizations can overcome common challenges like misalignment of leadership programs with real-world complexities, or ineffective application of developmental theories. Organizations leveraging academic models can build more effective, personalized leadership pipelines, grounded in research-backed evidence that tracks leaders' growth over time.

Customized Leadership Development Programs: Many academic institutions offer executive education programs designed around vertical development principles. These tailored programs allow organizations to integrate the latest academic research into their leadership development pipelines, ensuring alignment with evolving leadership demands. This customization helps organizations address barriers to success by providing programs that are directly relevant to their unique leadership contexts, overcoming generic, one-size-fits-all training programs that often fail to resonate with participants.

Opportunities for Action Research: Partnering with academic institutions provides organizations with the chance to pilot vertical development approaches, using empirical feedback to refine methodologies. This process allows for rapid testing of new strategies in real-time organizational settings, helping to overcome barriers such as slow adoption of new practices or lack of evidence for the effectiveness of developmental initiatives. The partnership with academia allows organizations to gather actionable insights that refine the approach, ensuring greater alignment with organizational goals and overcoming hesitancy about the effectiveness of vertical development programs.

Best Practices for Partnering With Universities

- Collaborate with faculty specializing in leadership development, adult learning, and complexity science to create programs that are both academically rigorous and practically applicable. This ensures that the program is aligned with cutting-edge research while meeting the organization's specific developmental needs.
- Integrate leadership maturity assessments (e.g., Action Logics or Leadership Development Profile) into executive education programs to track vertical development progress. This step helps organizations measure leadership growth and overcome the challenge of not knowing how to quantify developmental progress.
- Sponsor applied research projects, allowing graduate students and faculty to study leadership transformation within the organization. This collaboration results in highly relevant, context-specific data that can guide the refinement of internal leadership practices.

This kind of partnership can lend external credibility to the initiative, helping persuade skeptics internally who may respond better to academically endorsed programs. Alongside formal partnerships with institutions, fostering peer-based learning communities can further embed vertical development within the leadership cohort.

Building Communities of Practice and Peer Learning Networks

The Role of Peer Learning in Vertical Development

Peer learning groups—often facilitated by external experts or development firms—create dynamic environments where leaders can engage in collective sensemaking, challenge assumptions, and integrate new perspectives. These networks become essential for overcoming individual leadership barriers, such as limited self-awareness or resistance to feedback. These networks become essential for overcoming individual leadership barriers (like fear of feedback or siloed thinking) by normalizing continuous development among peers. By exposing leaders to diverse viewpoints and experiences, peer learning encourages them to broaden their thinking and deepen their understanding of complex leadership challenges.

Research by Garvey Berger (2012) shows that leaders involved in structured peer learning programs are more likely to sustain long-term developmental growth. They develop greater comfort with ambiguity and paradox, allowing them to navigate complex, unpredictable challenges with confidence. The research also shows that these leaders exhibit later levels of strategic agility and systemic awareness, making them more adaptable to changing business environments. These peer learning groups help break down barriers such as fear of failure or lack of confidence, encouraging leaders to embrace ongoing development without fear of judgment.

Best Practices for Peer Learning in Vertical Development

1. Create Cross-Functional Development Cohorts—Group leaders from different business units together to expose them to diverse organizational perspectives. This helps overcome siloed thinking and creates a more holistic view of the organization, fostering collaboration and breaking down barriers to innovation.
2. Use Developmental Inquiry Models—Action Learning, Polarity Thinking (managing paradoxical goals, etc.), and immunity-to-change circles are powerful frameworks for peer-driven vertical growth. These models help leaders challenge their assumptions and develop new, more adaptive approaches to leadership, overcoming limitations caused by habitual thinking.
3. Incorporate Facilitated Reflection Sessions—Structured debriefs and reflective sessions allow leaders to make sense of developmental experiences, reinforcing long-term mindset shifts. These sessions help leaders integrate learning from peer interactions and practical application, reducing the risk of stalling in development and ensuring continuous growth.

Peer learning groups and external facilitators can jump-start vertical development, but to ensure these efforts last, organizations need to develop their own internal capacity.

Ensuring Long-Term Sustainability of External Partnerships

Balancing External Support With Internal Capability Building

While external facilitators and partnerships are valuable, long-term success depends on building internal capacity for vertical development. Developing internal leadership coaches and integrating research-backed frameworks into the company's culture ensures that growth doesn't stop when external experts leave, overcoming the challenge of sustainability. This helps organizations avoid reverting to old mindsets and ensures continuous growth.

Key Strategies for Sustainable Growth

- Train internal leadership coaches to continue developmental conversations beyond external engagements. This ensures that the organization has the internal capability to foster leadership growth long after the partnership ends.
- Develop a knowledge transfer strategy, ensuring that best practices from consulting firms and universities are embedded within the organization's internal leadership frameworks.
- Gradually transition from externally facilitated programs to internally led vertical development initiatives. This helps organizations build self-sufficiency in their leadership development programs, overcoming dependency on external consultants.

Measuring the Impact of External Partnerships

To assess whether external partnerships are contributing to long-term vertical growth, organizations should track developmental assessment progress, including shifts in Action Logics or Global Leadership Profile (GLP) scores. Additionally, evaluating improvements in complexity-handling capacity, such as success in real-world leadership challenges, provides tangible evidence of growth. Long-term engagement in peer learning networks and coaching can also serve as important metrics for measuring the sustainability of vertical development initiatives.

Overcoming Resistance to Vertical Leadership Development

By strategically partnering with external experts, including academic institutions, coaching firms, and peer networks, organizations can overcome the common barriers to vertical leadership success—such as limited access to research-driven frameworks, siloed leadership thinking, and a lack of sustainable internal capacity. These partnerships provide critical expertise, structured developmental experiences, and research-backed frameworks to support transformation. Balancing external facilitation with internal capability building enables organizations to embed vertical development into their culture, so that leaders continue to evolve, adapt, and thrive in an increasingly complex world.

With these strategies and supports in mind, we can now turn to the future of VLD in Chapter 9.

References

Brown, B., Senge, P., & Isaacs, W. (2020). The power of storytelling in organizational transformation. *Academy of Management Review*, *45*(4), 789–812.

Day, D. V., Fleenor, J. W., Atwater, L. E., Sturm, R. E., & McKee, R. A. (2014). Advances in leader and leadership development: A review of 25 years of research and theory. *The Leadership Quarterly*, *25*(1), 63–82.

Garvey Berger, J. (2012). *Changing on the job: Developing leaders for a complex world*. Stanford University Press.

Iordanoglou, D. (2018). Future trends in leadership development practices and the crucial leadership skills. *Journal of Leadership, Accountability & Ethics*, *15*(2).

Kegan, R. (1994). *In over our heads: The mental demands of modern life*. Harvard University Press.

Kegan, R., & Lahey, L. L. (2009). *Immunity to change: How to overcome it and unlock the potential in yourself and your organization*. Harvard Business Review Press.

McCauley, C. D., & Palus, C. J. (2021). The state of leadership development: Trends and best practices. *Academy of Management Learning & Education*, *20*(3), 345–368.

Chapter 9

The Future of Vertical Development and Its Evolving Role in Leadership

Emerging Trends in Vertical Development

In this final chapter, we explore the future of VLD. As organizations face increasing complexity, rapid technological change, and evolving stakeholder expectations, Leadership Development must adapt to meet these demands. Leadership in the future will require higher levels of emotional intelligence, ecosystems thinking, adaptability, and ethical clarity. This chapter explores emerging trends in vertical development, including the growing emphasis on relational intelligence, the integration of holistic perspectives, the expansion of development to diverse leadership levels, and the importance of ethical leadership in a purpose-driven world. First, we examine several emerging trends shaping the future of vertical development.

Emphasis on Emotional Intelligence and Relational Skills

The Shift From Transactional to Relational Leadership

Historically, leadership development has focused on technical expertise and operational efficiency. However, research increasingly shows that relational skills such as emotional intelligence (EQ), empathy, and active listening are essential for leadership effectiveness in the modern workplace (Goleman et al., 2013).

> Leaders who develop strong relational intelligence foster environments where teams feel psychologically safe, motivated, and aligned with shared organizational goals.

DOI: 10.4324/9781003644941-9

The Role of Emotional Intelligence in Vertical Development

Vertical development focused programs are increasingly incorporating emotional intelligence (EQ) training, recognizing its critical role in supporting leaders to navigate the complexity and ambiguity of modern organizational life. Leaders who cultivate high emotional intelligence demonstrate a notable advantage in their vertical development journey, as emotional intelligence significantly enhances their capacity for deeper self-reflection, empathy, and effective interpersonal relationships (Day & Dragoni, 2015).

Enhanced self-awareness forms the foundation of this growth and development of leadership range, as emotionally intelligent leaders gain the capability to clearly recognize and articulate their own emotional triggers, biases, and assumptions. Through structured reflection and introspective exercises, these leaders become more adept at understanding how their internal emotional states and reactions influence their decisions and behaviors. This heightened self-awareness allows them to critically evaluate their actions and assumptions, opening opportunities to move beyond their habitual patterns and expand their meaning-making capacities.

Further, leaders with high EQ also exhibit greater social awareness. They develop an acute sensitivity to the emotions and perspectives of others, enabling them to respond more thoughtfully and effectively in varied interpersonal contexts. By understanding the nuanced emotional undercurrents within their teams and broader stakeholder groups, these leaders can adapt their communication and leadership styles accordingly. This capacity for empathy fosters environments of psychological safety, inclusivity, and mutual respect, which are essential for collective learning and development in organizations.

Lastly, emotional intelligence strengthens a leader's ability to manage relationships effectively, leading to improved team collaboration, trust, and cohesion. Leaders who skillfully regulate their emotions and respond constructively to interpersonal dynamics encourage a collaborative culture that enhances team effectiveness and adaptability. Their ability to nurture positive relationships and address conflicts constructively enables teams to achieve collective goals more effectively, ultimately facilitating organizational transformation and resilience.

Collectively, these areas of emotional intelligence—self-awareness, social awareness, and relationship management—create a reinforcing cycle that accelerates vertical growth and vertical range. By integrating emotional intelligence training into vertical development initiatives, organizations equip leaders with essential competencies required to thrive in today's complex and interconnected business landscape.

> As vertical leadership development continues to become more important in response to the increasing complexity and uncertainty of organizational environments, emotional intelligence is likely to become an even more central component.

Future trends in VLD indicate that developmental approaches will increasingly focus on cultivating not only cognitive complexity but also emotional and relational capacities. This holistic approach acknowledges that the leaders of tomorrow must skillfully navigate interpersonal dynamics, inspire collaborative problem-solving, and adapt responsively to rapidly shifting contexts. By emphasizing emotional intelligence alongside cognitive growth, future vertical development programs will better prepare leaders to engage with ambiguity, build resilient organizational cultures, and foster sustainable, transformative change.

Integrating Ecosystems Thinking and Holistic Perspectives

Why Ecosystems Thinking Is Essential for Modern Leaders

In today's highly interconnected and rapidly evolving global environment, leaders must move beyond traditional systems thinking to adopt an ecosystems approach as touched on in Chapter 1. While systems thinking encourages understanding relationships and interdependencies within organizations, ecosystems thinking expands this understanding even further, emphasizing dynamic interactions among organizations, industries, communities, and the natural environment. Leaders who can flex to advanced vertical developmental stages are uniquely positioned to cultivate ecosystems thinking, which equips them to recognize and thoughtfully respond to the complex interconnections that define the modern business landscape.

As industries increasingly operate within broader economic, social, and ecological contexts, the limitations of isolated or siloed thinking become more apparent. Traditional strategic approaches focused narrowly on internal operations or immediate industry contexts often overlook critical external factors, thereby limiting organizational agility and responsiveness. Ecosystems thinking provides a powerful antidote to this narrowness by enabling leaders to perceive and interpret complex patterns of interdependence extending beyond organizational boundaries. Such leaders are capable of identifying intricate relationships and reciprocal influences among diverse stakeholders, industries, and external environments. These leaders are capable of anticipating and addressing the broader and longer-term consequences of their decisions (McGuire & Rhodes, 2009).

> Ecosystems thinking strengthens leaders' capacity for multi-stakeholder collaboration. Leaders who adopt an ecosystem mindset actively foster partnerships and collaborations that span diverse sectors, industries, and communities.

Incorporating ecosystems thinking into vertical development programs fosters holistic leadership perspectives that move beyond isolated problem-solving toward integrated, sustainable strategies. Holistic leadership informed by ecosystems thinking compels leaders to explicitly consider how their organizations interact with external stakeholders, industries, regulatory environments, and broader communities. Decisions are informed not only by immediate operational goals but also by deep consideration of social equity, ecological balance, and long-term sustainability (Garvey Berger, 2012). Ecosystem-aware leaders deliberately weigh the ethical implications and broader societal impacts of their strategic choices, thus positioning their organizations as responsible participants within complex networks of economic and social systems.

Ecosystems thinking allows leaders to recognize that addressing contemporary challenges—such as climate change, technological disruption, or global supply chain vulnerabilities—requires collective action and coordinated strategies. Ecosystems-oriented leaders cultivate strong, trust-based relationships across multiple stakeholder groups, facilitating joint problem-solving efforts, innovation, and adaptive responses to complex global challenges.

Table 9.1 Systems Thinking Versus Ecosystems Thinking

Aspect	*Systems Thinking*	*Ecosystems Thinking*
Focus	Analyzes interrelated components	Analyzes the dynamic interaction between diverse, interconnected systems
Approach	Uses a structured, linear approach to problem-solving	Uses an adaptive, nonlinear approach to respond to change
Perspective	Views problems within a defined system with clear boundaries	Views problems as part of a broader context, recognizing interconnectedness across systems

Future-focused leadership development programs will increasingly embed ecosystems thinking as a core capability. Leaders skilled in ecosystems thinking will be better equipped to manage complexity, foster resilient organizations, and contribute positively to broader social and environmental systems. Ultimately, ecosystems thinking will become essential to leadership effectiveness, shaping the strategic mindsets needed to thrive in the interconnected world of the future.

Expansion of Development to Diverse Leadership Levels

Historically, vertical development programs have predominantly focused on senior executives, with organizations viewing advanced developmental capabilities as particularly relevant at top leadership levels. However, contemporary perspectives have significantly shifted, recognizing the benefits of democratizing vertical development across a broader range of leadership roles. Today's complex and rapidly evolving organizational environments demand vertical capacities at every leadership level. High-potential employees, mid-level managers, and even junior leaders can greatly benefit from cultivating vertical capabilities such as complexity management, enhanced self-awareness, and advanced perspective-taking.

> By providing developmental opportunities earlier in leaders' careers, organizations equip emerging leaders with critical tools to navigate ambiguity, handle increasing responsibilities, and effectively contribute to organizational adaptability and resilience.

Integrating vertical development throughout the leadership pipeline strengthens organizational capacity by building depth and agility across multiple levels. Organizations that systematically embed vertical growth into their leadership development frameworks create more robust and sustainable talent pipelines. Such intentional developmental strategies ensure that leadership bench strength is continually reinforced, which in turn supports smoother, more effective succession planning. When vertical development is not confined to senior ranks, mid-level and junior leaders are better prepared to step into positions of greater responsibility and complexity as organizational needs evolve.

Extending vertical development programs beyond senior executives promotes the cultivation of adaptive mindsets from the outset of a leader's journey. Early exposure to developmental practices like structured self-reflection, perspective expansion, and complexity management equips junior and mid-level leaders to proactively manage change and embrace uncertainty. These leaders become accustomed to adapting their approach in response to evolving circumstances, making organizations significantly more agile and responsive in rapidly changing markets.

Embedding vertical development across diverse leadership levels fosters a broader organizational culture characterized by continuous learning, self-reflection, and growth-oriented thinking (McCauley & Palus, 2021). When employees at all leadership stages engage with vertical development practices, organizations collectively build environments that prioritize curiosity, learning, and developmental risk-taking. Over time, this emphasis on growth and learning becomes ingrained in the organization's core culture, creating shared expectations that continuous development is both valued and essential for organizational success. As organizations increasingly recognize the strategic advantage of developing leaders vertically across all levels, this trend toward democratized vertical development will likely become standard practice, driving greater organizational resilience, adaptability, and effectiveness.

Focus on Ethical Leadership and Purpose-Driven Development

In recent years, organizations across industries have faced heightened scrutiny from stakeholders, investors, regulators, and the broader public, intensifying expectations for leaders to demonstrate transparency, integrity, and meaningful social responsibility. Vertical development plays an essential role in enabling leaders to meet these heightened expectations by guiding them through the process of clarifying their values, examining underlying assumptions, and cultivating the maturity required to navigate complex ethical dilemmas thoughtfully.

> Effective leadership goes beyond achieving financial and operational targets; it also involves aligning organizational actions and strategies with ethical standards and societal well-being.

As a result, VLD programs must embedding ethical decision-making frameworks into their core. One common method is the inclusion of value-driven leadership exercises, designed to help leaders critically explore their core beliefs, motivations, and potential ethical blind spots. By engaging in structured self-reflection, leaders become more conscious of their implicit biases and how their personal values shape organizational decision-making. This self-awareness fosters more deliberate, ethically consistent choices, even when faced with pressures from short-term demands or market uncertainties.

Further deepening their ethical capabilities, vertical development initiatives can incorporate ethical challenges (simulated tough dilemmas in training). These exercises present leaders with realistic, morally complex dilemmas that require them to practice applying ethical reasoning in high-stakes situations. Through these immersive scenarios, leaders sharpen their ability to analyze intricate moral dimensions, weigh competing interests, and ultimately arrive at decisions that align organizational strategies with integrity and accountability. Repeated exposure to such exercises enhances leaders' confidence and capability in managing ethical complexities within real-world contexts.

Additionally, vertical development programs increasingly emphasize stakeholder impact assessments as a central practice. Leaders are trained to systematically evaluate the broader implications of their strategic choices, ensuring a balanced consideration of profitability, environmental sustainability, social equity, and long-term organizational resilience (McGuire & Rhodes, 2009). This broader lens helps leaders understand and navigate tensions between short-term results and sustained ethical commitments, preparing them to balance organizational growth with responsible stewardship of resources and impacts.

Ultimately, the incorporation of ethics and purpose-driven leadership into vertical development reflects an essential shift toward more conscious and responsible leadership practices. As societal expectations continue to evolve, leaders with vertical development range will be increasingly well positioned to lead organizations that are not only effective and innovative but also deeply committed to ethical integrity and meaningful societal impact. In short, future leaders must be as adept at ethical reasoning as they are at business strategy.

A Growing Commitment to Human-Centered Leadership

As organizations navigate unprecedented change, uncertainty, and complexity, Vertical Leadership Development (VLD) is evolving toward a distinctly human-centered orientation. While traditional leadership frameworks primarily emphasized strategic or technical competence, the emerging emphasis in vertical development centers around cultivating leaders who prioritize human well-being, inclusivity, and genuine interpersonal connection. This evolution reflects a broader organizational recognition that enduring success hinges not merely on achieving business results but also on the leader's capacity to inspire, connect, and empower people within increasingly diverse and fluid environments.

Central to human-centered leadership is the cultivation of genuine empathy and a deep appreciation for the individual experiences and perspectives of team members. Rather than simply leveraging emotional intelligence as a strategic leadership skill, human-centered leaders integrate empathy authentically into their interactions, actively building cultures of belonging and psychological safety. They recognize that organizational effectiveness significantly depends on their capacity to nurture environments where individuals feel seen, valued, and fully engaged. Consequently, future vertical development initiatives will likely emphasize more experiential approaches designed explicitly to help leaders develop a deeper appreciation for individual and collective human experiences.

> Human-centered leadership emphasizes humility, openness, and the ongoing personal growth of leaders themselves.

Instead of positioning leaders as primarily authoritative or expert figures, this developmental approach encourages leaders to adopt a learner's mindset, actively seeking feedback and demonstrating vulnerability. Such leaders model openness to growth by acknowledging their limitations and continually striving toward self-improvement. Vertical development programs increasingly support leaders in cultivating these capacities through reflective practices, peer learning networks, and structured opportunities to explore their assumptions, blind spots, and biases within supportive contexts.

Further differentiating the human-centered approach is the prioritization of leader well-being and resilience, acknowledging the significant demands placed upon individuals who lead amid complexity. Human-centered vertical development increasingly includes strategies for self-care, stress management, resilience-building, and mindfulness practices. Recognizing the reciprocal relationship between leader well-being and organizational health, future-focused programs encourage leaders to view personal sustainability not as a luxury but as an essential practice that underpins long-term effectiveness, decision-making clarity, and organizational resilience.

The ongoing shift toward human-centered leadership signals a profound recognition of the intrinsic value of people at all organizational levels. By actively prioritizing empathy, humility, continuous learning, and leader well-being, organizations equip their leaders not only to achieve strategic objectives but also to create deeply human, inclusive, and resilient organizational cultures. This commitment ultimately positions both leaders and their organizations to thrive sustainably in the complex realities of the future.

Technological Innovations and Vertical Development

As leadership demands evolve in an increasingly complex and interconnected world, the role of technology in vertical development (VLD) has expanded significantly. Advancements in artificial intelligence (AI), machine learning, digital coaching platforms, virtual reality (VR), and data-driven personalization are reshaping how organizations assess, develop, and support leaders at all stages of their vertical growth. These technologies provide scalable, individualized, and immersive development experiences, enhancing accessibility and accelerating leaders' capacity for complexity handling, adaptability, and relational intelligence (Passmore et al., 2024). These innovations are not just novel tools; they fundamentally expand what's possible in vertical development, making it more effective and future-proof.

AI and Machine Learning in Developmental Assessments

The adoption of artificial intelligence (AI) and machine learning in leadership assessments represents a transformative evolution in the field of VLD. Traditional methods have long provided essential insights into leaders' strengths, capabilities, and developmental gaps; however, these approaches typically rely heavily on self-report questionnaires, structured interviews, and manual expert scoring, processes that can be both labor-intensive and subject to bias. In contrast, AI-powered assessments offer organizations a more dynamic, precise, and adaptive way of evaluating leadership capabilities. By harnessing vast quantities of behavioral and unstructured data, these advanced technologies can identify nuanced growth patterns, subtle indicators of cognitive complexity, and sophisticated measures of leadership maturity with far greater efficiency and depth than traditional assessment methods.

One notable advantage of AI-enhanced assessments is their ability to capture subtle behavioral and cognitive indicators of vertical development that traditional assessments often overlook. By analyzing rich datasets that include leaders' speech patterns, facial expressions, tone of voice, and decision-making processes, AI algorithms can identify patterns and markers associated with emotional intelligence, resilience, and cognitive complexity. This fine-grained analysis provides deeper and more objective insights into leadership potential, maturity levels, and growth opportunities (Hancock & Dethrow, 2022). AI systems can adapt in real time, tailoring their prompts, questions, and scenarios dynamically in response to each leader's unique responses. This personalized adaptability ensures that assessments remain relevant, engaging, and appropriately challenging, facilitating a deeper and more accurate evaluation of individual developmental trajectories. Imagine an AI assessment that notices a manager consistently hesitates when faced with ambiguous problems—it might dynamically introduce a new scenario to probe this, something a static test couldn't do.

AI-driven assessments also significantly enhance predictive accuracy, providing organizations with more precise forecasts of leadership potential and developmental needs. Unlike conventional assessments that primarily rely on static historical data, AI models leverage machine learning techniques to identify complex behavioral patterns across multiple interactions and contexts. By continuously analyzing large volumes of data, these models uncover relationships between leaders' past behaviors, decision-making tendencies, and relational skills, ultimately yielding powerful predictive insights into future leadership performance and developmental readiness.

The real-time adaptability inherent in AI-based assessments further distinguishes them from traditional methods. Through continuous machine learning, these assessments evolve dynamically to present personalized challenges and feedback based on each leader's progress and developmental stage. Rather than static snapshots, AI assessments offer ongoing, iterative developmental experiences, enabling leaders to engage in personalized learning paths aligned closely with their unique needs, strengths, and growth trajectories.

Finally, an essential advantage of AI-enhanced assessments is their capacity to reduce bias and increase fairness in leadership evaluation and development. Traditional assessment methods often carry inherent biases related to self-reporting or subjective rater interpretation. In contrast, AI-driven evaluations can be created to rely primarily on objective behavioral indicators and robust algorithms designed to minimize subjective influences. By assessing leaders based on objective data such as communication style, emotional responsiveness, and complexity of reasoning rather than potentially biased perceptions or interpretations, AI approaches can lead to more equitable developmental opportunities. This shift toward objectivity helps organizations foster inclusive leadership pipelines and supports a more diverse and representative leadership talent pool.

The integration of AI and machine learning technologies promises to fundamentally reshape how leaders are assessed, supported, and developed, enabling organizations to cultivate sophisticated leadership capabilities more effectively and equitably.

Digital Coaching Platforms for Scalable Leadership Support

Traditional executive coaching has long been recognized as an impactful approach to leadership development, providing personalized guidance and targeted interventions that significantly enhance leaders' vertical growth. However, recent advances in technology have paved the way for digital coaching platforms, transforming how organizations deliver coaching at scale. These innovative platforms leverage AI, video-based interactions, and sophisticated analytics to democratize access to high-quality coaching resources across various leadership levels, overcoming limitations inherent in traditional coaching methods, such as geographic constraints and coach availability (Boyatzis et al., 2019).

One of the primary advantages of digital coaching platforms is their enhanced scalability and accessibility. By eliminating geographical barriers, digital solutions ensure that leaders across the globe, including those in remote or geographically dispersed locations, receive consistent and timely coaching support. The asynchronous and on-demand nature of these platforms allows leaders to schedule coaching sessions around their personal and professional commitments, rather than being restricted by the availability of traditional executive coaches (Passmore et al., 2025). This flexibility encourages regular coaching engagement, reinforcing a continuous developmental process and enabling leaders at every organizational level—not just senior executives—to benefit from personalized vertical growth support.

Another significant enhancement offered by digital coaching platforms is their ability to provide highly personalized, data-driven feedback. Utilizing sophisticated AI-powered analytics, these platforms can continuously monitor a leader's developmental progress over time, analyzing patterns of behavior, engagement, and responses within coaching interactions. This robust analytic capability translates into targeted, individualized insights and recommendations tailored specifically to each leader's developmental stage, strengths, and growth opportunities. Such personalized feedback enables leaders to better understand their evolving capabilities, providing ongoing reinforcement that effectively accelerates their vertical growth and readiness to navigate complex organizational challenges.

Digital coaching platforms integrate seamlessly with existing learning management systems (LMS), vertical developmental assessments, and broader talent development programs, creating a cohesive and interconnected learning ecosystem within organizations. This integration allows for a continuous, feedback-rich developmental experience, in which coaching insights directly inform and enhance formal learning initiatives, developmental assignments, and leadership assessments. By linking coaching outcomes with broader organizational development efforts, digital platforms foster a holistic learning environment that promotes sustained growth and accelerates the practical application of new vertical capacities in leaders' daily roles.

Ultimately, the integration of digital coaching platforms into VLD represents a significant advancement, offering organizations the capacity to deliver effective, accessible, and scalable coaching solutions. Digital coaching platforms will likely become indispensable components of leadership growth strategies, enabling organizations to support broader populations of leaders with personalized and adaptive developmental experiences.

Virtual Reality (VR) and Immersive Learning Experiences

Virtual reality (VR) is rapidly emerging as a transformative tool within the realm of leadership development, providing highly realistic and immersive experiences that significantly enhance vertical leadership capabilities. VR technologies create lifelike scenarios where leaders can engage in high-stakes decision-making, experience authentic emotional pressures, and practice complex interpersonal interactions. These immersive learning environments allow leaders to develop critical skills such as cognitive adaptability, emotional resilience, and relational intelligence in a controlled yet profoundly realistic setting (Passmore et al., 2024).

One of the most significant advantages of VR-based vertical development is the capacity to simulate intensive "heat experiences." These scenarios place leaders directly into challenging environments that demand rapid adaptation, compelling them to navigate ambiguity, complexity, and uncertainty in real time. Such immersive simulations stretch leaders' cognitive and emotional capabilities, fostering deeper learning through firsthand experience of high-pressure conditions. By repeatedly confronting demanding situations in VR, leaders strengthen their systemic awareness and learn to quickly reframe problems, developing the mental flexibility and agility essential for effective leadership in complex organizational.

Another key strength of VR lies in its ability to facilitate multi-perspective role-playing experiences (Passmore et al., 2024). Leaders immersed in virtual scenarios can assume diverse stakeholder roles, actively experiencing the perspectives and motivations of others. This approach significantly enhances their relational intelligence by fostering empathy and understanding of complex stakeholder dynamics. By repeatedly practicing active listening, conflict resolution, negotiation, and influence strategies within these virtual settings, leaders internalize critical interpersonal skills that are directly transferable to real-world interactions. For example, in a VR module, a leader might have to navigate a virtual crisis—like a supply chain breakdown—making real-time decisions and then immediately see feedback on the outcomes. This kind of immediate cause-and-effect learning is hard to replicate in traditional training.

VR environments also provide leaders with psychologically safe spaces for experimentation, enabling them to test new approaches and behaviors without fear of real-world consequences. Unlike traditional training methods, VR scenarios offer immediate, actionable feedback, allowing leaders to quickly assess the impact of their decisions and behaviors. By iterating and refining their leadership strategies within these controlled virtual environments, leaders build confidence, competence, and a deeper understanding of effective leadership behaviors. This safe-to-fail learning (where mistakes carry no real penalty) approach significantly accelerates leaders' developmental growth, preparing them to translate refined skills and insights directly into their day-to-day organizational roles.

Collectively, the integration of VR into VLD holds enormous potential to accelerate leadership adaptability, enhance relational intelligence, and foster a culture of safe and reflective experimentation. As VR technologies become more accessible and sophisticated, organizations will likely increasingly leverage these immersive platforms as a strategic component of their leadership development initiatives, ensuring leaders are well equipped to thrive amid the complexity and dynamism of modern business environments. These immersive tools can dramatically accelerate vertical growth, making leaders better equipped to navigate complex change.

Data-Driven Personalization in Developmental Pathways

The increasing availability of big data, combined with advancements in AI and analytics, is revolutionizing the landscape of VLD. Traditionally, leadership growth initiatives have followed standardized curricula or generic development programs, offering limited tailoring to individual needs or circumstances. In contrast, today's AI-driven analytics allow organizations to deliver highly personalized developmental experiences by analyzing real-time behavioral data, historical performance trends, and nuanced indicators of growth potential. This innovative approach enables organizations to craft uniquely customized development plans, addressing each leader's distinct capabilities, challenges, and growth trajectories.

One powerful application of big data and AI in vertical development is the ability to craft individually customized leadership development plans (Passmore et al., 2025). By continuously analyzing real-time behavioral patterns, such as decision-making styles, interpersonal interactions, and responses to complex situations, organizations can pinpoint each leader's strengths, developmental needs, and unique learning preferences. This approach facilitates targeted growth interventions—such as personalized coaching sessions, adaptive learning modules, or scenario-based training—that precisely align with each leader's evolving developmental profile. The result is more effective, engaging, and relevant developmental experiences, which not only accelerate leaders' vertical growth but also ensure lasting retention and practical application of new capacities.

AI-powered data analytics enable automated, dynamic tracking of developmental progress and instant adjustments to learning pathways. Instead of static or one-size-fits-all approaches, machine learning algorithms continuously monitor a leader's performance and learning trajectory, dynamically adapting the content and challenge level of developmental exercises in real time. Leaders receive precisely calibrated growth experiences, ensuring they are neither overwhelmed nor under-challenged. By maintaining this optimal balance, organizations can significantly accelerate vertical growth, facilitating meaningful shifts in leaders' cognitive complexity and adaptive capacities in real time, and allowing leaders to fully engage with their development journey at a personalized, sustainable pace.

Additionally, leveraging big data and AI analytics provides powerful predictive insights for leadership succession planning. Organizations can proactively identify high-potential leaders by analyzing patterns across diverse datasets, including developmental assessment results, past performance, relational effectiveness, and adaptability in complex scenarios. With these predictive insights, leadership development initiatives become strategically aligned with organizational goals, ensuring emerging leaders receive timely, targeted support precisely matched to future role requirements. Early identification of high-potential individuals enables organizations to create robust succession pipelines, significantly enhancing long-term organizational agility, sustainability, and resilience.

Ultimately, integrating big data analytics and AI-driven personalization into vertical development practices represents a transformative shift. Organizations leveraging these advanced methods will cultivate more agile, responsive, and strategically aligned leadership talent pipelines, positioning themselves effectively to thrive amidst complexity, uncertainty, and rapidly evolving business landscapes.

Harnessing Technology for Enhanced Growth

The integration of AI, digital coaching, VR simulations, and data-driven personalization are transforming how leaders engage with vertical development. By leveraging technological innovations, organizations can provide scalable, customized, and immersive learning experiences, making vertical growth more accessible and effective than ever before.

Next, we explore how VLD can be adapted for global, remote workforces, ensuring that leaders across different cultural and geographical contexts can benefit from these advancements.

Adapting Vertical Development for a Global, Remote Workforce

As workforces become increasingly global and remote, organizations must rethink how Vertical Leadership Development (VLD) can be cultivated across diverse cultural, geographical, and digital contexts. Traditional leadership development programs have often been designed for in-person engagement, but the shift toward remote and hybrid work models demands new approaches that preserve the depth of vertical growth while ensuring accessibility and inclusivity.

This section explores the challenges and opportunities of adapting VLD for remote and global teams, focusing on cultural considerations, digital-first development strategies, and innovative methods for fostering deep leadership transformation across dispersed workforces.

Addressing Cultural Differences in Vertical Development

Cultural diversity profoundly shapes how leaders grow, so VLD programs must flex to different cultural norms. As VLD reaches across cultural and global contexts, it becomes increasingly important to recognize and adapt to cultural differences that influence leadership perceptions, communication styles, decision-making preferences, and developmental trajectories. Cultural diversity profoundly shapes how leaders interpret their roles, respond to developmental challenges, and engage with growth-oriented practices. For instance, in more hierarchical cultures, leaders may place greater emphasis on positional authority, status, and clear organizational boundaries, while in egalitarian or collaborative cultures, leadership expectations may prioritize openness, consensus-building, and inclusive participation. Similarly, leaders from collectivist cultures may value relational harmony, consensus-building, and communal achievements over individual recognition or autonomy, which may differ significantly from the autonomous, achievement-oriented tendencies frequently observed in more individualistic cultures.

To ensure Vertical Leadership Development (VLD) initiatives are globally effective, programs must thoughtfully address these cultural variations, explicitly incorporating flexible frameworks capable of adapting to diverse cultural contexts. Effective global VLD programs acknowledge the diverse ways in which leadership is perceived and enacted—for example, hierarchical versus egalitarian or consensus-oriented leadership styles—and create learning experiences that respect these distinctions. Rather than enforcing a one-size-fits-all approach, culturally adaptive programs deliberately offer multiple learning pathways, various developmental methodologies, and context-specific assessment tools. By accounting for variations such as preferred communication styles (direct vs. indirect), attitudes toward feedback (explicit vs. implicit), and comfort with hierarchical versus collaborative structures, these programs foster deeper engagement and more meaningful development for leaders worldwide.

One key strategy for cultural adaptation in vertical development is the incorporation of culturally tailored coaching approaches and assessments.

Coaches and facilitators trained in cross-cultural competence provide developmental support attuned to cultural nuances, making explicit efforts to adapt feedback and developmental plans to the leaders' cultural contexts. For example, coaching engagements might utilize cross-cultural assessments to identify culturally influenced strengths, potential developmental blind spots, or preferred styles of interaction among participants. Additionally, providing coach training and resources specifically focused on cross-cultural sensitivity and competence ensures that coaches can effectively adapt their approaches to diverse leader populations, enhancing both the effectiveness and global relevance of vertical development initiatives.

Another critical strategy for culturally sensitive vertical development involves the localization of learning materials, including tailored case studies, scenarios, and simulations. Instead of relying solely on generalized or universal case studies, effective vertical development programs integrate localized examples and scenarios that directly resonate with leaders from diverse cultural backgrounds. Region-specific case studies enable participants to engage with leadership challenges that authentically reflect their local business environments, cultural norms, and real world. Such tailored content fosters deeper understanding and facilitates practical application of developmental insights, significantly enhancing relevance, transferability, and long-term impact.

Creating structured opportunities for leaders to interact across cultural boundaries deepens their vertical development experience. By facilitating cross-cultural exchanges, peer mentoring, or multicultural cohort learning communities, vertical development programs encourage leaders to actively explore and appreciate diverse perspectives. Leaders exposed to these multicultural environments gain greater sensitivity to differences in assumptions, values, and decision-making patterns, enhancing their capacity to lead effectively in global contexts. Such experiences not only enrich individual leaders' development but also reinforce inclusive organizational cultures that value and leverage diversity as an asset in navigating global complexity.

Addressing cultural differences through thoughtful design and implementation of vertical growth programs enhances the relevance, effectiveness, and impact of leadership growth initiatives globally. By explicitly recognizing cultural influences, employing localized learning approaches, equipping coaches with cross-cultural capabilities, and promoting genuine appreciation for diversity, organizations ensure that their vertical development efforts resonate authentically across cultural boundaries, fostering inclusive, adaptive, and globally effective leadership. By addressing culture, organizations set the stage for a more cohesive development experience globally.

Creating a Cohesive, Development-Oriented Culture Across Regions

As organizations increasingly explore Vertical Leadership Development (VLD) at a global scale, they will inevitably encounter the significant challenge of ensuring consistent developmental growth across geographically dispersed and culturally diverse teams. One of the greatest risks in globalizing vertical development is fragmented or uneven growth—where regional differences, digital divides, and varying cultural norms lead to inconsistencies in leadership experiences, outcomes, and effectiveness. Leaders in different regions or remote locations may experience disparate developmental pathways, resulting in divergent leadership cultures, fragmented organizational cohesion, and diminished overall effectiveness. This fragmentation can dilute the shared vision of leadership excellence and compromise organizational resilience and adaptability in the face of global complexity.

To mitigate the risk of fragmented development, organizations must proactively create structured opportunities for connection, cohesion, and collective learning across dispersed leadership groups. One effective practice is hosting regular global or regional leadership "off site" experiences, which can occur annually or biannually, serving as unifying developmental events. These retreats or restorative off sites offer leaders from different locations, functions, and cultural backgrounds the chance to participate in shared experiences, structured reflection, and collaborative problem-solving (Day & Dragoni, 2015). Utilizing hybrid learning formats that blend in-person and virtual participation can significantly increase accessibility, ensuring that even geographically dispersed or remote leaders can engage meaningfully. Such experiences not only provide valuable developmental content but also foster interpersonal connections, peer learning, and cultural exchange, strengthening a common leadership language and a cohesive developmental culture across the organization.

To further mitigate the risk of fragmented leadership development, organizations can establish robust digital leadership communities or internal networks that facilitate continuous global connection and collective learning. These virtual leadership communities provide accessible platforms for leaders to share insights, developmental challenges, and best practices. Regularly engaging in these global dialogues encourages leaders to understand and appreciate diverse cultural perspectives, fosters consistency in applying developmental insights, and strengthens peer relationships across geographic boundaries (Zivkovic, 2025). By supporting ongoing peer coaching, structured reflection, and collective exploration of complex leadership challenges, these digital communities actively reinforce shared organizational values and developmental practices, helping mitigate the risk of fragmented leadership growth.

Additionally, actively recognizing and celebrating vertical developmental progress across diverse regions can further mitigate fragmented development and encourage cohesive organizational alignment. Organizations can implement company-wide recognition programs explicitly designed to highlight exemplary cases of vertical growth, ethical leadership, and adaptive intelligence demonstrated in various global contexts. For instance, establishing an annual "Global Leadership Impact" award can celebrate individuals or teams who exemplify advanced vertical capabilities such as ecosystems thinking, ethical decision-making, and relational intelligence within their unique regional contexts (Zivkovic, 2025). Publicly recognizing such achievements reinforces a shared understanding of organizational leadership excellence, motivates other leaders to pursue similar developmental growth, and clearly signals the organization's commitment to unified, purposeful, and culturally inclusive leadership practices.

Proactively addressing the risks associated with fragmented development requires intentional strategies designed to unite dispersed teams around common developmental experiences and expectations. Through deliberate integration of hybrid retreats, robust digital communities, and thoughtful recognition initiatives, organizations can ensure global consistency in leadership growth, cultivate cohesive leadership cultures, and effectively leverage diversity and interconnectedness as strategic advantages in a rapidly evolving global landscape. These practices reinforce a shared vertical development culture, so that leaders speak the same language of growth and maturity no matter where they are located.

Next, we will explore how evolving leadership demands—including rapid change, ethical complexity, and transformational leadership—are shaping the future of vertical development.

Future Leadership Demands and Vertical Development

The demands on modern leaders are rapidly evolving, shaped by factors such as economic uncertainty, technological advancements, globalization, and social transformation. As these challenges increase in complexity and unpredictability, traditional leadership models that rely on linear thinking, authority-based decision-making, and rigid hierarchical structures are proving inadequate (Petrie, 2018).

VLD is an important leadership factor to thrive in this Brittle, Anxious, Nonlinear, and Incomprehensible (BANI) world. Vertical Leadership Development (VLD) provides the cognitive, emotional, and relational growth frameworks necessary to prepare leaders for the future landscape of leadership. This section explores how vertical development prepares leaders to navigate uncertainty and rapid change—competencies that will define effective leadership in the future.

Preparing Leaders for Uncertainty and Complex Change

As organizations face accelerating uncertainty, rapid technological changes, and intricate global dynamics, traditional leadership approaches, characterized by linear decision-making and reliance on past experience, are increasingly insufficient. Modern leaders now operate in environments defined by volatility and unpredictability, requiring them to rapidly interpret ambiguous situations and respond strategically without the benefit of clearly defined precedents (Kegan et al., 2016). Leaders who rely solely on past solutions or rigid frameworks often struggle to address novel problems, leaving their organizations vulnerable to disruption and unable to effectively navigate complexity.

In this evolving context, organizations recognize the need for leaders who can confidently and efficiently make sound decisions despite ambiguity and rapidly changing conditions. Effective leadership in these complex environments involves more than traditional analytical skills—it demands a sophisticated ability to hold multiple perspectives simultaneously, skillfully managing tensions and contradictions that arise from conflicting viewpoints. Vertical development programs specifically equip leaders to broaden their cognitive complexity, enabling them to understand the nuanced interplay between diverse perspectives, stakeholder interests, and emerging organizational challenges.

The ability to adapt dynamically without defaulting to familiar solutions is increasingly central to leadership effectiveness. Leaders who can dynamically reframe challenges in real time, experiment with novel approaches, and adapt their strategies fluidly are significantly better positioned to drive organizational resilience and innovation. Traditional reliance on historical solutions can limit leaders' effectiveness in environments where contexts change too rapidly for past experiences to remain relevant. Vertical development cultivates the mindset of flexibility, emotional adaptability, and openness to new information that allow leaders to pivot dynamically, creating innovative responses to emerging challenges.

By intentionally cultivating advanced vertical capacities, organizations help leaders significantly expand their ability to manage complexity. Leaders who progress vertically become increasingly comfortable with ambiguity, enabling them to recognize patterns, anticipate systemic implications, and respond effectively even in highly uncertain scenarios. Through structured reflection, complexity simulations, and experiential learning opportunities, vertical development programs empower leaders to enhance their decision-making agility and confidence, better positioning them to handle fast-moving and unpredictable environments with clarity and poise.

Ultimately, as complexity and uncertainty become defining characteristics of organizational life, the cultivation of advanced vertical development capacities—such as complex problem-solving, multi-perspective engagement, and dynamic adaptability—will become essential. Organizations investing proactively in these capabilities through vertical development will not only enhance individual leadership effectiveness but also strengthen collective organizational agility, responsiveness, and sustained competitive advantage in the face of unprecedented global challenges.

Next, we explore practical recommendations for ensuring the long-term success of vertical development programs, focusing on sustainability, scalability, and continuous innovation.

Recommendations for the Future of Vertical Development Programs

Organizations must ensure that their leadership programs remain relevant, sustainable, and impactful. The complexity of globalization, digital transformation, climate change, and shifting workforce expectations requires organizations to rethink how they structure and implement leadership development (Petrie, 2018). To future-proof VLD, organizations must adopt a flexible, technology-integrated, and research-driven approach that enables leaders to grow continuously. To future-proof VLD, organizations should consider the following strategies.

Adopting a Flexible, Continuous Growth Model

Traditional leadership training has typically been delivered as discrete, one-time events, assuming that meaningful leadership growth can be encapsulated within short-term programs or isolated training workshops. However, contemporary research underscores that vertical development—the advancement of a leader's capacity for complexity, relational intelligence, and adaptive thinking—is most effective when approached as a continuous, iterative process rather than as a finite intervention. Leaders do not evolve uniformly or on predictable timelines; each individual experiences distinct developmental trajectories influenced by personal readiness, professional context, and ongoing experiences. Thus, sustained vertical growth requires organizations to continuously offer opportunities for structured reflection, meaningful experiential learning, and strategically assigned stretch challenges to accommodate leaders' evolving developmental readiness.

To support ongoing vertical growth, organizations should intentionally develop robust, self-directed learning ecosystems. Such ecosystems enable leaders to continuously engage with personalized developmental resources aligned to their individual growth paths. Providing access to comprehensive digital libraries, curated leadership case studies, interactive (and immersive) scenario-based exercises, and reflection prompts empowers leaders to pursue their growth flexibly, according to their own developmental pace and unique challenges. Complementing these resources, organizations can leverage micro-learning techniques—brief, targeted learning interactions delivered through digital platforms—to foster habitual reflection, continuous self-assessment, and incremental skill building. These regular, accessible learning engagements reinforce ongoing vertical development by consistently prompting leaders to pause, reflect, and incorporate new insights into their daily leadership practices.

Vertical development must become seamlessly embedded within leaders' daily workflows rather than being treated as a separate or additional activity. Effective organizations strategically integrate developmental feedback loops directly into everyday leadership practices, ensuring continuous real-time refinement of critical leadership capabilities. Rather than isolating leadership development from daily responsibilities, organizations assign authentic, real-world business challenges to emerging and experienced leaders alike, encouraging them to apply advanced cognitive, relational, and adaptive capacities to actual organizational problems. By situating developmental growth directly within the context of meaningful organizational work, leaders rapidly internalize new skills, test their expanded capacities in authentic scenarios, and visibly connect their growth to organizational impact.

Cultivating a culture of peer accountability and reflection is vital to sustain ongoing vertical growth. Organizations should actively promote the creation of structured peer coaching networks and leadership cohorts where individuals regularly share insights, challenges, and progress in their developmental journeys. Peer groups provide psychologically safe environments for leaders to discuss developmental setbacks, reflect collaboratively on growth opportunities, and hold each other accountable for their personal evolution (Edmondson & Kerrissey, 2025). Additionally, implementing regular developmental check-ins within leadership cohorts encourages sustained engagement, reflection, and mutual support, reinforcing long-term commitment to continuous learning and self-awareness. Such peer-driven, reflective cultures strengthen individual and collective growth, building robust developmental momentum across the organization.

> Organizations that embrace Vertical Leadership Development as a continuous, embedded process—supported by self-directed learning ecosystems, integration into daily workflows, and peer-driven accountability—are better positioned to nurture adaptive, resilient, and continually evolving leaders.

This sustained, iterative approach ensures that leaders maintain relevance, responsiveness, and capacity to effectively navigate the complexities and uncertainties characteristic of today's organizational landscape. In sum, treating vertical development as a continuous journey rather than a checkbox event ensures leaders keep evolving in step with the demands of their environment.

Emphasizing the Integration of Technology With Human Support

As digital technology continues to reshape leadership development, organizations face the important task of integrating digital innovation with meaningful human connection. While advanced technologies such as artificial intelligence (AI), machine learning, and virtual reality (VR) significantly enhance accessibility, scalability, and precision, effective leadership development still fundamentally relies on authentic interpersonal engagement, trust-building, and deep reflective dialogue. Purely digital approaches, though scalable, risk losing the relational depth essential for facilitating transformative personal insights and behavioral shifts. Conversely, purely face-to-face approaches can be costly, resource-intensive, and limited in scalability. Consequently, the future of VLD lies in thoughtfully designed hybrid models that strategically blend digital innovation with human interactions to maximize both developmental depth and organizational scalability.

Hybrid coaching models exemplify this integrative approach. AI-driven digital coaching platforms provide scalable, real-time feedback and analytics, identifying patterns and developmental needs that traditional coaching methods may miss (Passmore et al., 2025). These digital solutions offer leaders timely and personalized feedback, helping them track their progress, refine specific behaviors, and reflect on developmental challenges continuously. However, to achieve genuine vertical growth—where deep shifts in mindset and behavioral transformation occur—human coaching remains indispensable. For now, professional coaches add essential depth by guiding reflective dialogue, challenging underlying assumptions, providing empathetic support, and facilitating deeper meaning-making. Combining AI's capacity for scalability and real-time responsiveness with human coaches' nuanced understanding of emotional dynamics and behavioral change creates a powerful and holistic developmental experience.

Similarly, integrating digital and synchronous development experiences balances convenience with meaningful interpersonal connections. By offering flexible options for virtual and person-to-person interactions, organizations can accommodate diverse leader preferences, schedules, and geographic locations while maintaining authentic human engagement. Digital platforms can provide ongoing developmental prompts, reflective exercises, and real-time personalized feedback, while in-person or live-virtual sessions offer richer relational experiences, deeper reflection, and space for nuanced developmental conversations. This approach ensures leaders benefit from continuous developmental interactions, balancing convenience with substantive, personalized coaching relationships.

The use of AI-driven predictive analytics further enhances hybrid developmental approaches by precisely identifying leaders' readiness for advanced or targeted growth experiences. By continuously analyzing historical performance, real-time interactions, and leadership behaviors, AI tools predict developmental readiness and highlight when leaders are prepared to advance to more challenging or nuanced developmental interventions. Such predictive insights empower human coaches and facilitators to deliver precisely timed, contextually relevant developmental experiences, ensuring that each leader receives targeted interventions aligned with their current capabilities, developmental trajectory, and unique organizational context.

Additionally, incorporating virtual reality (VR) into leadership development further enriches hybrid learning models. VR technology provides realistic, immersive experiences that closely simulate real-world scenarios, allowing leaders to practice decision-making, ethical reasoning, crisis management, and interpersonal skills in psychologically safe yet highly realistic contexts. These simulations offer leaders safe-to-fail environments in which they can test strategies, experience emotional and cognitive pressures, and explore the consequences of their decisions without real-world risk. The subsequent integration of reflective dialogues facilitated by coaches further enhances experiential learning, allowing leaders to internalize critical insights, experiment with new behaviors, and effectively translate virtual experiences into practical growth and tangible leadership improvements.

By intentionally blending AI-driven technologies, VR simulations, and human-centered coaching interactions, organizations achieve an optimal balance between scalability, developmental rigor, and authentic relational connection. Such integrated developmental approaches prepare leaders comprehensively to navigate complexity, cultivate deeper emotional intelligence, and engage authentically with their teams. As the landscape of leadership continues to evolve, hybrid models promise to become the standard for organizations seeking to maximize both developmental impact and operational scalability, fostering deeper, lasting vertical growth among their leaders.

Continuing Research and Innovation in Vertical Development

The future effectiveness of VLD hinges on a robust commitment to evidence-based practices. As organizational environments continually evolve, becoming more complex and interconnected, it is crucial that leadership programs remain agile, responsive, and firmly anchored in rigorous empirical research. Continuous inquiry ensures that developmental initiatives stay relevant, data-driven, and effective in addressing emerging leadership challenges. To sustain their strategic relevance, vertical development programs must continually integrate findings from contemporary research, systematically testing, refining, and evolving their methodologies based on empirical insights and practical experience. In this context, ongoing research is not simply desirable; it is essential for ensuring programs remain impactful, valid, and appropriately tailored to leaders' real-world needs.

A critical strategy for keeping VLD at the forefront of practice involves creating robust partnerships with universities, research institutions, and think tanks actively conducting leadership and adult development research as discussed in Chapter 8. Academic institutions and think tanks play pivotal roles in advancing the field by exploring emerging leadership theories, validating new developmental models, and rigorously evaluating leadership interventions. By engaging in active collaboration, organizations gain early insights into innovative theories, methodologies, and assessment tools, and can integrate these insights directly into their leadership programs. Such academic-practitioner partnerships can also support field research, allowing organizations to test new interventions in real-world contexts, thereby ensuring continuous validation and refinement of vertical development approaches.

Additionally, organizations must intentionally integrate partnerships with specialized research centers and research experts dedicated explicitly to leadership development or vertical growth research. By maintaining connections with institutions conducting cutting-edge research—such as Harvard's developmental research centers, the Center for Creative Leadership, or vertical development-focused institutes—organizations remain at the cutting edge of emerging theories, methods, and best practices. Through regular engagement in research initiatives, thought leadership events, and collaborative studies, organizations stay informed of the latest scientific findings, emerging trends, and innovative approaches in the leadership development domain. Leveraging this external research expertise ensures organizational programs remain dynamically aligned with contemporary understanding and evolving developmental theories.

Organizations must actively pilot, iterate, and evaluate developmental approaches in collaboration with academic and research institutions to keep their vertical development methodologies innovative and responsive. By systematically experimenting with innovative methods—such as AI-powered leadership assessments, immersive VR simulations, or novel approaches to assessing cognitive and emotional complexity—organizations gather valuable empirical data about which interventions are most effective. Structured experimentation allows organizations to validate the efficacy of new methodologies, refine developmental strategies in response to real-time feedback, and continuously improve their leadership programs based on actual organizational impact rather than theoretical assumptions alone.

Creating communities of practice or thought leadership forums, such as regular seminars, webinars, or industry roundtables, further reinforces organizational alignment with evidence-based, cutting-edge vertical development practices. These forums, ideally conducted in collaboration with academics, researchers, industry thought leaders, and practitioners, provide platforms for exchanging insights, disseminating emerging research findings, and collectively exploring future challenges and opportunities. They allow leaders and practitioners to learn directly from innovators in vertical development, ensuring that the organization continuously adapts and incorporates new insights into its leadership programming.

By embracing ongoing research, rigorous evaluation, and continuous learning through strategic academic and industry partnerships, organizations ensure their VLD initiatives remain innovative, effective, and positioned to respond adaptively to the demands of an increasingly complex future. In essence, organizations must themselves adopt a learning mindset—continuously learning about learning to keep their leadership development effective.

Creating an Organizational Legacy of Vertical Growth

For vertical development to become a lasting component of leadership strategy, organizations must embed continuous learning, technological integration, inclusive access, and evidence-based practices into their leadership cultures.

By embracing a flexible, technology-enabled, and research-backed approach, organizations can future-proof their leadership development efforts, ensuring that leaders at all levels continue evolving to meet the complexities of tomorrow's world. VLD grew in importance as a response to a complex world, and as complexity escalates, its importance only grows.

By committing to ongoing growth and innovation in development, leaders can navigate the complex and colliding change curves—ensuring that what got us here truly won't be the only thing that carries us into the future. This legacy-minded approach means each generation of leaders cultivates the next—creating a self-sustaining cycle of growth.

A Lifelong Journey of Growth and Impact

> Vertical development is not just a journey but the most future-oriented investment we can make in ourselves and in those we lead.

Committing to this ongoing journey equips us to navigate the complexities of tomorrow with resilience, insight, and purpose. The path of growth, adaptation, and transformation never truly ends, as the demands of leadership evolve alongside the world. By committing to this ongoing journey, we equip ourselves to navigate the complexities of tomorrow with resilience, insight, and purpose. The leaders of the future will be those who embrace this continuous evolution, who dare to grow beyond their limits and inspire others to do the same. This is the future of leadership—dynamic, interconnected, and always in motion. Let us choose to invest in it, to continue growing, and to shape the world with the power of our collective potential.

References

Boyatzis, R. E., Smith, M., & Blaine, T. (2019). The impact of digital coaching platforms on leadership development outcomes. *International Journal of Coaching in Organizations*, *17*(3), 250–265. https://doi.org/10.1108/IJCO-06-2018-0045

Day, D. V., & Dragoni, L. (2015). Leadership development: An outcome-oriented review. *Annual Review of Organizational Psychology and Organizational Behavior*, *2*(1), 133–156.

Edmondson, A. C., & Kerrissey, M. J. (2025, May–June). What people get wrong about psychological safety. *Harvard Business Review*, *103*(3), 52–59.

Goleman, D., Boyatzis, R., & McKee, A. (2013). *Primal leadership: Unleashing the power of emotional intelligence*. Harvard Business Review Press.

Hancock, L., & Dethrow, K. (2022). Leveraging artificial intelligence to analyze unstructured data for leadership assessment. *Journal of Leadership Analytics*, *8*(1), 34–50. https://doi.org/10.1007/s12345-022-00012-3

Kegan, R., Lahey, L. L., Fleming, A., & Miller, M. L. (2016). *An everyone culture: Becoming a deliberately developmental organization*. Harvard Business Review Press

McCauley, C. D., & Palus, C. J. (2021). The state of leadership development: Trends and best practices. *Academy of Management Learning & Education*, *20*(3), 345–368.

McGuire, J. B., & Rhodes, G. B. (2009). *Transforming your leadership culture.* Jossey-Bass.

Passmore, J., Diller, S. J., Isaacson, S., & Brantl, M. (Eds.). (2024). *The digital and AI coaches' handbook: The complete guide to the use of online, AI, and technology in coaching.* Routledge. https://doi.org/10.4324/9781003383741

Passmore, J., Olafsson, B., & Tee, D. (2025). A systematic literature review of artificial intelligence (AI) in coaching: Insights for future research and product development. *Journal of Work-Applied Management.* https://doi.org/10.1108/JWAM-11-2024-0164

Petrie, N. (2018). *Lessons in vertical leadership development.* https://dragonfly-recorder-nty9.squarespace.com/s/Lessons-in-Vertical-Leadership-Development_Nick-Petrie.pdf

Zivkovic, S. (2025). Leadership and cultural intelligence: Past, present, future. *Dynamic Relationships Management Journal*, *14*(1), 23–38. https://doi.org/10.17708/DRMJ.2025.v14n01a02

Glossary

360-Degree Feedback: An evaluation method where a leader receives performance and behavior feedback from a full circle of sources (supervisors, peers, subordinates, and sometimes self-assessment). It provides comprehensive insight into a leader's strengths and development areas, often used to inform personal development plans.

Achiever (Action Logic): A stage in Bill Torbert's Action Logics model characterized by a results-driven mindset. Leaders at the Achiever level set ambitious goals, seek measurable outcomes, and begin to integrate strategic thinking with teamwork. They are proactive and resilient, though they may still focus heavily on short-term results.

Action Logics Model: qA framework developed by Bill Torbert that describes distinct stages or "action logics" of adult leadership development. Each action logic (e.g., Opportunist, Diplomat, Expert, Achiever, Individualist, Strategist, Alchemist) represents a way leaders interpret challenges and make decisions, with later stages reflecting greater complexity and adaptability.

Adaptive Capacity: The ability of a leader to adjust and thrive amid complexity, uncertainty, and change. It reflects a leader's capacity to handle new challenges, learn continuously, and modify their approach as situations evolve—a core goal of vertical development.

Adaptive Thinking: A thinking approach that emphasizes flexibility, learning, and adjusting strategies in response to changing conditions. In the context of future leadership needs, adaptive thinking enables leaders to navigate novel problems and rapidly evolving environments with agility.

Adult Development (Theory): The field of psychology that examines how adults continue to grow and mature cognitively, emotionally, and socially beyond childhood. In VLD, adult development theories (such as Kegan's or Erikson's models) provide the foundation for understanding how leaders can progress through more complex stages of meaning-making and perspective-taking over time.

AI-Driven Assessments: Leadership assessment tools enhanced by AI to provide data-driven insights. These may analyze behavioral data, language, or performance patterns to determine a leader's developmental stage or competencies. AI-driven assessments make evaluating leadership growth more scalable and personalized.

Alchemist (Action Logic): The highest stage in Torbert's Action Logics model, representing a transformative and visionary leadership mindset. Alchemist leaders integrate multiple perspectives, drive systemic change, and lead with a strong ethical and global awareness. They are adept at managing complexity and fostering innovation for long-term societal and organizational benefit.

BANI: An acronym for *Brittle, Anxious, Nonlinear, Incomprehensible*. It describes a contemporary world context highlighting fragility and unpredictability, succeeding the VUCA concept. BANI emphasizes the need for leaders who can cope with systemic breakdowns, anxiety-inducing challenges, nonlinear events, and incomprehensible situations with resilience and creativity.

Behavioral Observations: A method of assessing leadership growth by watching and noting a leader's behaviors in real situations. This includes observing how a leader handles complex problems, interacts with others, and makes decisions. Behavioral observations complement formal assessments by capturing real-world indicators of vertical development progress.

Coaching (Executive Coaching): A development practice where trained coaches work one-on-one with leaders to enhance their self-awareness, challenge their thinking, and support their growth goals. In VLD, executive coaching is used as a tool to help leaders reflect on assessments, confront personal assumptions, and reinforce vertical growth through guided feedback and support.

Collaborative Decision-Making: An approach to making decisions that actively involves multiple stakeholders or team members. Leaders practicing collaborative decision-making leverage diverse perspectives and collective intelligence, which aligns with higher vertical development stages that value interdependence, inclusivity, and systems thinking.

Colliding Perspectives: A developmental condition in which leaders are exposed to differing, often conflicting, viewpoints. By intentionally bringing together diverse perspectives, organizations challenge leaders' assumptions and expand their cognitive flexibility. This process deepens relational intelligence and encourages leaders to develop more integrative, inclusive approaches to problem-solving.

Competency Framework: A structured set of defined leadership competencies (skills, behaviors, mindsets) that an organization values. Aligning VLD initiatives with the competency framework ensures that as leaders grow vertically (in mindset and capability), those developments match the organization's strategic needs and role requirements.

Constructive-Developmental Theory: A perspective in developmental psychology (notably advanced by Robert Kegan) that looks at how people construct meaning through evolving stages of mental complexity. In VLD, this theory underpins the idea that leadership growth is not just about adding skills but transforming how leaders make sense of the world—shifting from external definitions of reality to internal, more complex ones.

Continuous Learning (Culture): An organizational environment that encourages ongoing learning, curiosity, and development at all levels. A culture of continuous learning supports VLD by making growth a daily expectation—leaders are consistently challenged and supported to expand their capacities rather than settling into static skill sets.

Dependent Stage: The earliest phase of vertical leadership growth where leaders rely on external guidance, rules, and approval. In the dependent stage, decision-making is shaped heavily by established norms and authority figures. Leaders at this stage are consistent and loyal to the status quo but often struggle with ambiguity and innovation due to their reliance on others for direction.

Developmental Assessments: Specialized evaluations used to gauge a leader's stage of development (beyond skills and performance). These assessments—such as maturity profiles or stage quizzes—measure cognitive complexity, self-awareness, and other qualitative shifts. They help identify a leader's current vertical development level and track growth over time through subsequent reassessments.

Developmental Assignments: Planned work experiences or projects designed specifically to stretch a leader's capabilities. These assignments place leaders in unfamiliar or challenging situations (e.g., leading a cross-functional project or an overseas stint) to push them beyond their comfort zone. They serve as "heat experiences" that catalyze vertical growth by prompting new learning and perspective shifts.

Diplomat (Action Logic): An early stage in Torbert's Action Logics model, marked by a leader's emphasis on maintaining harmony and gaining others' approval. Diplomat leaders excel at upholding group norms and creating stable, cooperative environments. However, their strong need for acceptance can make them avoid conflict and struggle with initiatives that require challenging the status quo.

Elevated Sensemaking: A higher-order reflective process in which leaders deeply interpret and learn from their experiences. Elevated sensemaking involves synthesizing different insights, questioning one's assumptions, and deriving strategic lessons from challenges. It is one of the core conditions for vertical growth, enabling leaders to transform experiences (especially difficult ones) into wiser action and new mindsets.

Emotional Intelligence (EQ): The ability to recognize, understand, and manage one's own emotions and to empathize with others' emotions. In VLD, developing higher emotional intelligence is crucial as leaders progress, since advanced leadership stages require self-awareness, empathy, and strong interpersonal skills to navigate complex human dynamics and foster trust.

Erikson's Psychosocial Model: A theory of development (by Erik Erikson) outlining stages humans go through across the lifespan, each defined by a central psychosocial conflict (e.g., identity vs. role confusion). It extended developmental understanding into adulthood and highlighted that adults continue to face growth challenges. In the context of VLD, it reinforces that leadership maturity builds through successfully navigating life's stages and challenges.

Ethical Leadership: A leadership approach that prioritizes integrity, ethical standards, and the consideration of broader societal impacts in decision-making. As an emerging focus in the future of VLD, ethical leadership involves leaders acting with transparency, fairness, and a moral compass, especially important in advanced development stages where decisions can affect diverse stakeholders.

Expert (Action Logic): A stage in the Action Logics model defined by a leader's reliance on personal expertise and logic. Expert-level leaders pride themselves on technical mastery and solving problems with precision. They tend to work independently, using established knowledge to drive results. While effective in clear problem domains, they may have a narrower perspective and can struggle to see beyond their specialization or accept ideas outside their expertise.

External Facilitators: Outside experts or partners (such as executive coaches, consultants, or specialized leadership development firms) engaged to support a vertical development initiative. They bring expertise in adult development, provide neutral guidance, ensure psychological safety, and help sustain momentum. External facilitators can lend credibility and structured experience to overcome internal resistance or capability gaps in implementing VLD.

Fear of Change: An emotional and psychological resistance common among individuals facing new ways of thinking or working. In VLD initiatives, fear of change can manifest as leaders feeling threatened by the need to alter their long-held mindsets or behaviors. This fear often stems from uncertainty and vulnerability, and it must be addressed through supportive strategies to enable growth.

Global Leadership Profile (GLP): An assessment instrument that charts a leader's developmental stage along a continuum of maturity. The GLP reveals how a leader makes meaning of experiences and relationships—for instance, whether they operate from external approval (dependent) or internal principles (independent). It provides insight into the current vertical stage of a leader and what growth areas exist to reach more complex ways of thinking.

Heat Experiences: Intense, stretch assignments or situations that push leaders beyond their comfort zones. These experiences (like crisis management or high-stakes projects) challenge a leader's current capacities and force them to develop new approaches. In VLD, heat experiences are deliberately used to accelerate growth, as they often trigger significant self-reflection and shifts in perspective.

Heat-Seeking Mindset: A term describing a leader's attitude of actively seeking out challenges and stretch experiences rather than avoiding them. Leaders with a heat-seeking mindset embrace difficult tasks that test their limits, understanding that these situations catalyze growth. Cultivating this mindset helps embed vertical development as a continual personal pursuit.

Horizontal Development: Traditional leadership development that focuses on broadening skills, knowledge, and competencies within the same level of complexity. It's about "learning more" or "learning new skills" without fundamentally changing how one thinks. Horizontal development is valuable (improving what a leader can do) but differs from vertical development, which transforms how a leader thinks and sees the world.

Immunity to Change (ITC): A concept and process developed by Robert Kegan and Lisa Lahey that explains why individuals resist deep change. It refers to subconscious, competing commitments that act like an "immunity," protecting a person from perceived dangers of change. In VLD, immunity-to-change mapping is used to uncover hidden fears and assumptions that hold leaders back, so they can be addressed and overcome.

Independent Stage: A developmental stage where a leader has grown beyond reliance on external authority and operates from their own values and principles. In the independent stage, leaders develop self-authorship—they make decisions based on an internal compass. They take initiative, accept accountability, and can handle ambiguity better, focusing on personal and team achievements guided by their own judgment.

Individualist (Action Logic): A stage in the Action Logics model where a leader starts to question norms and appreciate multiple perspectives. Individualist leaders become more aware of their own and others' unique viewpoints and are willing to challenge standard procedures. They value creativity and authenticity, often leading them to innovate, although they may still be somewhat independent in how they operate, setting the stage for greater collaboration later.

Interdependent Stage: A leadership development stage characterized by a shift to collaboration and systems awareness. Leaders at the interdependent stage recognize the value of integrating their efforts with others and seeing the bigger organizational and systemic picture. They seek diverse input, foster teamwork across boundaries, and make decisions with a broader, long-term perspective, balancing various stakeholders' needs.

Kohlberg's Stages of Moral Reasoning: A framework by Lawrence Kohlberg describing how individuals progress in ethical thinking, from basic self-interest to principled, conscience-driven reasoning. It underscores that moral judgment evolves in stages. In VLD, this model illustrates that as leaders develop vertically, their ethical reasoning and values can deepen, influencing more socially responsible leadership decisions at higher stages.

Leadership Maturity Framework (LMF): An assessment tool or model (influenced by adult development research, such as the work of Susanne Cook-Greuter) that evaluates a leader's stage of mental complexity and maturity. The LMF provides a profile of where a leader stands developmentally by examining elements like cognitive complexity, emotional resilience, and values orientation, offering a baseline to guide vertical growth efforts.

Leadership Pipeline: The structured pathway and process through which organizations develop employees into higher leadership roles. Incorporating VLD into the leadership pipeline means that promotions and leader preparation emphasize not just skills and performance but also the growth of mindset and capacity to handle complexity. This ensures future leaders are vertically ready for greater challenges.

Longitudinal Data Tracking: Collecting and analyzing data over time to monitor changes in a leader's development. In VLD programs, longitudinal tracking might include periodic assessment scores, behavioral indicators, and feedback results to see how a leader is evolving. This long-term view helps in understanding the trajectory and sustainability of vertical growth and in adjusting development strategies as needed.

Mentoring: A professional development relationship where a more experienced leader (mentor) guides and supports the growth of a less experienced leader (mentee). Within VLD, mentoring provides ongoing feedback, role modeling, and encouragement, helping emerging leaders reflect on experiences and potentially speeding up their progression through developmental stages by learning from the mentor's insights and challenges.

Misconceptions (about VLD): Common misunderstandings that can impede the adoption of vertical leadership development. Examples include thinking VLD is too abstract or impractical, or confusing it with traditional skill training. Such misconceptions may lead skeptics to dismiss the approach. Clarifying what VLD truly entails—a change in thinking capacity, not just knowledge—is crucial for gaining buy-in.

Opportunist (Action Logic): The most basic stage in Torbert's Action Logics model, driven by self-interest and immediate gains. Leaders at the Opportunist stage often operate reactively and competitively, seeking to win or assert control. They may handle crises with quick action, but their short-term, egocentric view can undermine trust and teamwork. This mindset is effective for survival situations but limited in collaborative or complex environments.

Organizational Inertia: The tendency of an organization (its culture, structures, and processes) to resist change and continue on its current trajectory. In VLD contexts, organizational inertia can be a barrier, as existing systems and mindsets may push back against the new practices and shifts in perspective that vertical development requires. Overcoming inertia often involves change management efforts and strong leadership commitment.

Peer Learning: A development approach where leaders learn collaboratively with colleagues, sharing experiences and feedback. Peer learning communities or networks allow leaders to reflect on challenges together, expose each other to diverse viewpoints, and support mutual growth. In VLD, peer learning is valuable because it leverages collective insight and reinforces that development is a shared, social process.

Psychological Safety: A climate in which team members (or program participants) feel safe to take risks, admit failures, and express themselves without fear of punishment or ridicule. Psychological safety is essential for VLD because leaders need to be honest about their growth areas and experiment with new behaviors. In a safe environment, they're more likely to embrace vulnerability, seek feedback, and thus develop vertically.

Recognition Programs: Initiatives that acknowledge and reward leaders for growth and development, not just performance outcomes. In sustaining VLD, recognition programs might highlight leaders who demonstrate learning agility, increased complexity in thinking, or innovative problem-solving. Recognizing these behaviors publicly helps reinforce the importance of vertical growth and keeps leaders motivated to continue developing.

Reflective Practice: The habit of regularly examining one's experiences, actions, and thought processes to derive deeper insight and learning. Reflective practices such as journaling, meditation, or debriefing conversations enable leaders to convert experience into wisdom. In VLD, structured reflection is a critical tool for elevated sensemaking and helps leaders internalize lessons from heat experiences or challenges.

Relational Intelligence: The capability to understand and manage relationships effectively, often considered an aspect of or complement to emotional intelligence. It involves skills like empathy, active listening, and building trust. As emphasized in emerging leadership trends, high relational intelligence becomes increasingly important at advanced development stages, enabling leaders to navigate complex stakeholder networks and team dynamics.

Resistance to Change: Pushback or reluctance to alter established behaviors and mindsets. In vertical development, resistance to change can occur at the individual level (leaders clinging to familiar habits) or the organizational level (people questioning the value of VLD). This resistance is natural but must be managed through communication, education, and small wins that demonstrate the benefits of embracing vertical growth.

Risk-Taking Culture: An organizational atmosphere that encourages experimentation and accepts failures as learning opportunities. Such a culture supports VLD by allowing leaders to undertake heat experiences and novel approaches without fear of punitive consequences. In a risk-taking culture, leaders are more willing to step outside their comfort zones—a necessary condition for vertical development.

Self-Authoring Mind: A term from Kegan's constructive-developmental theory referring to a stage where an individual forms their own beliefs, values, and goals (rather than simply adopting those of others). Leaders with a self-authoring mind operate with an internal guidance system, making them more independent and principled decision-makers. This mindset aligns with the independent stage of VLD, where leaders start charting their own course.

Self-Transforming Mind: In Kegan's framework, the highest adult mindset where a person can examine and reinvent their own ideology and integrate multiple worldviews. A leader with a self-transforming mind is highly adaptable, sees themselves as part of a larger system, and constantly learns from interactions. This mindset underlies the self-transforming stage of leadership, enabling unprecedented levels of flexibility, insight, and ability to manage complexity.

Self-Transforming Stage: The most advanced phase of vertical leadership development, where a leader transcends individual or organizational agendas to focus on broader, systemic change. At this stage, leaders demonstrate exceptional cognitive and ethical development: they can handle paradoxes, unite conflicting perspectives, and drive innovation with a global, long-term outlook. They lead with vision, humility, and a dedication to the greater good.

Socialized Mind: A mindset described by Kegan in which an individual's thinking and self-worth are largely shaped by external expectations and norms. People with a socialized mind tend to align with the opinions of authority or their group. In leadership terms, operating from a socialized mind corresponds to earlier development stages (similar to dependent leadership) where external validation guides decisions.

Stakeholder Buy-In: Securing agreement and support from key individuals and groups (such as executives, managers, and sometimes employees) for a new initiative. For a VLD program, stakeholder buy-in means leaders and decision-makers understand the value of vertical development and actively support its implementation. It is crucial in the early phases of rolling out VLD to ensure adequate resources, participation, and cultural acceptance.

Subject-Object Theory: Robert Kegan's theory explaining how people progress through stages by shifting what they are embedded in (*subject*) to what they can see and manage (*object*). As applied to leadership, it means qualities that once unconsciously drove a leader's thinking (subject) become things they can consciously reflect on (object). This progression enables the leaps in perspective that define vertical development—moving from being controlled by one's assumptions to examining and changing them.

Succession Planning: The process of preparing high-potential employees to fill key leadership roles in the future. Incorporating VLD into succession planning ensures that successors are chosen and groomed not only for skills and experience but also for their capacity to grow into more complex leadership roles. This helps organizations maintain leadership that can meet future challenges with higher-level thinking.

Systems Thinking: A way of understanding and analyzing complexity by viewing organizations or problems as interrelated wholes rather than isolated parts. Leaders with strong systems thinking see connections between various elements (teams, departments, external factors) and anticipate how changes in one area affect others. VLD emphasizes developing systems thinking because advanced leadership stages require navigating and influencing complex systems rather than just managing silos.

Talent Management: The integrated strategy of recruiting, developing, and retaining employees to meet an organization's current and future leadership needs. Embedding VLD in talent management means that leadership programs, career paths, and performance evaluations all consider vertical growth. This ensures a pipeline of leaders who have not only skills but also the mental sophistication to lead in complexity.

Transformational Leadership: A leadership style focused on inspiring and effecting significant change in organizations or teams by engaging others' higher ideals and motivations. In the context of VLD's future trends, transformational leadership qualities (visionary, empowering, innovative) are increasingly crucial. Leaders who are transformational often operate at higher vertical development stages, as they transcend self-interest to elevate their team and organization.

Vertical Leadership Development (VLD): A process of growing a leader's capacity by advancing how they think, interpret experiences, and understand complexity. Unlike horizontal development (adding skills), VLD is about "growing taller" in mindset—moving through progressive stages of meaning-making and perspective. It enables leaders to handle greater ambiguity, see broader systems, and adapt to challenges that exceed their previous scope of understanding.

VUCA: An acronym for *Volatile, Uncertain, Complex, Ambiguous*. It describes the challenging conditions of the modern world that traditional leadership methods struggle to address. The concept of VUCA highlights why vertical development is needed: to prepare leaders who can be agile and effective despite rapid change (volatility), unpredictability (uncertainty), multiple variables (complexity), and lack of clarity (ambiguity).

Index

Note: Page numbers in *italics* indicate figures, and page numbers in **bold** indicate tables in the text.

For Product Safety Concerns and Information please contact our EU representative GPSR@taylorandfrancis.com
Taylor & Francis Verlag GmbH, Kaufingerstraße 24, 80331 München, Germany

www.ingramcontent.com/pod-product-compliance
Ingram Content Group UK Ltd.
Pitfield, Milton Keynes, MK11 3LW, UK
UKHW022352190926
475702UK00015B/2242
* 9 7 8 1 0 4 1 0 8 3 3 7 5 *